MY B

OTHER ANIMALS

GUY PRATT

The right of Guy Pratt to be identified as the author
of this work has been asserted by him in accordance
with the Copyright, Designs and Patents Act 1988.

First published in hardback in Great Britain in 2007 by
Orion Books
an imprint of the Orion Publishing Group Ltd
Orion House, 5 Upper St Martin's Lane,
London WC2H 9EA

1 3 5 7 9 10 8 6 4 2

A CIP catalogue record for this book is available
from the British Library.

ISBN: 978 0 7528 7631 3

Printed in Great Britain by Mackays of Chatham plc,
Chatham, Kent

The Orion Publishing Group's policy is to use papers
that are natural, renewable and recyclable and made from wood
grown in sustainable forests. The logging and manufacturing
processes are expected to conform to the environmental
regulations of the country of origin.

Every effort has been made to fulfil requirements with
regard to reproducing copyright material. The author and
publisher will be glad to rectify any omissions
at the earliest opportunity.

www.orionbooks.co.uk

CONTENTS

For Gala

'If you can't take a joke,
you shouldn't have joined'
Mike Pratt

INTRODUCTION

This book is not meant to be an autobiography proper, or a cautionary tale, although it does probably contain a few. It's simply a collection of hopefully entertaining, half-remembered half-truths from a carefree and rather out-of-control young life, with perhaps a soupçon of middle-aged hindsight.

I started trying to write a book in 2003, as my professional life had all but ground to a halt.

I had a studio at the legendary Townhouse – legendary meaning it's now closed down – but not a lot to do in it. My TV composing work had dried up, the musical I'd written with Gary Kemp and Shane Connaughton had stalled, and my attempts at being a pop songwriter had been fruitless. Hardly surprising really, as to be a successful pop writer you have to genuinely like Westlife records. Apart from the odd bass session I was at a standstill.

Trawling through the dusty attic of my addled memory, I found that I'd been in rather a lot of daft and amusing situations, so I set about writing them down. The only problem being that I was a lot better at telling stories than writing them, probably because telling them involves a lot less typing and a lot more shouting.

In the end I decided to try telling them in front of an audience, organizing a members' dinner at the Groucho Club. This is where people buy tickets, have dinner and listen to a talk on whatever the speaker's subject is – usually their new cookery book. The only problem was that half the people I was going to talk about came along.

I scanned the room, looked at my notes and thought, Can't do that one . . . Can't do that one . . . Can't do . . . till I thought, Sod it, if you can't say it in front of them, you shouldn't be saying it at all.

Despite being one of the most nerve-wracking and unenjoyable experiences of my life, it went down surprisingly quite well. One thing led to another, and within a few months I was at the Edinburgh Festival with a one-man show.

In the meantime, something else odd happened: I became a working musician again, landing the dream job of bassist for Roxy Music and for the reactivated David Gilmour. It seems that when you get up on a stage and poke fun at pop stars, you start getting hired again – not that those acts had much to worry about, I'm not that stupid.

The next thing I knew, people started telling me I should write a book, so here we are, back where I started.

I've tried to keep it true to the spirit of my show, meaning it's about the stuff that's happened to and around me, rather than about me. I don't see the appeal of my personal life, or any of the depressing bits that are part and parcel of any life, but as a result, there's a lot that's been left out, and some of my closest friends don't even get a mention. All this book is meant to include is the funny stuff, usually involving people you've heard of, which is pretty much what I'd like to hear if I was sitting round a table with anyone vaguely interesting, or not even.

*

Through a combination of luck, ability, and perhaps a bit of wit and charm, as well as a distinct lack of common sense or willingness to think things through, coupled with a complete disregard for my own wellbeing, a terrible fear of missing out and no idea that you can in fact occasionally say no to things, both professionally and personally, I spent fifteen years careering around the world in the company of some of the finest, daftest and most iconic musicians of the post-sixties era.

It was never my intention to be a session musician – in fact it's only recently occurred to me how low an aim that is – but people I really wanted to play with just kept offering me money. Admittedly back in the eighties 'session musician' wasn't the dirty word it is today; we were fêted and sought after, and received most of the trimmings, if not all the trappings, of global pop success.

At various times during my career, I made pathetic half-hearted stabs at getting my own thing going, but in truth that's not where my heart lay. I've never had a manifesto or the conviction to stand up and be counted as an artiste.

Most musicians are people who fall in love with music in their formative years and decide, That's what I want to do. They then go and find like-minded people and start the next generation of bands.

I, on the other hand, fell in love with music in my formative years, but when I decided, That's what I want to do, I meant just that. I wanted to play that music with those people. Playing 'Comfortably Numb' with Pink Floyd, or 'Kashmir' with Jimmy Page, getting to play Bernard Edwards's bass guitar which he used to played 'Good Times' with him in the room and having Joe Strummer record a vocal in my house were good enough for me, as opposed to, say, starting the Stone Roses.

If it wasn't for the fact that Johnny Marr was literally stuck in the room in front of me, I would probably never have realized his genius, for by the tender age of twenty-four, having already worked with the likes of Robert Palmer, Bernard Edwards and Bryan Ferry, my icons were set in stone, and I simply didn't feel the same dumbstruck awe for artists of my own generation.

Take Live8, for instance. It was quite probably the greatest live music event ever. Well, since Live Aid anyway. Then again, it depends on your taste, maybe neither of them rocked your boat. I mean, it's pretty subjective, isn't it? Morrissey was hardly jumping up and down about either of them.

But I digress. Everyone, it seemed, was either thrilled about going, thrilled about performing, thrilled about watching it, thrilled about everyone agreeing to donate their tax dollars to Africa, despite not paying tax themselves, like Bono, or simply thrilled to have something to slag off, like Damon Albarn. I was far from thrilled, though. I was in a pit of despair. After eight years without a decent live gig, I suddenly had to choose between playing with Pink Floyd in London or Roxy Music in Berlin.

My obvious loyalty was to Pink Floyd. The keyboard player is my father-in-law, my family had just got back from a rather delightful holiday with their guitarist and the drummer had just got me a rather fun if bizarre job that entailed recreating the *Top Gear* theme tune using only car exhaust noises.

No band has ever impacted on my professional and personal life in the way Pink Floyd has, ever since they asked me to take the bass player's spot vacated by Roger Waters. A spot that was no longer vacant. That was the whole bloody point, wasn't it? Roger was back! Hurrah! That'll show those miserly old G8 finance ministers. If Roger Waters can be persuaded to leave the golf course, surely they'll *have* to cancel Africa's debt! Roger, however, wanted to play acoustic guitar on two songs, so David, quite rightly I thought, suggested I play bass.

The problem was, I was already booked to play with Roxy Music, something I'd wanted to do pretty much all my adult life. If I hadn't been playing for Mr Ferry back in 1987, I probably wouldn't have been considered for the Floyd gig in the first place.

In the end I plumped for Roxy Music. Ironically, I was apparently the last thing you saw on TV before Floyd came on. Ironic because, if I'd taken the Floyd gig, you wouldn't have seen me at all.

*

Most of the stories in this book are about people, places and events, not about music itself, since that's one thing I do tend to take seriously, and is intended for anyone who has ever enjoyed music in even the most casual sense, as opposed to the serious fan, anorak, obsessive, stalker or even musician.

Having been forced to revisit my younger years, it seems extraordinary that I'm here at all, let alone a reasonably well-balanced – despite the occasional lapse – father who's just celebrated his tenth wedding anniversary.

Rock music now has such a long history that it can't possibly impact on young people in the same way it did on me. Today it's just an accepted part of the landscape of growing up, a soundtrack to your favourite video game and a way to sell mobile phones. For the last twelve years, all rock music has done is look backwards, though that's not to say that some great music hasn't been made, as clearly it has.

Back in the eighties, music was driven by technology. Practically every week there was a new 'box' to get excited about, and studios were magical temples of science and art, to which access was an exclusive privilege. Nowadays your laptop comes with a recording studio included, which makes it all a bit less precious. But it seems odd that whilst musical technology has moved forwards at the same speed as lighting and video technology, the music itself has stopped and turned around. At most gigs today you'll listen to music you could have heard at the Riki Tik club in 1964, while the lighting and staging have become totally space age, which strikes me as a tad incongruous. But then I'm just a grumpy old man, what do I know? Read on and you'll find out how little . . .*

---

*   Actually, that's all bollocks, the only reason I'm writing a book at all is in the vain hope of getting it published in America so I can appear on *The Daily Show with Jon Stewart*.

1

I didn't want to put in *too* much about my childhood, as this isn't really meant to be a proper grown-up autobiography. Besides, you're probably not that interested, so I've just dug up the funny bits.

I'm always suspicious of books that contain endless chapters describing impoverished but bucolic summers spent on uncles' farms in Ireland, rummaging around beaches and bombsites, being kidnapped by Basque separatists or riding on elephants to meet maharajahs. I've yet to meet anyone who can recall their formative years in anything like the detail people do in books, and I certainly remember precious little about mine. I read an interview with Pete Townshend recently in which he said he can remember everything from eighteen months up to four years old, but then there's a gap until he's six. Everything from eighteen months! Are you kidding?

What I do know is that I was born to Tessa and Mike Pratt in a flat above a shoe shop, eighteen months after the birth of my sister Karin. We lived opposite the pie and mash shop R Cookes, which is sadly no more, in The Cut, Waterloo. It's the dividing line between Lambeth and Southwark, as well as being home to the Old and Young Vic Theatres.

On a quiet day, with the wind in the right direction and if you strain hard enough, you can probably just about make out the chimes of Bow Bells, so I could assume the mantle of being a true cockney, but if you've ever heard me speak, you'll know that's patently absurd.

I was meant to arrive on Christmas day 1961, and my dad always swore he was going to call me Jesus. Thank God I was late, as Pratt is quite enough of a cross to bear, thank you very much.

I nearly arrived much earlier, on 5 November, when my parents attended a bonfire party thrown by Tommy Steele's manager John Kennedy. A load of fireworks went off in the living room, the house caught fire and Mum had to jump out of an upstairs bathroom window, almost triggering a premature birth. Years later, Mum told this story to someone who jokingly replied, 'Don't tell me, you had a son and called him Guy!'

The neighbours used to say she drugged her babies so she and dad could have parties, and it's true that the whole Count Basie band came and jammed at her twenty-fourth birthday, with Karin and I allegedly drugged asleep upstairs. The next day in the local supermarket a neighbour told her she'd been kept awake all night by the most beautiful sax playing she'd ever heard, which was from Joe Harriott, a criminally overlooked British saxophonist.

As you may have gathered, Dad was quite a fearsome drinker in his younger years, and would think nothing of coming home at two in the morning with Dizzy Gillespie and his band or several inebriated thespians who were always welcome to crash. On one such occasion, Tubby Hayes allegedly rolled a huge joint out of newspaper, causing an immediate attack of the munchies. Mum was duly dispatched to Waterloo Station to get some chocolate from the vending machine there, but returned empty-handed, saying, 'It kept telling me I weigh seven stone.'

Mum also tells me I once ran into my parents' bedroom at four in the morning having been woken by a noise and gone to the front room to investigate. I was screaming, 'Mummy, Daddy, there's a tramp sleeping on the sofa!'

After much soothing and consoling, my parents managed to convince me they had in fact invited Peter O'Toole to stay the night.

When I was two, we moved around the corner to a little *Corrie-* type terraced house in Whittlesey Street. It was just behind the South Bank, and I spent my whole childhood there in a very secure, loving environment.

Mum now lives with my stepdad Martin Clarke out near Buckingham, having retained the house in Waterloo, which they bought in 1971 for £7,000. Like everywhere in central London, the area's now extremely chichi, so they rent it out lucratively to media types.

I go down to the South Bank quite a lot these days, as in my opinion

Karin, Mum, Me

it's one of the best bits of London. What with the Tate, the London Eye and the Imax, it really makes me think of London as a thrusting modern European city, which is more than slightly annoying. When I was a kid it was an oppressive, deserted, futurist, Kafkaesque nightmare landscape, although good fun for exploring.

As a kid I was allowed to wander as far as I liked on my own or with friends from about the age of seven, which would be unheard of in today's paedo-frenzy climate of parental hysteria. Despite being south of the river, I was in easy striking distance of old Covent Garden, the West End, and the City, which was a favourite haunt of mine, as my mate Lawrence Blampied and I would spend whole weekends exploring the vast *Omega Man* emptiness of the Square Mile.

I still have a scar above my left eye, which is a trophy picked up in the crypt of St Paul's cathedral on one such trip. My companion, schoolfriend Paige Almond, who later changed his name to Stewart England and played guitar for mod revivalists Long Tall Shorty, smacked me into a pillar for some reason, and I was dramatically carried off to St Bart's by a gang of passing Benedictine monks.

As young boy, I was in thrall to anything to do with planes, space travel, Formula 1 and the usual TV shows of the day, my favourite being *The Saint*.

I was a big fan of Roger Moore, although there was one thing about him that annoyed me: he seemed to beat up my dad quite a lot, and on one occasion even went so far as to kill him.

My dad, Mike Pratt, was a songwriter turned actor, who did a very good Russian accent, which got him a lot of work on TV playing KGB agents, often with Bert Kwok playing his Red Chinese counterpart. It was nice steady work, but the downside for me was that he was always on the losing side.

For a short time dad was really quite famous, when he played Jeff Randall in *Randall and Hopkirk (Deceased)*. My parents had separated by then, and Dad had moved into the lower two floors of 66 Eaton Place in Belgravia, the house where they filmed *Upstairs Downstairs*.

It was the first place I encountered such exotic things as frozen concentrated orange juice and Perrier, and in 1969 I was presented with a newfangled contraption from New York called a skateboard. I whizzed up and down the mews beside Dad's house for a couple of weeks and then got bored of it. Shame really, as I had the jump on the rest of the country by about five years.

I remember going to visit Dad in St George's Hospital, where my wife Gala would be born the following year. He'd come home from celebrating his thirty-eighth birthday, forgotten his keys and tried to get in the window. Being pissed, he'd misjudged the distance, fallen into the basement and broken both legs. They were still filming *Randall and Hopkirk* at the time, and had to quickly run up a script that involved him being in a hospital bed for an entire episode.

We used to get to visit the set of *R&H*, which was shot at Elstree along with all the other ITC shows, such as *Department S, The Champions, Man in a Suitcase* and, of course, *The Saint*.

Watching the show on TV I finally understood why, during filming, they'd occasionally stop, and everyone had to stand really still while Kenneth Cope in his white suit ran off the set really quickly, after which they'd carry on the scene as if nothing had happened.

We were having lunch in the canteen one day when who should walk in but Roger Moore. Dad asked him to come and say hello to me, knowing that I was a fan, and Roger kindly said he'd be happy to.

He came over to our table and sat down with a look of suave satisfaction, then Mum said, 'Guy, do you know who this is?'

'No,' I replied curtly.

He'd beaten my dad up once too often.

Telly fame is different and more insidious than other types of fame, as people don't have to go out of their way to be a fan. If you like a particular movie star, you go to the cinema and pay money to see their work. Likewise with musicians; you have to make the effort to obtain their music, even if all that requires nowadays is typing their name into a computer, or get off your arse to go see them live.

People on telly just turn up in your living room at the same time every week, so you can take them or leave them, and it shows in people's attitude towards TV actors. It was by turns flattering and upsetting to go out with Dad and have people come up and tell him *exactly* what they thought about him, good or bad.

This is probably part of the reason I've always been content to be a sideman, and didn't actually get up on a stage on my own and say, 'Look at me!' until I was forty-three.

Although I have often wondered whether the thespian path may have been my true calling, it had no appeal when I was young. Actors have to get up early in the morning when they're working, whereas, apart from catching planes, musicians generally don't – or rather didn't. In the new lean, mean accountant-led music business, things are much more nine to five.

I always found my most creative moments happened in the wee small hours and it's the ability to stay up late and lie in pretty much all of the time that I thought separated musicians from the bourgeoise masses, making it seem like the life for me. Conversely, it could be that I'm just trying to disguise the fact that I'm bone idle, since most truly successful artists I've ever known work at least as hard as anyone in the 'real' world.

The fact that I ended up a session musician does show a serious lack of aspiration or direction on my part, as it's a career that gives you very little control over your life as you're completely dependent on the whims of the artists you're working with, and we're talking serious whim here. Trevor Horn once hilariously described Seal to me as having a 'whim of iron'.

On the other hand, when it's good, it's got to be one of the best jobs in the world. Like now, for instance, as I sit writing this while enjoying an exquisite six-course Tuscan dinner in the garden of the five-star

Regency Hotel in Florence, having flown in on a private jet this after-noon from Belgrade, where Roxy Music played an absolute stormer last night to a delirious sell-out crowd that included the President of Serbia.*

*

From 1965 until 1973 I attended Friars Primary School in Webber Street, just off Blackfriars Road.

There was a bench in the playground where girls would go and sit during playtime, and the boys, myself included, would endeavour to entertain them with renditions of the latest pop hits, complete with air guitar. The big favourites for the boys were T. Rex and Alice Cooper, although I was a Slade man myself, while the girls liked The Osmonds, Donny Osmond, David Cassidy, Bay City Rollers and Jackson 5. There were very clear gender-based divisions about music, and I suffered the first of many crises of confidence when I came under the spell of 'Crazy Horses' by The Osmonds, an irresistible piece of *faux* heavy rock by a decidedly girl's group.

Recently I found myself back in the area with a bit of time to kill, so I wandered down to the school and explained I was an ex-pupil. The staff couldn't have been more friendly and helpful, looking up my records and such, although they persuaded me that letting a middle-aged man in a parka have a poke around the school on his own was hardly a good idea. I was thrilled to discover that our old classroom attendant, a sweet old Jamaican lady, had just been honoured with an OBE, for no other rea-son than that she'd been a really nice helpful person for a very long time. Either that or she'd somehow managed to scrape together a couple of million to lend to the Labour Party.

At the age of eleven I was packed off to Kingham Hill School, a boarding school in the Cotswolds between Stow-on-the-Wold and Chipping Norton†. I was happy to go, as I already had friends there and Lawrence Blampied was coming with me. Plus my choice of schools in Lambeth was terrifying for a rather small, vulnerable, if lippy, well-spoken smartarse like myself. Apparently my eleven plus results had

---

* Although for environmental reasons I would never endorse the use of private jets.
† Then twee but now media whore fashionable.

been very good, so I was given a very limited choice of schools as an 'experiment'. Nice one ILEA.

Kingham Hill was hardly a grand public school, having been founded by Charles Edward Baring Young, of Barings Bank fame, as a home for orphaned or wayward boys. Originally boys would go there from the age of six to fifteen, before being packed off to the Baring farm in Canada in the hope of making something of their wretched lives. They even had a warden rather than a headmaster, for Christ sakes.

The school also had an arrangement to take on boys from Vanbrugh, the RAF benevolent fund prep school, and it took me a while to get used to all these kids waking up screaming every night because they'd seen their dad at the end of the bed.

I did once see a ghost there, in 'The Planney', the dark scary wood one had to walk through to get from Plymouth, the junior house, up to top school. The legend was that sometime in the 1950s an RAF fighter – we were surrounded by airbases – had crashed, and the pilot was never found . . .

Everything was fine until I turned thirteen and suddenly realized that I could really do with girls in my life. From that point on it was downhill all the way, including two attempts at running away. The first was a straightforward sneak out of school, get on a train to London and plead with my parents to send me somewhere else. Needless to say it didn't work. The second involved walking the thirty or so miles to my mate Matthew Johnson Jones's house. His folks were away and we planned to live it up there for a few days before deciding on our next move. Unfortunately his parents had returned early, so we spent two days hiding out in his little sister's wendy house before being finally apprehended and returned to school, tails between our legs.

2

FIRST BASS

t was on a family holiday in Holyhead that my life irrevocably changed course. Having been bullied into smoking by an older cousin, I'd gone upstairs feeling sick and faint after my first properly inhaled cigarette. The fact that I was suffering a nicotine overdose could explain what happened next as my first drug-induced experience.

I was lying on my cousin's bed, starting to feel a bit better, when I noticed the cassette player on the bedside table. Although quite interested in music – I'd grown out of Slade and moved on to David Bowie, and liked fifties rock'n'roll, *Tubular Bells* and the 2001 soundtrack – I was *very* interested in cassette players and audio technology in general, so I pressed play.

The opening synth loop of Baba O'Riley cascaded out into the room, followed by those chords, then the drums and that bass line. It was extraordinary. Suddenly a bloke started singing about being out in the fields and he sounded really angry. He wasn't talking about some baby or other; he was talking about his life. It was all too much for me, and my head resumed spinning, but my epiphany was far from over, because what I heard next threw everything I thought I knew and cared about out the window: Pete Townshend playing that riff.

It was hardly the biggest, most distorted or in any way macho or deliberately impressive bit of guitar playing I'd ever heard. As a matter of fact, it was the most basic 1, 5, 4, chord sequence possible, without even a hint of embellishment or flourish. I'd just never heard a song with so much intent. I couldn't believe it was possible to actually *mean* anything that much. I didn't even care what it was, if anything, that he meant. In fact, come to think of it, I still don't know exactly what it does mean.

I listened to the next track, 'Getting In Tune', which did my head in as well. Then for some reason I can't fathom, I turned the tape over, it being about ten minutes from the end of side 2 (ah, cassettes, God rest 'em), and listened to 'Won't Get Fooled Again', which was, and remains, the best thing I have ever heard in my life.

That a song can be so angry and vicious, but at the same time utterly joyful, seems to me the very definition of perfection in art. It's at this point that I could really do with Nick Hornby stepping in for a few paragraphs, as he really knows how to express this stuff.

Years later I would sit in a Philadelphia hotel bedroom with David Gilmour while he told me how he had stood next to Pete Townshend on stage and played 'Won't Get Fooled Again' with him, then ask me if I could imagine how amazing that was. The answer was yes, I could actually. The fact that David was even slightly impressed struck me as a great affirmation of my younger self's taste. Although to be fair, we were both appallingly drunk at the time.

For the rest of the holiday all I wanted to do was listen to The Who, and Led Zeppelin, who I'd also discovered and thought were incomparable for groove, riffs and sheer weight, though their appeal was limited by the singer banging on about this 'baby' all the time, whoever she was. Pete, on the other hand, had no time for her, he just wanted to get things done, see action and a change. Quite right, I know I did, still do really. Just never seem to get round to it.

From then on I spent all my half-terms and holidays mooching around the guitar shops on Charing Cross Road. My friend Lawrence and I would gape and drool in awe and wonderment as we wandered through this new and unbelievably exciting world.

Japanese copies of guitars had got well up to speed by this point, and though they looked like the Gibsons and Fenders we lusted after, they were cheap enough for the surly, rollup-smoking hippy behind the counter to begrudgingly let us have a go. I would spend whole days in Macari's and Andy's, painfully picking out 'Can't Explain' and 'Substitute'. Later I progressed to 'Stairway To Heaven', but I swear on my life, never, ever 'Smoke On The Water'.

In all that time, though, I only once picked up a bass. It was a Rickenbacker 4001 if I remember correctly, and had it not been for my sheer desperation to obtain an electrified instrument, things could have turned out very differently.

Because my birthday is so close to Christmas I've always been in the unfortunate position of receiving a present that's bigger than an individual Christmas or birthday present, but of slightly lower value than the two combined. As a child I had to employ extraordinary cunning to gain maximum value from said gift, and so it was that I asked my mum if perhaps she and Dad would join forces and get me an electric guitar for Christmas and birthday. Being no fool, she had quickly responded with, 'Oh darling, why don't you get a nice Spanish guitar, and if you get on all right with that, we'll see about getting you an electric one.' Her well-founded concern being the God-awful din that would doubtless emanate from my bedroom at all hours of the day and night, our house in Waterloo being far from palatial.

Spanish guitar? Fuck that! I wasn't interested in the guitar; it was the *electric* bit I was after, and so a plan had to be devised. Then it came to me. Eureka! I thought. I'll ask for a *bass* guitar, knowing, or at least assuming, that the acoustic equivalent – i.e. a double bass – was way too big and expensive.

At the time I knew nothing about the bass guitar and how it differed from its counterpart, I'm not sure I was even aware that it had four strings rather than six. All I knew was that it was *electric*, and therefore what I was after.

So it came to pass that on Christmas Eve 1975, my father arrived carrying a very long slim case. I remember the moment exactly. He walked in the door and I exclaimed, 'What's that?'

'It's a bass guitar,' he replied coolly. 'What you gonna do with it?'

Dad had been very encouraging about my recent discovery of rock-'n'roll, having been a songwriter himself, penning most of Tommy Steele's early hits with Lionel Bart, and even winning an Ivor Novello award for 'Handful Of Songs'. (Both of my son's grandfathers are Ivor Novello winners, whereas I've just been nominated twice. No pressure there then.)

Along with the bass, he gave me an album he knew I wanted: *Dark Side of the Moon* by Pink Floyd. Anyone reading this who has lost a parent early will know how easy it is to invest meaning in the smallest of things. However, assuming the reason you're reading is in the hope of juicy Pink Floyd stories, I expect you can see how this particular gift would have great resonance in later life. I'd like to be able to say I still have it, but I haven't. Some time later, back at school, I swapped it for *Made in the Shade* by the Rolling Stones, which at least is another album with a pyramid on the cover. Well, *everyone* had *Dark Side of the Moon*.

I still remember the smell. Guitar cases don't smell like that to me any more, in the same way that cars don't smell like old Jags did. It was a mixture of Pledge, leather and some indescribable thing that was just rock'n'roll, as opposed to, well, furniture, and it completely intoxicated me.

I loved my bass like nothing I'd ever owned, and I still have it today. It's a copy of a Fender Jazz Bass made, I think, by a Japanese company called Grant. I say think because it has no markings or brand name on it, and in 1981 when I stripped it down and made it fretless, I discovered the body is made of bloody plywood! When it came to insuring it, I stuck a Judge Dredd badge on the body and said it was a 'Dredd Custom Fretless Bass'. I'm sure it's why the Jazz is still the only bass for me. The slim tapering neck, the curve of the waist, the tonal possibilities of the two pick-ups – it always comes back to girls, doesn't it? Although I'm not quite sure where the tonal possibilities come in. The Fender Jazz Bass has got to be one of the most perfect things ever designed by man. It's right up there with cling film and Sky+.

I realized very quickly that I'd overlooked one very important part of the equation: an amplifier. Playing the bass guitar on its own is quite dull enough, but when you can't even *hear* it, it's bordering on masochism.

I devised a way to plug it into my stepdad's hi-fi, which was an achievement in itself, as anyone who grew up in the seventies will attest to. It's hard to describe the reverence that surrounded the family stereo back in those days; it was as if the obelisk from 2001 had suddenly materialized in the front room.

My stepdad Martin was the proud owner of £200's worth of Scandinavian excellence, and about three seldom-played albums, including Neil Diamond and something by Sky. I'm being a bit unfair here, as Martin's long-forgotten copies of Crosby, Stills, Nash and

Young's *Déjà vu*, Cream's *Disraeli Gears*, Bob Dylan's *Highway 61* and Jimi Hendrix's *Smash Hits* were to provide great succour in my fledgling days. I would spend all day playing down in our basement, while Mum sat in her office upstairs doing accounts, occasionally shouting down encouragement as I finally mastered the national anthem or some other basic melody designed for another instrument.

I got myself a 'how to' book, which came with a flexi-disc – remember them? – of 12-bar blues-type backing tracks without bass for you to play along to. Unfortunately I couldn't have the turntable and the bass playing at the same time, so I'd listen to the record, desperately trying to glean what I could, then play along from memory. It had supposedly helpful photos of a man with a bass, showing you the correct way to sit, hold it, finger it, etc. The only snag was that the man holding the bass was an enormous, psychedelically dressed black dude with the biggest Afro I'd ever seen; it made me think I could spend a million years practising but would still never look like that.

The book offered to teach you in either standard music notation, which I knew a little, having grappled with the clarinet for a year or so, or 'TAB', which uses string and fret numbers and is way too boring to go into at this point. It took me about an hour to figure out that I wanted nothing to do with either of them, and that was the extent of my formal musical training.

When I got back to school, I knew I was going to need an accomplice, since playing the bass on your own has its limitations. In fact, that's pretty much all it has, especially when you haven't got an amp and only know how to play 'Hey Joe', the national anthem and something off Mike Oldfield's *Hergest Ridge*.

The previous autumn at school, I had moved up from the junior house (Plymouth) to one of the six senior ones (Bradford). Friendships and gangs had all gone into flux since we'd been allowed to wear long trousers and been thrust into a world of bigger and seemingly cooler boys, and it forced one to reconsider one's place in life, putting away childish things in favour of, well, slightly less childish things.

Martin Glover was very cool indeed. He was in Sheffield House, which was generally regarded as the most yobby and rebellious. A year above me, he was a known Led Zeppelin fanatic, but, more importantly, the owner of an electric guitar.

I always wanted to be friends with my elders and betters – I assume it's the same for most boys – which wasn't easy as few people, other than those of a certain bent, aspired to be mates with their juniors.

I can't remember if we'd made contact before, but I think turning up at school in January 1976 with a bass certainly changed things.

No one had a bass guitar at school in those days. Being a *type* of electric guitar but not an *actual* electric guitar meant it was *almost* the coolest thing in the world, but not quite. I like to think it hinted at hidden depths and sophistication, but then I would.

When I started playing, most gangs of kids thrashing away in their bedroom or garage had a roadie before they had a bass player. That's being kind, actually, they had a lawyer before they had a bass player.

Possessed of neither the obvious vainglorious sexiness of the lead guitar, nor the sheer muscular fundamentalism of the drums – I'm not quite sure where the keyboards fit into this equation – the bass guitar was always rock music's poor relation.

The players you knew of, you knew because they supplemented their income by doing something else, such as writing the songs and singing them, such as Paul McCartney with The Beatles, Sting with The Police, Phil Lynott with Thin Lizzy, Jack Bruce with Cream and Roger whatever-his-name-is with Pink Floyd. There were always the bass virtuosos to look up to, for sure, but even they usually had another string to their bow, like John Paul Jones for instance, who was also a gifted keyboard player and string arranger of note – or notes, even. We all know, of course, that the success of The Who's heady mix of art-school pretentiousness and sheer rage was only made possible by the fact that their bass player, the legendary John Entwistle, was also a one-man colliery brass band. Incidentally, I bought my most treasured bass – a 1964 Fender Jazz that I call Betsy – from him, though admittedly, owning a bass guitar that once belonged to John Entwistle is about as rare as owning a Tracey Emin that belonged to Charles Saatchi . . .

The whole oeuvre of rock music and what it meant was very different back then. Nowadays you can learn the history of pop at school. You can even go to college and learn how to play rock'n'roll. We, however, were taught that rock music was simply noise made by cretins, and it's only now after over twenty years in the business that I'm starting to think my music teacher may have had a point.

It was a secret world and it only existed outside the gates or in your head. With the coolest bands not bothering to put out singles, just *Top of the Pops* or *The Old Grey Whistle Test* on telly – which we hardly ever got to watch anyway – and Radio 1 being pretty useless, apart from John Peel under the pillow and Alan Freeman on Saturday – 'Bitta Quo, bitta Heep, bitta Tull, bitta Floyd, bitta Zep, but first . . . Eberson Laig ag Ballber!' – we were totally reliant on the music press for information. The undisputed king of the music press was the NME, with MM as the slightly more grown-up paper, and *Sounds* as the brash little brother. Bob Geldof once said, quite rightly, that punk basically happened in the music press, as there was practically no other outlet for it. There was also *Beat Instrumental*, which was aimed at musicians – you had to learn to read between the lines with that one, or you'd find yourself going out and buying a Robin Trower live album, like I did.

Essentially what we were experiencing was the fag end of the sixties. It was at about this time that I remember the audience at a Faces concert having to wait two and half hours, as the band wouldn't go on until Princess Margaret got to her seat. An act of spectacular crassness for which I hold Rod Stewart entirely responsible, Woody, Mac and Ronnie being above reproach. The Who and the Stones would do a round of stadiums and arenas every two years while Zeppelin didn't bother playing Britain at all for five years, as everyone just wanted to be laid-back rich and mellow in LA. Man.

Much as I loved *Wish You Were Here*, being the first Floyd album I bought on release, the trouble with Pink Floyd was that you had to listen to the whole bloody album, and we had neither the time nor the pot. It was getting ridiculous, and something had to give. The only really interesting new music in Britain was being made by Roxy Music and David Bowie – although he was actually making his in Berlin at the time.

Whilst I loved the swampy funk of Little Feat and Robert Palmer, only one chap from Asbury Park, New Jersey, was addressing my penchant for angry underdogs. Pete Townshend had just turned thirty, and although still fabulously angry, his current woeful tales of being a rich drunk weren't quite what I was after to get me through the nightmare onset of adolescence, which was annoying as few records have served me as well as *Quadrophenia*.

There was good fun stuff like The Sensational Alex Harvey Band and Dr Feelgood, with a valiant gaggle of misfit bands such as the Kursaal Flyers trying to fill the void, but there was no real meat and no one less than fifteen years older than us to relate to.

It was against this backdrop that Martin and I started our band, A Nice Pear. Martin somehow managed to procure the use of the attic above the gym as a rehearsal space and general den. We covered the walls with posters and record ads cut out from NME, and somehow concocted bass and guitar amps using two knackered old Dansette record players and copious amounts of Blu-Tack.

Over the next couple of months we tried out several drummers, although none impressed us enough to get the coveted stool, which is hardly surprising as for a start we didn't have a stool and our drum kit comprised of used catering-size baked-bean tins in varying states of decay.

We struggled manfully – well, childishly – with Martin's earnest tunes, but towards Easter I was informed that my father was ill, and would be 'for about six months'. What I wasn't told was that once the six months were up he'd be dead.

The day my father died I was sent to join my sister, Karin, who was in Ramsgate staying with Dad's friends John and Joan Le Mesurier. It seemed like the right place to be, everyone was very good to us, and John made hilarious attempts at being paternal – I still try to live by some of his pearls to this day.

'If they're going to worry about your shoes, don't bother going.'

'Don't let anyone make you play cricket, unless you really want to.'

But the greatest of them all was, 'When you grow up, Guy, be a mass murderer, be a fascist dictator, but don't ever, ever, ever be a bore.'

It's only in middle age that I can see how much my father's death shaped me, and the fact that the bass guitar was the last thing he gave me probably explains why that's what I went on to do, as he wasn't there to give me any other instructions to the contrary.

I also fell completely under the spell of David Malin, Joan Le Mesurier's son, a budding songwriter and general roué who'd left school at fourteen, and who I thought was the coolest person I'd ever met. I immediately thought the cool thing was to get out of school ASAP, something I now bitterly regret, as my total lack of qualifications means

I'm condemned to living off my wits for the rest of my life. As a result, my offspring will probably be imprisoned in places of further education until their mid-thirties.

One of the first rock books I read was Barbara Charone's hands-on biography of Keith Richards, in which she tells of Keith's two-day sleep cycle. In my youthful naivety I thought his extended wakefulness was an interesting lifestyle decision, rather than the result of massive and prolonged stimulant ingestion. I hadn't really been exposed to anything on that front, and it was at about this time that I discovered spliff, which was amazing for the vistas it opened up and the fact that music just sounded so good when you were stoned. It also helped you cross the line from being 'straight' to the exciting realms of underground culture. It seemed much more illegal and criminal back then, and everyone I knew who smoked had incredibly elaborate 'stashes', little hiding places under the floor or behind boilers that hopefully would elude discovery by the 'pigs'.

It's easy to forget, in an age where cocaine jokes are the norm on TV, that thirty-odd years ago the Rolling Stones had policemen coming through the window practically every day.

Sadly I can't smoke any more, as it just makes me paranoid and fearful, partly because, with the advent of hydroponics, it's just so bloody strong. I always liked weak pot, which was just as well as that's all I could afford.

With the advent of punk, I assumed that pot would be eschewed, being such a hippy accessory – surely only speed would help if you were going to play that fast. I was shocked and surprised to learn of Joe 'n' Mick's legendary intake. Especially as, when I later encountered Martin Glover in his punk persona as Youth, he was hitting on a hookah of staggering proportions. When he'd first seen me smoke a spliff two years earlier he'd chastised me for being a hippy. Ooh, get her.

My first proper engagement as a bassist was accompanying David Malin at my father's benefit show at the Aldwych Theatre.

It turned out that a couple of years before he died, Dad had decided he didn't want to pay tax any more, so he didn't. Unfortunately for us, that meant that when he died, leaving no will, of course, the only inheritance Karin and I received was an outstanding demand from the Inland Revenue. (Which is why whenever I hear 'Papa was a rollin' stone', I always hear the follow-up line as 'All he left us was a loan'.)

Luckily, Dad had been amazingly well-liked, and a ridiculous line-up came together to put on a show to help pay off his debts and give Karin and I a little something in our pot. (It's true, you know, there's no people like show people.) It included Glenda Jackson, the cast of The Brothers, Barbara Windsor, Lionel Bart, Annie Ross, John Le Mesurier, Gordon Honeycomb, performing 'No one loves a fairy when she's fifty' with Rita Webb, Richard O'Brien, as well as messages of support from Peter O'Toole, John Hurt and Kenneth Cope. John Junkin and Barry Cryer wrote sketches and links pretty much on the spot, but sadly I can only remember one gag:

'It's not right, it's not fair, and it's not British!'

'What isn't?'

'Eartha Kitt's left tit!'

Boom boom!

I turned up at the stage door with David Malin, and the guy on the door duly went through the list to check us off. David was on the list of performers but I wasn't. In fact, there was only one name left on the list, a Mr Mike Sun. Obviously when they were doing the list someone had said, 'Oh, Mike's son is doing something or other . . .'

I didn't even warrant a name. It was incredibly upsetting, and I felt thoroughly patronized, which is fair enough really, as I'd only been playing for about six months and was hardly competent enough to get on a West End stage under any other circumstances.

We performed one of David's California singer-songwritery numbers, with me dutifully plodding away at the simplified part that the real bass player had written for me. I was so scared I don't think I even dared look at the audience once.

My name did stand me in good stead when punk came along, though, and I first ventured down to legendary punk venue The Roxy, fifteen years old, alone and really quite scared. I was most relieved when an equally young punk came up and engaged me in conversation, chatting happily and exchanging ideas for about ten minutes before I asked him about himself. Turns out he'd come all the way down from somewhere in Yorkshire for the gig, and was called something unlikely like Phlegm Ratbite or perhaps Jimmy Pus. He asked me my name, so I told him.

'Guy Pratt.'

He paused for a second before exclaiming, 'That's brilliant!'

If it hadn't been for punk and what followed I doubt I would have stuck at the bass, because the whole idea of demythologizing rock, spurning musical prowess and the idea of the guitar hero put the bass on a much more equal footing. And more to the point Paul Simenon was just the coolest-looking bass player I'd ever seen.

Thanks to the likes of Simo, Bruce Foxton and JJ Burnel, when I made my regular visits to the music shops of Tin Pan Alley I'd actually see guys trying out basses as well as guitars – even in front of their girlfriends! I knew then how the suffragettes must have felt when they got the vote. All right, maybe that's pushing it a bit, but you know what I mean. Punk lifted the bass from its lowly role as rock music's Cinderella and brought it squinting into the glorious sunlight of acceptability.

As a rule, there was little room for actual basslines with punk, as everything was played so bloody fast. The best most bassists could do was hang on and try to keep up with the guitarist, with the notable exceptions of 'Peaches' by The Stranglers, and The Clash's 'Police And Thieves' and the sublime 'White Man In Hammersmith Palais'. In fact, more than anything it got me into trying to cop reggae licks.

That same year I somehow contrived to play in a recording studio with a band, having got permission from my housemaster to come down to London to make a record with a mad Californian girl David Malin had introduced me to. She'd made a fortune out of health food-type chocolate bars, then decided to be a singer.

The band was called The Lil-Lettes and the songs had typical *faux* punk titles like 'Glands Outta Control' and 'I Don't Feel Nothin'' and featured Mike Thompson from Donovan's band, Open Road, on guitar – punk you say? – and a drummer whose name I don't recall but whose dad owned the Rainbow Theatre in Finsbury Park, which was one of the top venues in London then, giving him as good a qualification as any to be in a band. What was really exciting, though, was that no less than John Cale (or was it Cage?) was meant to be producing. Sadly neither of them showed up, but we did record a track, and the cassette is still mouldering away in a box somewhere.

Back at school the band got a keyboard player in the form of one

Bernard Baker, and I stopped playing with them as I was more interested in just learning to play the bass. Years later, Bernard Baker informed me I was actually kicked out. Hey, it's a tough business.

3

MOD BAND SEEKS BASSIST

In 1979 the back pages of the weekly music papers made for hilarious reading. They were a law unto themselves and had long been a source of amazement and mirth, not least for the radical change in the small ads section over the preceding two years

Let me explain. Before punk, 'musician wanted' ads would read something like this:

'WANTED, GUITARIST, NOT ON HEAVY TRIP,
NO BREADHEADS OR TIME-WASTERS'

The temptation was to call up and say, 'Hi, look, I'm a bit of a breadhead and something of a timewaster, but like, when's the audition man?'

In the post-Pistols world, things were much more succinct.

'GUITARIST WANTED. NO BEARDS'

Rock music had been through a huge cultural upheaval over the preceding three years, for my generation anyway, and very definite lines had been drawn in the sand, not that you'd have guessed it from the 'singers wanted' section, which was always a real treasure trove, featuring such classics as:

'SINGER WANTED
MUST HAVE OWN PA AND VAN'

Or:

'MUST LIKE CLIFF RICHARD AND LIVE NEAR NEASDEN'

The clothes on offer in the back pages had also been swept along on a tide of art students' new-found access to screenprinting. In the days before bondage trousers, in amongst the Black Sabbath iron-on transfers were 'humorous' T-shirts with slogans like 'Fly United', 'Makin' Bacon', accompanied by cartoon animals engaged in comedy coitus, and who could forget the classic 'I'm With Stupid'. Now it was all '18 Pleat Bowie Pegs!' and 'JAM SHOES!'.

However, one week, in between the Joy Division bootlegs, 'anarchy' T-shirts and vinyl ties, I spotted what seemed the very thing I was looking for:

'MOD BAND SEEKS BASSIST'

I'd spent every spare moment of the last three years learning how to play bass and thought I was now good enough to put myself to the test. I just wanted to be in a band, any band. Obviously not one with members who liked Cliff Richard, although they could live as near Neasden as they liked. Youth had joined a band called The Rage, and the rumour back at school was that he'd *actually shagged Gaye Advert!* I had to get me a band.

I'd left school in June the previous year and spent three months hitch-hiking around Canada and the States with a schoolfriend, David Seymour. Ending up in LA, I'd blagged my way into designing a logo for a rollerskate company, and on my return had got a job as a junior graphic designer/cartoonist for a little design company in Belsize Park.

I quit to pursue my bass-playing dreams, perhaps a tad prematurely. Although that may have been more to do with the fact that everyone I worked with, although lovely, was gay. I drank in gay pubs and was taken to gay parties. I was *never* going to get laid around that lot.

Although not technically a mod, the embryonic mod revival brewing at the time certainly suited my sensibilities, as turning the clock back to 1964 seemed a logical step after punk's year zero. You also got to wear nice smart clothes and didn't have to hate everything, plus you could be as big a Who fan as you liked, which suited me fine.

I was seventeen years old and a bit naive to say the least. I had a Gibson Les Paul Triumph bass guitar, which I'd bought the previous week from Jake, a hairdresser at the Great Gear Market in the King's Road, who also kept me in Bruce Foxton proto-mullet haircuts for the next year or so. More to the point, I had my stepfather's modtastic 1968 tailor-made pin-stripe suit, complete with working four-button flared cuffs, which fitted me like a glove.

The auditions were held at Alaska Studios, a mouldering fleapit of a rehearsal space just around the corner from my home in Waterloo, which was a good start as I'd already developed an intense dislike of carrying instruments on public transport. I was yet to develop my intense dislike of rehearsal studios.

I arrived and was greeted by Roger Allen, the band's manager. He was dressed in a leather coat, mohair suit, loafers, red socks and a Fred Perry shirt. Nice. He turned up at one of my stand-up shows last year and looked *exactly* the same.

Another potential bassist was just coming out. He was wearing a parka, carrying a McCartney-style violin bass and apparently knew the bass solo from 'My Generation' note for note. Fuck! Why hadn't I thought to learn that?

Speedball – for that was their name – consisted of Rob Buelo on guitar and lead vocals, with Dave Dyke on drums. Rob was a gifted writer and player and generally lovely guy. He was only really interested in music, the mod bit being Roger's idea, which he was happy to go along with.

Dave was a slightly scary, more rock'n'roll character who'd been a child-prodigy drummer, appearing on *Nationwide* at the age of seven. He was one of those blokes that girls go mad for, but you can never quite figure out why.

All my playing since leaving school had been alone in my bedroom, and I was totally new to being in a room with a band.

Luckily for me, they didn't want me to play 'My Generation', and instead Rob suggested he show me one of his simpler songs. It was then that I discovered the gift that was to be one of the lynchpins of my career: show me a song once, and nine times out of ten I can pretty much play it. Though this doesn't extend to anything as involved as solos, and I've still never got round to mastering John Entwistle's blistering fretwork on The Who's aforementioned anthem.

'One, two, three, four . . .' and we were off into 'Don't You Know Love By Now?'. It was the most exhilarating things I'd ever experienced, apart from my first wank, probably. The first thing I played became the bass line for that song from then on. I couldn't believe it, they couldn't believe it and it was a done deal.

Rob asked if I fancied joining them and I replied, 'Of course! Why do you think I came?' It didn't even occur to me that it was a two-way equation, and that I had to like the band too. I was going to say yes to anyone who'd have me. Like I said, more than a little naive.

Five minutes earlier I'd been a sad, spotty teenager (well, not that spotty), living at home and riding a moped, now I was a bass player in a band and my stepfather was never going to see that suit again.

What the ad had neglected to mention was that the band were based in Southend, which was a bit arse about face, as let's face it, people from Southend move up to London to be in bands, not the other way round, not that I cared. They were a band and I wanted in. They packed up their gear and I got into Roger's car with them and headed for Essex.

There are two things I remember about the journey, the first being that I had a load of those joke cap things you put in cigarettes to make them explode, which I put into my fags and offered around. It's not really the sort of gag you pull on people you don't know when they're driving you away from home to an unknown destination, especially when your mum doesn't know where you've gone.

The second thing is that I had no idea how often young people with dyed hair got stopped by the police, for the crime of 'Being young people of a particular youth cult who surely can't afford a car.' Or, more accurately, 'Being exactly the sort of twat my daughter wants to go out with.'

One of the band, Dave I think, had just moved into a house at the back of the main shopping precinct, which he shared with about a million other people who wanted to move out of their parents' homes but couldn't realistically pay the rent, usually because that would involve either getting a job, or getting up before the dole office closed at 4 p.m. This was to be my surrogate home for the next few months.

It was complete and wonderful chaos, a sanctuary for every misfit in Southend who was too young, poor, or stoned to leave home. Things degenerated pretty quickly, and soon most of the furniture had been burned, broken, nicked, or quite possibly smoked. There were regular fires, noise complaints, visits from the police and bailiffs. It hadn't taken long for most of the occupants to figure out that you could buy a lot more beer and speed if you stopped squandering money on rent. When I saw the film *Dogs in Space* years later, I wept with fond recognition, and if you've seen it, that's where I lived, well, without the heroin anyway.

Southend seemed incredibly foreign to me, even though I'd spent a large proportion of my childhood in Essex, as all my grandparents lived there, either in Dunmow or Frinton-on-Sea. My recollections of it are as a genteel, slightly posh county, unsullied by the onslaught of Essex jokes that became an eighties hallmark.[*]

There was a big mod scene in Southend, Canvey Island being one of the spiritual homes of R&B in England, the others being Eel Pie Island and, um, Wigan, I suppose. The only snag was that there was an even bigger, in fact enormous, Teddy boy scene there, too. This posed quite a problem for a slightly effete out-of-towner like myself, as the Teddy boy lifestyle seemed to comprise of dancing weirdly, combing sump oil into your hair and beating up mods. Consequently, in all the time I spent in Southend, apart from one 4 a.m. raid on an amusement arcade to nick coffee from a vending machine, which I bottled out of once we got there, I never once visited the seafront.

After a few days going through Rob's songs with him in whatever bedroom had the least shagging, fighting or fire in it, subsisting on a diet of Heineken and the odd bag of chips, I was deemed ready for unveiling.

[*]   While I was a mod, my granny and her husband Ken came to stay with us for a while, and Ken and I had an odd moment of sartorial overlap, when we would admire each other's Hush Puppies, Sta-Prest and Prince of Wales check suits.

Speedball had been the subject of some local controversy, having recently competed in a talent contest where they were apparently so far ahead of the other contestants it was embarrassing, and yet somehow failing to secure victory.

The reason why was no great mystery. As it turned out Speedball had been a four-piece, formerly known as Idiot, with Barry Godwin on rhythm guitar and Paul Dunne on bass. Their dedication to the band was absolute, supplying them with top-of-the-range new equipment, although no one could figure out how they could afford it. As it turns out, they couldn't.

Southend had an inordinate number of music shops back then, and Barry and Paul had been systematically knocking them off, in ever more ingenious ways. For one of the raids, they backed the band's van up to the shop front, then Barry, having covered himself from head to toe in gaffer tape, cartwheeled the length of the van and through the shop window. For another, they literally took out the side wall of the shop, brick by brick.

By the time of the talent contest, Barry and Paul were pretty firmly in the frame for the robberies, and their latest victim was one of the judges. Ah. Their subsequent incarceration was the reason for my instatement, although the band decided to dispense with the notion of two guitarists – or burglars even.

My first gig was at the Takeoff 6 on a Friday night. The band had a big local following, and I was naturally viewed with suspicion as an outsider.

I was so nervous and excited I nearly fainted, although admittedly that could have been brought on by my diet of beer, speed and chips. I still remember that feeling of butterflies in my stomach, which I got right up until I started playing stadiums regularly; it's a great shame when it goes; it's probably the cue to pack it in and do stand-up. Now there's an idea . . .

We ran onstage to a huge cheer and literally exploded into the first song. Riding a wave of euphoria, I jumped up, did a scissor kick, landed, spun round and immediately knocked out some bloke at the front with the end of my bass.

I didn't know the songs that well yet, so it was quite tricky to keep playing while leaning over to yell apologies. The gig was a storming

Speedball

success, though, and afterwards we celebrated with 600 or so people back at the house until about Monday.

I'd been a hit. It had finally happened, I was in a band, and surrounded by girls, loads of them! Trouble was, having been in an all-boys school, I didn't know how to deal with them. Most of my flirting up till then had been with my mother's friends and their children, for God's sake.

The band noticed this and, taking pity on me, decided to circulate the rumour that I was Bruce Foxton's brother, the idea being to render me so attractive I wouldn't actually have to say anything. This turned out to be very effective, but I couldn't keep up the pretence, and within a few days I was getting pretty frosty treatment from several of the local modettes.

My sister Karin had been going out with one Nigel Bennett, lead guitarist of up-and-coming band The Members, who I thought were fantastic – not only were their songs great tunes, they were also very funny. This was one of the great things after punk as English rock seemed to rediscover its, well, Englishness; dragging along a whole legacy of music hall knockabout humour, which probably reached its peak with Madness.

One night Karin, who'd been banging on about her brother's band, dragged JC, The Members rhythm guitarist and songwriter, along to see us play at the Notre Dame Hall off Leicester Square. (Bear in mind there can be few things less inviting than a fellow band member's girlfriend banging on about how you've got to see her brother's band.) He came, he loved us and we became friends. When The Members had their one biggish hit, the classic 'Sound Of The Suburbs', he even went so far as to pay for and produce our first demos.

Speedball went through the usual ups and downs, slogging around the country in Barry's van once he was released, usually followed by another old Transit containing the ragtag bunch of punks, mods, skins and bikeless bikers that constituted our following. I found out years later that one of them was apparently a biker chick known as 'Fat Alf', who grew up to become Alison Moyet.

Not being a big van man, I used to travel with Roger the manager in his old Riley, which was crammed full of luxury items like windows, ashtrays and seats.

Roger was forever getting things out of the glove compartment – cassettes, although I don't think the luxury extended as far as a cassette player – and I couldn't help noticing the unopened half bottle of Bell's whisky.

One night, coming back from a gig out in west London, we got stopped just past the Hogarth Roundabout, as Roger was quite pissed and had hit the kerb. The procedure in those days was for the copper to come to your window, inform you that you were going be breathalysed, then ask you to follow him back to his car, which is just what happened. But as soon as his back was turned, Roger did something extraordinary: he reached over to the glove compartment, pulled out the whisky and downed practically the whole thing in about five seconds. I was aghast, Roger was obviously going to lose his licence anyway, but what the fuck was he playing at?

It transpired that there was a method to his madness. He held a mouthful of whisky until he reached the police car, took the breathalyser, swallowed, then released a huge lungful of air into it. The subsequent blood alcohol reading was so high he couldn't possibly be alive, meaning the breathalyser was faulty, so they had to let him go. It was incredibly audacious, brazen and stupid, and it left me with the problem of being driven home by arguably the most drunk person I had ever seen in my life.

Our high point was probably securing a Monday night residency at the Trafalgar, a pub in the middle of the Shepherd's Bush shopping centre. It was there that I got reacquainted with one Tony Fletcher, who I knew through tenuous family connections and used to see every Boxing Day. A fellow Who nut, he had started a fanzine called *Jamming* and a band called Apocalypse, who supported us. Unlike other fanzines, which mainly interviewed little-known bands like us, he'd decided to do it properly, obtaining audiences with McCartney and Townshend. He'd got to know Paul Weller and took me along to meet him at the Townhouse Studios when The Jam were recording *Sound Affects*. Weller was apparently going to back Tony's record label, Jamming Records, and we were going to be the first signing.

It was my first visit to a proper first-division studio, and I was in awe at all the roadies and gear everywhere. While we were chatting to Paul in the control room, the band Japan came in to have a look round. Paul made a dig at their coiffured, made-up appearance, which of course I indicated was the cleverest and funniest thing I'd ever heard. The Jam were playing a secret gig at the YMCA in Woking, as a sort of hometown thank-you, and he invited Tony and I to join them for the encore for some obscure reason. We went to the show, which was plagued with problems from the start, and after half a dozen or so songs, Paul smashed his guitar and stormed off stage. Maybe it was the prospect of being joined by two overly keen fans. It had all seemed a bit too good to be true, so I wasn't too gutted. Likewise when the label failed to materialize, though Tony went on to become a very successful writer, with *Dear Boy*, the definitive Keith Moon biography, to his credit.

Speedball sputtered out eventually, and it seems like someone else's life now, which in a way it was. The band was something of an anomaly, and I was just a confused young lad with no sense of his place in the world.

I had no idea where anyone from that part of my life had got to, or even who was still alive until I started doing stand-up, when occasional faces from the mod scene started showing up. It turns out that some of the old bands are still going, and there's a small die-hard mod scene still chugging away. I wish them all the best. Keep the faith, lads.

4

THE HUNGRY YEARS

Any young wannabe musician in 1980 worth his salt eventually wound up in Notting Hill, although some went to Camden, the poor demented fools. I did because my mum got fed up with me moping around the house and kicked me out. I got the tube to Notting Hill Gate and have lived thereabouts on and off ever since.

It seemed to be the last bastion of bohemia, where the days were long and the harsh realities of the big city rarely encroached. There were a few pubs, the Churchill, the Frog and Firkin, the Gold, and the Lonsdale, where you could always find a friend to stand you a pint. Everyone ate cheaply and well, bar the odd life-threatening tropical disease, at Mike's Café or the plethora of Indian restaurants that adorned Westbourne Grove. The only smart restaurants this side of Notting Hill Gate were Monsieur Thompson's, where you got taken if Virgin signed you, and L'artiste Asoiffe, which was famous for its belligerent parrot rather than its cuisine. You went up West to go clubbing or visit one of the major record companies, who at that point maintained grand offices in Mayfair and St James, and there was a fair few bob to be had from blagging promo copies to sell at the Record and Tape Exchange. The cooler Indy labels, however, such as Virgin, Stiff, and Rough Trade, abided in W11.

Other than the odd sortie down to Chelsea for posh girls' parties, we were pretty much self-contained, the idea that places like Hoxton or Aldgate would one day even *exist* seems absurd. It was as cool a place as you can imagine, at least through the rose-tinted glasses of memory, and a million miles from the tacky *faux* Beverly Hills it is today. When I first moved there it was the only part of London apart from Earls Court that had an all-night shop. Now it's about the only part that doesn't.

It seemed as though everyone living around Ladbroke Grove was in a band, as this was before DJ or stylist became compulsory career choices for the less usefully inclined. There were also lots of empty houses to squat in, this being the domicile of choice for most aspiring rock stars. The term 'trustafarian' hadn't yet been coined, but I certainly knew plenty of people who lived in 'squats' that Daddy had bought them.

I only squatted once, when a singer called Dan-I, who'd had a hit with 'Monkey Chop', invited me to crash at his place, which turned out to be a very politically motivated 'squat against sales!' in a council block on Elgin Avenue. There were police with dogs on the landings and apparently we were going to bring down the government. My room was barren apart from a horrid old mattress and a chest of drawers, which I'd come across on the Great West Road late one night. While I was standing there thinking what a shame it was that I couldn't carry such a beast on my own, some nutter came up to me, speeding off his trolley. I engaged him in conversation and he was so grateful for someone to talk to, I don't think he even noticed lugging a bloody great piece of furniture half a mile up the road.

I was never cut out for squatting, although I know several people who've pulled it off with great style and panache, so when the most terrifying Scotsman ever – and I've met a few – burst into my room to inform me that I'd said he could borrow my guitar, even though I'd never seen him before in my life, it was obviously time to go.

I shared a flat on Elgin Crescent with the sax player Adam Maitland, his girlfriend and a couple of other people, including Kevin, the stage manager at Richard Branson's the Venue, in Victoria. This proved particularly fortuitous, as it meant I could always get in free. The Venue was the best gig and general hangout I've ever known in London, and I'm sure anyone who was around at the time would at least partially agree. I ended up doing little odd jobs around the place, like lights and sound, for which I was beyond unqualified. When Harry Chapin played, I was drafted in to man the follow spot, so when he died two days later I took it as an omen and have never touched a spotlight since.

I'd bumped into my 'old' schoolmate Youth on Kensington Park

JC and Chris Payne at Risk

Road and it transpired that he was living directly opposite. He'd become something of a local figure with his dreadlocks and indescribably filthy once-white fifties dinner suit. He had also joined the fantastic Killing Joke, who were all really tall and frightening, until you got to know them (except Jaz, who remained frightening for several years).

The Grove was a great melting pot of rich, poor, black, white, punks, hippies, drug-dealing gangsters, and well-to-do pretty girls called Camilla or Sophie, who usually went out with the drug-dealing gangsters until Daddy hauled them back to Chelsea. It was like the NME come to life – every day you'd see Paul Simenon coming out of Dub Vendor, or Aswad copping spliff on All Saints Road.

Once Gene October of Chelsea stopped me on the street and asked if I wanted to join his band. He neglected to ask if I played an instrument, which made me slightly suspicious, so I declined. Most of The Members had relocated to Notting Hill, and JC and I ended up working in the same clothes shop on Saturdays. Called Risk, it was up the top end of Portobello, next to Better Badges and Honest Jon's Records. It was owned by one Chris Derham, who had a great knack for finding brand new fifties and sixties American clothes in the back of New York warehouses. I didn't know at the time that working in a cool clothes shop was actually a compulsory part of a musician's CV, unless of course they went to art college.

JC used to play great music in the shop, bluebeat, soca, cajun and disco. I remember bouncing up and down while minding the coat rail outside, partly because the tunes were so good, but mainly to keep warm, especially as I'd seldom troubled my bed on the Friday night. I can't remember how or when it happened, but suddenly we weren't listening to any rock'n'roll – at least nothing later than 1958 – at all.

One day, while listening to Narada Michael Walden's 'I Should Have Loved Ya', which features one of the finest bass lines ever written, JC turned to me and said, 'If you learn to play bass like that, I'll start a band with you.'

So I did.

By this time I was living in the little back room of a flat belonging to two freebase addicts, a sort of early middle-class crack house. It was a place of frayed nerves, with a definite sell-by date. My mother once rang up to talk to me at three o'clock on a Sunday afternoon and was greeted with, 'WE'RE TRYING TO FUCKING SLEEP! WHAT DO YOU THINK THIS IS?'

People – some surprisingly well known – would come round to buy a pipe or two, score some coke and leave. Hearing me practising away on my little amp, the more compassionate among them would pop their heads round the door and offer words of encouragement, and as often as not some charlie. This is probably why in less than two weeks I'd mastered all of Chic's secrets, weighed about 6 stone and was very tetchy indeed.

Few things on earth can express sheer *joie de vie* like a good disco bass line. Once you've mastered the bubble, for that is the key, you'll want to do precious little else, assuming you're a bass player and not a serious muso or rock dunderhead. In my mind, the Zeus-like Bernard Edwards of Chic gazed benevolently down on us from his Olympian perch; his playing was the absolute pinnacle of the instrument. On the home front, Norman Watt-Roy of Blockheads fame had me trying to cop his relaxed yet frenetic style till my fingers froze up.

I had fallen in love with music originally because of the whole package, the intent, social comment, revolution, trousers, etc., but the for the first time I was just interested in music. The great British bands of the sixties had started out imitating the black music of the day – or older in the case of the blues – and now it seemed my generation were going to do the same thing all over again.

Hip hop was it at that time, and we were all clamouring for mix tapes of Shep Pettibone's show on Kiss Radio in New York. Everyone was, as The Clash put it, 'overpowered by Funk'. The grove was alive to the sound of beats, we'd all go to shebeens, drink Special Brew and smoke sensi all night while drowning in a sea of dub. It was a great time to be young and poor. Well, young anyway.

It's impossible to overestimate the role of the girlfriend in the struggling young musician's life. She is his rock, his counsel, his stylist, his shrink, his fan, and, usually, his meal ticket. I used to find it very sad, if somewhat predictable, that every time someone I knew got a record deal or a decent gig, their long-suffering, dutiful girlfriend who had supported, fed and most importantly *believed* in their spoilt charge, would be unceremoniously dumped, usually for a model. When Killing Joke became a bona-fide hit band, Jaz said coldly in an interview, 'We're all upgrading our boilers.' (All right, so my next girlfriend was a model, but that was a *long* time after we'd split up, honest.)

In the hungry days of 1980 and 1981, pretty much every musician I knew was supported to some degree by his girlfriend – except for the female ones, of course, who were more than capable of looking after themselves.

If said girlfriend wasn't a model, she usually worked at a record company or was a waitress at either a trendy Mexican or burger restaurant. This would enable access either to records and gigs, or food and drink, all essential items for the struggling artiste.

My girlfriend, the wonderful and quite extraordinarily tall Emma Bagust, went one better and actually became manageress of Tarts restaurant, on the corner of Pembridge Road and Kensington Park Road. Not only did this give her unlimited access to food and drink, it meant she could get me the occasional shift as cocktail barman, which worked very well until the day she begged me to fill in at the Chiswick branch when I was two hours into a very strong acid trip.

I went in and did my valiant best, concocting previously untested combinations of luminous multicoloured booze, until by sheer coincidence my mum and sister – Karin lived in Chiswick at the time – came in for dinner. I soon became hopelessly paranoid, lost my nerve and was never asked to work there again.

Luckily, I still had my job at Risk, which had a little rehearsal room in the basement. JC and I would go downstairs and jam when the newly formed Big Country weren't working in it on endless versions of that one song of theirs. I showed JC my new-found prowess and he was duly impressed. The Members had just got a deal with Martin Rushent's Genetic Records, but JC was keen to form a splinter group. This became a reality when, one night, while babysitting for my friend Oona, I wrote what was to become my first recorded and released track. (Quite what I was doing babysitting is a mystery, as I wouldn't have had a clue what to do if my charge had woken up or needed anything.) But when I played the track for JC, he immediately got to work writing a song on top of it.

Solidarity was the buzzword of the moment, what with Lech Walesa kicking off in Gdansk, and everyone in left-wing politics desperately expressing solidarity with everyone else. So that became the title of our song. We knocked it up at Alvic Studios in Olympia. Lead vocals were ably handled by Chris Payne, The Members' bassist, and The Children Of 7 were born. I liked the name because it sounded arcane and mysterious, but JC's reason for liking it was far funnier, the line being that he'd played our songs to his mum, who'd said, 'That could've been done by a monkey or a child of seven.'

Literally the day after we recorded it, tanks rolled into Gdansk and we had a hot property on our hands, with every label in town expressing interest. The only snag was that as The Members were signed to Genetic, we had to invent fake band members. One of my first lessons in handling A&R men came when sax player Simon Lloyd and I went to see a label. We had a cassette with the song on it twice. We played it, and before the guy could say anything, Simon said, 'Hang on, there's a different mix', and played exactly the same track again. He then asked which one the man preferred.

'The second one,' came the authoritative reply.

'You're right,' concurred Simon.

Thus flattered, the A&R man offered us a deal there and then.

We signed to Stiff, and I did the round of music papers with their press officer, the delightful Andy MacDonald (later to found

Independiente Records). I even got my picture in *Jackie*, which was quite a thrill, I can tell you.

I got a £300 publishing advance, which JC paternally suggested I use to buy a proper bass, rather than robot shoes and Fullers ESB. I duly went and bought an Aria Pro 2 from my mate, Funkapolitan's Tom Dixon.[*]

Funkapolitan were the trendy band in the area, certainly for all the Camillas and Sophies, as they were all pretty posh and well connected – the first gig I saw them play was a garden party for Charles and Diana's wedding, for Christ's sake. I'd become friends with some of them, and when Tom broke his leg as a result of riding his motorbike into the back of a Tory MP's car – while ogling a girl, apparently – he asked me to fill in for him on their upcoming tour.

They were managed by Rick Cunningham, designer Antony Price's partner, and were all kitted out in Antony's suits, which were also sported by Roxy Music and soon to be Duran Duran's weapon of choice. I would be required to wear one on stage. I still had a bit of the old mod in me, and these puppies came in at £300 a pop. No complaints there then.

The Funkapolitan tour was a great laugh, if something of an eye-opener, for these boys were not accustomed to life downtown, even sending the 'brothers' in the band out to score their weed for them.

Driving up to Sheffield to play at the Comet, we stopped at a road-side burger shack as we were starving, but on seeing what was on offer the band opted out. I tucked into an admittedly disgusting cheese-burger while everyone scoffed and laughed at my lack of discernment. It was clear that only one of us had a future on the road. These guys would starve to death.

The gigs were great fun as the drummer and percussionist were proper, and guitarist Sagat was technically amazing, if infuriating, being seemingly unable to play the same thing twice – 'That was great, Sag, do it again.' 'Do what again?' It was the first time I ever got to play out-and-out funk live.

---

[*] Tom went on to become one of the most influential furniture designers in the world and ended up running Habitat, for which he received an OBE. You know you're middle-aged when the bass player from Funkapolitan has an OBE.

One of the most memorable gigs was the Retford Porterhouse, where due to the low ceiling the lights had to be placed right up against the side of the stage. When Sagat changed guitars and put down his vintage Gibson, it was leaning right against them and the heat started to melt the pick guard, causing the stage to fill with smoke, much to the delight of the audience. It wasn't until we started choking that we realized the effect hadn't been scheduled by Smart, our charming lighting man, and by that point the Gibson was in flames. It was both terribly sad and unbelievably comic seeing Sagat boot his beloved, newly purchased and very expensive guitar out into the crowd. It probably set a couple of them alight, but hey, nothing much happens in Retford, as I found out when I was making one of my rare and pathetic attempts to chat up a girl afterwards. Finding conversation something of a struggle, I'd resorted to, 'So what do you do then?' She told me in a thick northern accent, 'I make parts for army radios in Worksop.'

Funkapolitan fell apart soon afterwards, when keyboard player Toby Anderson decided to turn an NME interview into a band meeting and let everyone know *exactly* what he thought of their rapper Cyberman, which I'm sure the journo loved. They were more at home with *Harpers & Queen* or *Tatler* really.

London was awash with nightclubs at the time, what with the new romantics having just been and gone, although I must say I never went to Blitz or any of that ilk. That scene was more of a north London/LSE thing. A girl once asked me along to Club 21, and had I gone I may well have ended up donning a tea towel, and, who knows, my whole life could have turned out differently.

Thursday was Gaz's Rockin' Blues, in fact, it still is, and it's a comforting thought that in twenty years' time I'll probably still be able to go down Wardour Street and shuffle along to 'Ain't Nobody Here But Us Chickens'.

The aforementioned Tom Dixon, another band member Nick Jones and Simon Oakes ran the first rap club in London, called the Language Lab, on Mondays at the Nell Gwynne Club in Meard Street. At Tom's request I put together a little jazz combo to play in the theatre upstairs, comprising of Chrysta Jones (vocals), Simon Lloyd (sax), Justin (percussion) and Andrew Crawford (keyboards). Andrew had recently saved my life by getting me out of the freebase hell house, literally the day before the police raided it, and moving me into his family home, where he now lived alone.

It was a beautiful house overlooking Queen's Park, complete with a grand piano in the upstairs sitting room, where we would hone our jazz funk and reggae skills till the wee small hours, when we got back from pub or club. The Nell Gwynntet, as we were known, would go on at midnight, which was when the strippers finished, and as a result we shared a dressing room with them. There was much blushing, apologizing and averting of eyes. We weren't very rock'n'roll – not at all actually, we were supposed to be a jazz band after all.

Some pretty interesting acts joined us at the club over the following months, it being where I first encountered two key players in my later life, the embryonic Dream Academy and one Keith Allen, who I threw a pint of beer over when he pulled me out of the audience for heckling. The next week he got knocked out by Youth's girlfriend Sally with an expertly aimed high-heeled shoe.

The only official way into the club involved squeezing into a tiny and far-from-trustworthy lift. To avoid the interminable queuing and flagrant breach of about a hundred fire regulations, not to mention entrance fee if you weren't playing, we worked out ever more ingenious ways of gaining access. JC once burst through a fire exit and found himself on stage at the beginning of our set, cleverly covering himself by grabbing a mic and introducing the band: 'Ladies and gentlemen, the Nell Gwynntet, umm, playing all your old favourites from . . . before you were born!'

By the time the place had been going for a few months, Funkapolitan guitarist Sagat and myself had worked out a route that involved climbing a fire escape half a mile away, then crossing Soho rooftop by rooftop before swinging in through the upstairs window of a Russian restaurant, all the while carrying our guitars. And perhaps a box of Milk Tray.

I'd also been doing some gigs with Gaz's Rebel Blues Rockers, who are still going today under the tidier name of the Trojans, and we actually garnered a favourable review in Harpers by bringing Portobello Road to a standstill when we played outside Honest Jon's Records one Saturday afternoon. As soon as we finished, I was back working the coat rail. I love jump blues to listen and dance to, but as far as playing goes, it was just good practice.

Interesting things had been going on in the Killing Joke camp. Their star having been in the ascendant for some time, their gigs were monstrous, muscular, terrifying onslaughts, driven by Geordie's awesome guitar and Big Paul's powerhouse tribal drums. My view of them was probably influenced by the fact that I was still pretty scared of Jaz and could only really talk to him when we were both drunk, which luckily was quite often.

He and Youth shared a basement flat on Ladbroke Grove, which was a big hang, with Youth inviting all and sundry over for his experimental curries. One day something odd happened: Youth got up and Jaz wasn't there. He'd vanished, which was pretty strange, as Killing Joke had a single creeping up the charts and had just secured their first appearance on TOTP. I was suggested as a stand-in, but was ineligible as I wasn't a member of the Musicians' Union, so Jaz's place was instead filled by the Risk shop dummy.

Jaz eventually surfaced, in Reykjavik (of course!), having had some sort of vision about an island at the end of the world surviving the apocalypse. (It's worth bearing in mind that throughout the eighties we lived in the shadow of Armageddon. Ronnie, Maggie and their evil empires ensuring that all our dreams were mushroom cloud-shaped.)

It all turned out to be a long-winded way of getting Youth out of the band, as a few days later Geordie vanished as well, only to reappear in . . . Reykjavik! Youth sprang into action and decided to start a new band, Brilliant, with Big Paul. They had the novel but totally unworkable idea of getting two bass players and two drummers, plus singer, without such useless ephemera as guitarists or keyboard players – after all, it was them who'd got them into this mess in the first place.

I was recruited as 'lead' bassist, a post I accepted with great glee. A singer, Marcus Myers, was found, though not a second drummer, thank God, and we decamped to Cheltenham, where their soundman had an 8-track studio. We came up with something, but soon afterwards Big Paul was lured back to Killing Joke and I got involved with something else. I don't remember leaving or being kicked out of the band, but for years afterwards journalists used to quiz me about having been in Killing Joke.

Brilliant soldiered on, Youth recruiting one Jimmy Cauty, and when they got a record deal their A&R man was none other than Bill Drummond – thus are legends born.

I was very much feeling my way, for although a Londoner born and bred, I had no peer group from school and basically had to invent myself as I went along.

5

SYLVAIN SYLVAIN

The next gig to come my way was with the fabulous Sylvain Sylvain, ex-New York Dolls and therefore with excellent punk credentials. He'd decamped to London with his wife/drummer Rosie and their two children, feeling his past would serve him better here, and maybe he was right.

Rosie was Puerto Rican, and had a drum kit with timbales rather than tom toms, and came complete with Latin groove and sexiness, a kind of proto Sheila E. (She also had a fine way with Puerto Rican cooking, and I still salivate remembering her fried green beans with salt and lemon.)

They needed a sax player, so I drafted in my mate Simon Lloyd. We rehearsed in the attic of their Golders Green flat, and then ventured out to gig around London. Then something amazing happened, we got offered gigs in Paris and Stockholm. I couldn't believe it. TOURING ABROAD! This was it.

This wasn't touring as I would come to know it, more of a family excursion really. Sylvain and Rosie packed up the kids, the drums, and all the gear they could fit into their little sports car, leaving Simon and I to get the train/ferry and meet them in Paris.

The gig was incredible, I was gobsmacked by just how cool the audience looked. Chic punks, Algerians in zoot suits and African rockabillies with topiary quiffs; it was like a living Serge Clerc cartoon.

The return trip was something of a disaster though. I lost my ticket, and Simon had to go on ahead. Alone, carrying my bass, I managed to get the train to Calais and board the ferry without detection, which was fine apart from the fact I had no money, and no idea how I'd get back to London.

I must have been looking particularly disconsolate as a group of ten-year-old schoolgirls came and sat with me, asking what was wrong. I explained my predicament, and in what has got to be one of the sweet-est gestures I've ever known, one of them gave me ten pounds, a fortune for a little girl back then. Stupidly, it didn't occur to me to take her address, but if she's reading this I'll gladly refund it at today's value.

Stockholm was a different matter. We flew out, and stayed in the Grand Hotel. The gig was a big club, with a more purist audience, who didn't take so well to Rosie's salsa feel and our cover of Rick James's 'Superfreak'. The show was recorded for radio and during my bass solo you can clearly hear someone shout, 'Stop it, you're terrible!'

I was jumped on by a girl, which was fantastic until the next morn-ing, when she spent two hours on the hotel room phone, chatting away whatever money I'd made.

Having risked everything on the move to London, Sylvain came to the conclusion it wasn't really going to happen for him and Rosie. I think he was right, had he got there a couple of years earlier it may have been different.

He's still out there doing his thang, and long may he.

6

L ife continued to be pure slacker bliss in leafy Queen's Park with Andrew.

It was like living in some wonderful conservatoire, only with more pot, and it was here that I outgrew my childish rock aspirations and properly learned my instrument.

I had a wonderfully supportive girlfriend in Emma, the DHSS were paying my rent and life was idyllic, if spectacularly lazy. For example, when Andrew and I decided to give up smoking and sugar, it was decreed that we could still smoke pot. As a result, we got so stoned that all we could do was go and see Tron at the Odeon Marble Arch every day for a week. In the end we decided to go back on the tabs just so we'd get something done, but I'm proud to say I haven't taken sugar in my tea since.

My attempts with various bands had come to nothing. I'd even auditioned for Adam Ant when he disbanded the Ants. I didn't get the gig – no one did in the end – so when Andrew's brother spotted guitarist Marco Perroni outside his window the next day, he filled a paper plate with shaving foam, ran outside and 'pied' him.

One evening I got a call from a man called Ray Hearn. He managed a band, and wondered if I'd be interested in going on tour. I said of course. He'd be in town soon and we'd meet and talk then. He said he'd call back with more details after lunch.

'Lunch?' I said. 'Its half past ten at night!'

'I should explain,' he replied. 'Icehouse is an Australian band. I'm in Sydney.'

Australia didn't really exist back then for us, apart from flying-doctor jokes, Barry Humphries and cricket. Admittedly the official first punk single was '(I'm) Stranded', by The Saints, and there was AC/DC, but let's face it, I was way too cool to be listening to them. People only went down under if they weren't coming back. There was, of course, Split Enz, who'd had a great single out – 'I Got You' – but they were from New Zealand, which back then might as well have been middle earth.

Ray came to London with Iva Davies, who was, and still is, Icehouse, to all intents and purposes.

I don't remember having to audition. I think Iva took one look at me and thought, He'll do.

They'd had trouble finding a bassist in Oz, as the only ones around were of the neolithic rock variety, whereas in London we were all wrestling with The Funk, and in the post-new-romantic world, having an able bassist was actually quite important.[*]

It might also have had something to do with my rather flash Antony Price suit, which I'd got as part payment for the Funkapolitan tour. I do remember being on hand to try out loads of drummers at Hammersmith Studios with him, though, none of whom fulfilled his strict criteria. Just as well, I thought. I'd never come across session drummers before, and the ones we auditioned were far from inspiring.

Whilst in London, Iva also acquired a keyboard player, the delightful Andy Qunta, previously from Hazel O'Connor's band. His nickname was Roots, because of his surname – Kunta Kinte being the protagonist of said story – something I always found amusing as he's one of the whitest black men I've ever met, who although a truly talented keyboard

---

[*] After I'd been with Icehouse for about a year, an English bass player became the must-have accessory for any moderately successful Aussie band – God knows how many lucky pub-rock dossers found themselves lapping up Bondi surf thanks to me.

player, if left to his own devices would go off and make the most AOR music imaginable.

Another reason for Iva's trip was to shoot the video for what was to be Icehouse's one proper UK hit, 'Hey Little Girl'. It was directed by another Australian, the soon-to-be video legend Russell Mulcahy. Suddenly they were everywhere! I was invited to be an extra and it was shot in Sadlers Wells Theatre and featured a ballerina. There was a checklist of essential items for videos back then: ballerina, men fencing, bloke in evening dress, girl with painted body looking through quickly opened Venetian blinds, 1950s-style photographers popping flash-bulbs, horses . . . I could go on.

It was here I realized I was crossing a line. This was the music business. These people were making, or at least had access to, money. Iva carried a briefcase, which whilst impressive in itself, even more impressively seemed to contain nothing but a spare packet of Dunhill's. Spare cigarettes! Imagine being able to buy cigarettes you weren't even going to need for a while!

Ray told me to get taxis to my various appointments, give him the receipt and he'd reimburse me. I'd never seen anyone get a receipt for a cab and didn't know it was standard practice. I was too scared to ask for them and as a result spent my days swanning around London in taxis I couldn't afford, squandering my entire precious dole on them, probably giving Ray the completely inaccurate impression that I was a guy who wasn't after sponging anything.

He and Iva were staying at the Pembridge Court Hotel which, as it was in Notting Hill, reflected well on them, I thought, and Iva had taken quite a shine to me, so I found myself eating dinner with him in a different restaurant – of my choice! – almost every night.

The only demand I'd made for the tour was that they buy me a Trace Elliot bass amplifier, which was the amp at the time. (Youth had one, so I wanted one.) They looked like serious military hardware and were only available from Sound Wave in Romford.

I duly got the train out to collect it, carrying the heavy-duty flight case I'd ordered specially. My excitement upon gaining my prize was immeasurable, but I hadn't given any thought to how I'd lug it back to the station. I had no cash to get a cab and it was so heavy I could only carry it a few yards at a time. It was a journey of nigh on half a mile, raining, obviously, and I was literally sobbing by the time I got it onto the train.

Apart from the two European shows I'd done with Sylvain Sylvain, I hadn't been out of England since I'd hitch-hiked across America three years previously, so going to the other side of the world was quite daunting. However, going to the other side of the world to play in a successful band and get *paid* was quite a different matter. I'd been staggered when Ray told me what my wages would be: $300 (Australian, granted) a week for rehearsals, going up to $500 once we were on tour. It seemed an absolute fortune. I could afford to buy spare cigarettes and even drink vodka at home.

I sublet my room to Rudi, the sax player from X-Ray Specs and The Members, who was, come to think of it, another bloody Aussie, so I was rent free, but still had a home to come back to. As I was going to be away for three months, on my last night I splashed out on a trip to the theatre and dinner with Emma. Unfortunately, The Children Of 7 had managed to blag some studio time, so after dinner poor Emma had to sit around Gateway Studios till three in the morning while I laid down bass and piano parts. They weren't letting me go until they'd wrung every last note out of me, so they could crack on once I'd left the country. Standing on Ladbroke Grove in the freezing rain trying to find a cab with Emma, who was bored and completely knackered but still dutifully smiling, is one of my most enduring memories of the time.

The flight was going to be twenty-eight hours – more than a day. It was beyond comprehension to a neurotic like myself. Chrysalis Records sent a nice car to collect me, and en route to Heathrow I got it to stop at Z. Punjani, the newsagent and post office at the bottom of Ladbroke Grove, where I cashed what was to be my last ever dole cheque. Well, hopefully.

Luckily, as Australia was so far from pretty much anywhere, Qantas were well versed in the art of long-haul travel. If the cabin crew had a motto it would've been 'Get 'em drunk, keep 'em drunk.'

At least the flight meant I had plenty of time to get to know Andy, who, being a long-serving professional muso, was the ranking officer.

I slept through the Dubai stopover, drank my way out of the hangover at Singapore, had another nap and awoke just as the sun was coming up over central Australia. It was the most beautiful, barren, alien landscape I'd ever seen. It was also high time this flight was over.

When we landed at Sydney, that wasn't it as we then had to sit on the runway for an hour waiting for Ministry of Agriculture officials to come and spray the plane because us filthy foreign scum were all riddled with fruit fly, apparently. Smart move. You haven't even arrived and you already want to bring down the government.

We were to be met by Jane, from Icehouse's management company Dirty Pool, but she couldn't spot us when we arrived, despite me walking up and down the arrivals hall with a sign saying,

'GUY PRATT AND ANDY QUNTA FROM LONDON MEETING JANE FROM DIRTY POOL', and the fact that black people were about as common as hen's teeth in Sydney at the time.

We eventually made it to our flat on the famous Bondi Beach, which we were to share with the lighting designer, another Pom who was charmingly named Richard Burton. The moment I saw the traffic sign at the end of our street, which had been altered to read 'GIVE HEAD', I knew everything was going to be fine.

Sydney was a funny old place. There were rows of neat English suburban houses, temperance halls and Masonic lodges. But there seemed to be a revolution going on, as if everyone had suddenly woken up and said, 'Wait a minute, this place is paradise! We don't need this uptight colonial bullshit!' and gone off to start surf-wear companies, nightclubs and INXS.

On our first night we were taken to Kinselas, a nightclub in a converted morgue, where we saw the hysterical Los Trios Ringbarkus. If there's one thing Australia does well, it's laugh at itself. We went on to a party afterwards and a very nice girl insisted on coming home with me. I love that town.

My sexual exploits over the next few months were severely limited by two things: guilt, obviously (as I was still going out with Emma, but being on the other side of the world in a hit band . . .), but also herpes. I'd just heard about it and it had struck the fear of God into me. Once you had it, you had it for ever. AIDS was a couple of years away, and the notion of using condoms for anything other than birth control had yet to dawn on anyone. There was no such thing as safe sex, which turned the whole thing into a game of Russian roulette as far as I was concerned. I once got myself in such a state that I willed a condition into existence, went to the doctor, and explained to him how I had definitely, 100 per cent, without a shadow of a doubt contracted the dreaded herpes simplex virus. It took him twenty minutes to convince me I hadn't.

The next morning we went to the office to meet the rest of the band. The office was in a new complex deep in the heart of Sydney's smut district, King's Cross, just opposite was a shop proclaiming, 'Show her you care this Xmas, give her a dildo!'

Icehouse was originally a four-piece called Flowers whose first album, Icehouse, had been a phenomenal success. After threats of legal action by an American band called Flowers – they certainly took the world by storm didn't they? – they neatly changed their name to the title of the album, so there was no need to reprint the album sleeves. However, after their American tour, things had gone pear-shaped and the band had split, so Iva went and recorded a second album Primitive Man on his own. This was the record we were there to promote. Flowers had originally been a new wave covers band, Iva garnering the title 'The Punk Jukebox'. When they outgrew that circuit, he'd started writing, wearing his influences very much on his sleeve. You could hear bits of Bowie, Roxy, Talking Heads, Eno, Reed and Iggy Pop in many of Iva's songs, although he was obviously a brilliant and very accomplished songwriter.

Having failed to find a drummer in London, Iva re-enlisted the services of John Lloyd. I'm not sure why he left/was pushed, as he was a sterling chap and a perfectly good drummer. Bob Kretschmer was on lead guitar, having been poached from Melbourne art rock band ManMachine, not to mention his job as a make-up artist for ABC Television. He was really arty, trendy and pretentious and I loved him. He prayed to the gods of Scorsese, Eno, Truffaut, Pop and Reed. I needed someone to reintroduce me to the other elements of contemporary culture, as I was so ensconced in music everything else had ceased to exist for me. His brilliant use of effects and sonic textures was not only inspired but a bloody good way of hiding the fact that he couldn't actually play the guitar that well.

Then there was the other keyboard player, Michael Hoste. He was extraordinary. Fantastically intelligent, studious, with a degree in eurhythmics – no, not them, although I'm sure nowadays there's a college somewhere offering a two-year course on Annie 'n' Dave – bordering on genius perhaps. He was, however, utterly incapable of social niceties, empathy, or indeed most forms of human interaction, I really liked him, when he wasn't being overbearingly logical and cyborg-like.

Before rehearsals started in earnest, we each had a day with Iva at his home, the idea being that he could take us through any tricky bits as he'd played practically everything on the album himself. Already displaying the shoddy it'll-be-fine devil-may-care attitude that was to become my trademark, on the day I told Iva, 'Sod this, let's write a tune!' he went along with me, although I don't think he was that happy about it, but I've still got the cassette somewhere.

Our rehearsal studio was above a BMX bike shop in Bondi Junction, the country's youth currently being in the grip of BMX fever. The band were impressively equipped, so I used to stay behind to noodle on the various keyboards and guitars when everyone went to the pub at the end of the day. Ah the keenness of youth!

It was here I was to have my first brush with the Australian media. Donny Sutherland was the host of Saturday Superstore, the Oz equivalent of the English Saturday morning TV show. The new-look Icehouse was to be unveiled on his show, and Donny was due to come down and get an exclusive behind-the-scenes peek at our rehearsals. I was a little taken aback to discover that I was to be sat at Iva's side and be interviewed alongside him – the token new lad.

After Iva had waffled on a bit, Donny turned to me and asked, 'So, Guy, how d'ya come to be here in Sydney playing with one of our top bands?'

To which I said something along the lines of being transported to Botany Bay to serve a sentence with Icehouse for some crime or other. CUT! End of interview. Oops! I hadn't yet learned that, for all their self-deprecating humour, Aussies can still be a bit touchy about their history.

There was a great routine to those first few weeks. Andy and I would get the bus to work, come home via the pub, then dine at one of the many local restaurants. Then we'd either head home to watch some staggeringly foreign Australian TV, or into town to the Manzil Room, a filthy fleapit late-night rock club in the Cross, unless there was a gig on.

Gigs in Sydney were hilarious as they were all played in pubs, whether it was Simple Minds, Orchestral Manoeuvres or The Pretenders (when you're far from home, any British band or film seems great). I'd been told that Icehouse was going to tour pubs around the country before embarking on a proper concert-hall tour. Beggars can't be choosers, but I was a little disheartened, to say the least, that I'd spent over a day on a plane just to go and play pubs. The reason for my disappointment was that music pubs in Britain hold between twelve and forty-seven people and are where you go to see your boyfriend/girlfriend's brother's punk/goth band, and have lager poured down your back.

Music pubs in Australia, on the other hand, hold up to 5,000 people and are where you go to see bands that usually play in major sporting facilities.

The approach to going to see bands was different in Australia, too: in London people tended to go out and see a band, or go out and get twatted, or maybe go out, see a band and then go on and get twatted. Some people, of course, don't get twatted at all. In Australia, though, you'd combine the two, so most of the audience were so bladdered by the end of the gig that they were only capable of two possible responses: you were either the best thing they'd ever seen, anywhere ever in their whole life ever, and would you like to meet their sister? Or they had no idea you'd actually been on at all. I remember one occasion when a bloke got really upset with me because I wouldn't come down off the stage in the middle of a song to give him a light. I'd never seen such carnage –

every Friday was like New Year's Eve in Glasgow.

Australians have a reputation in England for being fearsome drinkers, but this wasn't borne out by what I saw. Closing time at most gigs was like the aftermath of Paschendale, as countless broken men were carried out wailing.

Our weekends were spent lying around Bondi Beach or perusing the markets (one of those annoying cultural things in Oz you go to the markets, not market). On Sundays I would write letters home, a hangover from my years at boarding school: girlfriend and mother every week, friends and relatives every two or four, depending on closeness and level of affection. What a nice well-brought-up young man! It seems unbelievably quaint, I know, but phone calls were *really* expensive and treated with a deference that's hard to explain now.

I spent most of my spare time with John, as after the first couple of weeks, Andy had all but disappeared, having met a girl of dubious profession who appeared to be bringing him great joy. I never met her, though, so maybe she didn't exist? Bob was off with his arty mates, which was fair enough, and Michael just didn't get out much.

We'd occasionally hook up with Iva, but these would be very much official dinners; he was busy after all. Iva lived in the then surprisingly downmarket suburb of Leichhardt with his schoolteacher girlfriend, Jill. She used to make him mark her pupils' homework, and I always loved the thought of some thirteen-year-old girl with his poster on her wall getting a 'could do better' from her idol.

John shared a flat in north Sydney with Paul Hester, who was then drummer for Deckchairs Overboard and later for Crowded House; he sadly hung himself in 2005. I remember ending up round there at 7 a.m. one Sunday, John and I chopping out coke and talking bollocks – this would have been a rare occasion as coke was rubbish and mind-numbingly expensive in Australia at the time. I recall that the video for John Cougar Mellencamp's 'Jack and Diane' was on the telly, it being an enormous hit at the time, though I hated it. Paul appeared in the doorway in his underpants, surveyed the scene and shouted, 'You thrill-seekers you!' Just a random memory.

I was very much out of step with Australia, musically speaking, as they liked their music butch or arty, but not, alas, funky. They liked rock, and at that time I liked anything but, although I was deeply influenced by Tony Levin's playing with Peter Gabriel. In retrospect there was a fantastic music scene, with tons of great bands. Split Enz, Hoodoo Gurus, Divinyls, Midnight Oil, Hunters and Collectors, and of course INXS (they were Oasis, we were Blur). I remember going to see them and thinking, that is one proper world-class rock star – and five very lucky Australians. Men at Work had just had a huge worldwide hit with 'Down Under' and Rose Tattoo returned bragging about how they'd conquered England. When Iva said that doesn't say much for England, I replied honestly, 'Sorry, Rose who?' Australian music was feeling confident, and all eyes were on Iva . . .

Our first professional engagement was on the TV show *Countdown* in Melbourne.

This was the big one, Australia's TOTP. It was presented and run by Molly Meldrum, a huge bushranger hat-wearing poof of a man who wielded undue influence over Australian music and would later try to wield undue influence over me.

I can't remember much about it, except that Chris Bailey from punk legends The Saints was on. Four years earlier I would have been in awe, but I now just thought he was sloppy and his band were rubbish.[*]

Molly introduced us with, 'This is Icehouse, remember The Beatles? Need I say more?' Meaning he expected every man, woman and child in Australia to buy the new record. Wahey.

Then the phoney war was over it was time to hit the beach.

Our tour was to begin on the Gold Coast in Queensland, at the Playroom to be precise.

I'd never been to the Costa del Sol, but even that couldn't have prepared me for the high-rise beer-and-chips nightmare that is this particular stretch of tropical Queensland.

Our hotel was just over the road from the gig, so we walked there. The streets were rammed with pissed holidaymakers, and as we crossed the road in the middle of this huge shouting, staggering throng, it became apparent that I was going to collide with a rather brassy-looking blonde. I decided to make the best of it and jokingly spread my arms, as if to embrace a long-lost lover, and got one of the best

[*]   I met him years later at Michael Hutchence's house in the south of France, and he did have the air of the desperate genius Irish poet about him, but Christ he could waffle.

put-downs of my entire life: 'Come off it, mate, you're not spunky and ya know it!'

I can't remember the gig, except that I was terrified before we went on and electrified the second we hit the stage. The first gig of any tour is always fantastic, for no matter how under- – or over- for that matter – rehearsed you are, how many bits of songs you're not sure of, or tricky technical things you have to pull off, the gods smile down and everything comes out right. The second or third night is where all the cracks show and you get found out. For years I had a terrible fear of things going wrong and would go into a blind panic if a keyboard went down, someone fluffed an intro or broke a string. It wasn't until I saw David Gilmour's state of absolute calm when Pink Floyd's sound and lights packed up in front of 75,000 people that I realized it was pointless worrying.

Post-gig we were all euphoric, partly because the Playroom had given us a few cases of their appalling own-brand champagne – or 'charmagne' as I believe the label said.

Everyone ended up in John's and my room, including a bevy of girls. We were too pissed and pleased with ourselves to know what to do with them, though, and I remember John sitting up against the wall shouting, 'GIRLYGIRLYGIRLLLLYYY!' which was as near as we got to any interaction.

The next couple of weeks were a mad blur as we travelled the country, playing pubs and RSLs. These were the Returned Servicemen's League clubs, which would comprise of a dance hall, where we'd play, a Chinese restaurant – I don't know why but it was always Chinese – a couple of bars, and huge halls full of 'pokies' (fruit machines).

We'd soundcheck in the afternoon while the pokies were in full flight as hundreds of old dears who'd risked life and limb for their country chucked their pensions into the ever-hungry beasts. At four o'clock every day there'd be a minute's silence for fallen comrades and I always found it slightly obscene that at about 58 seconds past the machines would roar back into life, the ageing warriors unable to resist their need to lose money.

Having two guitars and two keyboards gave the band a lush, full sound unlike anything I'd ever known. I was also singing backing vocals, something I hadn't done since Speedball, and which I love. Iva had written most of the bass parts and, given his classical training, they were harmonically complex and very satisfying to play. I even got to play keyboard bass on the song 'Icehouse'. A couple of the tunes were already quite funky, and several more were by the time I'd finished with them. On the new album, 'Mysterious Thing' had a full-on slap-fest bass part, played by the legendary Abraham Laboriel, which I had to wrestle with. Then there was our encore, the surprising 'Gimme Some Lovin'' by The Spencer Davis Group, in which I had a solo that was so manic from the off I usually found myself with nowhere to go after only a couple of bars. Iva kept telling me, 'Well, if you will start at the top of the mountain . . .'

We were playing to packed houses full of people who genuinely loved the band, and I couldn't have been happier. We went around the country a second time doing theatres, and it was at the Capitol in Sydney that I had my life's one pop-star moment. Halfway through the set, a gaggle of girls managed to get on stage and start running towards us. Aye, aye, I thought, Iva's going to cop it, this should be amusing. He braced himself for impact, but to his (and my) surprise, they ran straight past him and jumped on me. After the show I pretended to be totally freaked out by the incident, in the pathetic hope of getting a sympathy shag from a girl in the office who I had the hots for – it worked.

Then came New Zealand, which sticks in my mind as quite possibly the happiest three weeks of my life. The band had totally come together as a unit, thinking and acting as one; we were an unstoppable band of brothers. We went literally the length and breadth of the country, all the way down to Dunedin Town Hall, where we broke the house record set by The Beatles in 1964, possibly because we were the first band to play there since The Beatles in 1964.

John and I had a suite in the hotel, which was so rammed full of incredibly chintzy furniture and objets d'art that it was nigh on impossible to entertain more than a couple of people at a time. This was clearly no good, so we emptied the room out a bit, by throwing the excess furniture and bric-a-brac out of the window. Unsurprisingly, the hotel management were less than impressed with our rearranging tactics, and it took much pleading and promises of better behaviour to avoid ejection. Things calmed down, for about twenty minutes, after which, as an elderly couple bent down to sign the guest register, Bobby our monitor engineer was sent hurtling over their heads by the rest of the crew, coming to rest on top of the hotel's assistant manager. The funny thing is that rather than being a Primal Scream-type bunch of out-of-control rock-'n'roll animals, we were actually a pretty mild-mannered bunch of nice middle-class boys.

As everyone knows, New Zealand has more sheep than people, they are absolutely fucking everywhere, and pretty much everything, barring heavy machinery, is made of sheepskin. As a result, there were a couple of occasions where displeasure with, say, someone from the record company was registered by coaxing a sheep into their room and leaving it to be discovered at bedtime.

The gigs were fantastic, and we played mainly in theatres, opera houses or sporting arenas. It felt like the big time, apart from the fact that we were in New Zealand, obviously.

One time we had an overnight drive in a bus so cold that we were forced to tear off the inevitable sheepskin seat covers to try and stay warm. We spent most of the drive stuck behind a lorry full of pigs, bearing the immortal legend 'Pick your own porker!'. We also discovered the many uses of gaffer tape, such as sealing lift doors, attaching furniture to ceilings and, of course, people to furniture.

We visited the thermal spring town of Rotorua, one of those places that stinks of sulphur and is meant to be really good for you as long as you don't live there. We visited one of the many spas, where I was allocated my own personal hot tub room. You're not meant to stay in them for more than half an hour, but after a liquid lunch I was easily overcome by the mineral-rich fumes and my limp body was dragged out by the staff a couple of hours later and I was given strict instructions not to attempt anything strenuous, like moving, as it could easily engender a heart attack.

One day, in Hastings I think, practically everyone in the party received bad news. It was as if there was some terrible planetary alignment at work, or we were being punished for having too much fun. I got a letter from my girlfriend informing me that my grandmother had died, John had a similar family disaster and it transpired that The Angels, Dirty Pool's other big act, had had to flee the studio they were recording in when it caught fire, leaving their almost completed album's tapes to perish in the inferno. Needless to say, there was much drowning of sorrows in the hotel bar, and then the owner informed us that if we wished to continue drinking in our rooms, we would have to purchase bottles at shot prices, which worked out at around $100 a bottle. Well that was the last straw. There then commenced the most savage and unforgiving shaving foam, fire extinguisher and water fight I've ever witnessed or taken part in, leaving the entire hotel sodden, ruined, but with an unmistakable lemony freshness. We fled in the early hours, having to outrun the police, and were temporarily banned from staying in any other hotel in the country.

When we played our first arena, it was the first and last time I did a gig stoned – at least intentionally. Someone had given us some incredibly strong weed, and Bob and I shared a spliff just before going on. The gig seemed to go on for ever, and I remember thinking, I don't know how much longer I can keep playing, then realizing that we were only halfway through the second song.

We returned to Sydney triumphant and I had a couple of days off before flying home for Christmas. I was put up in the Coogee Bay Hotel, which was right by the sea, so I'd go out clubbing till six in the morning, come back and pass out on the beach, only to be woken a couple of hours later, drenched in sweat with the soles of my feet practically on fire. It wasn't particularly healthy, but I went home with a cracking tan.

7

ICEHOUSE EUROPE

I returned triumphant from my Antipodean adventures just in time for Christmas, which was lovely, what with being the prodigal son back in the bosom of family and friends, and having a few bob to play with to boot. Everyone got opals, boomerangs, corked hats and, inexplicably, desk calendars in the shape of Australia with coins of the realm stuck in them. I treated myself to a decent stereo and for some obscure reason an electric double bass, which has only just earned its keep as, for the first time ever in 2006, I played it on tour with Mr Gilmour.

The band was scheduled to come over in February as the album was being released in Europe, and we were booked to trawl around the continental TV-show circuit. Our promotional tour took in Scandinavia, Holland and Germany. For some reason we always got the grittier northern climes – the lands of harsh-sounding languages, mild mustard and fierce pornography – and more often than not in winter, too. I never got to visit the sexier parts of Europe with Icehouse. We went to France, but never Spain or Italy; I guess they felt Iva's moody Bowie/Ferryesque stylings wouldn't set Latin hearts aflame.

The beauty of promo jaunts, at least when you start doing them and the crushing ennui has yet to set in, is that the record company rather than the band are paying, so the hotels are better, you're endlessly wined and dined, flown rather than driven, and only ever have to mime the one song, so apart from reasons of decorum, you don't *have* to be sober at all. Well, the band don't anyway. For the actual artiste – Iva in this case

– it's a never-ending grind of life-sapping interviews, but hey, that's why he got the big bucks.

There was also often an attractive girl from the local record company in attendance, and in smaller countries she would represent several labels. At least a couple of the band would inevitably try it on with her, me included, which was usually pretty pointless, as within the last fortnight she'd probably had Duran Duran, Paul Young's band, Southern Death Cult, Culture Club, the Thompson Twins, Spandau Ballet, All About Eve, Billy Idol, China Crisis and Simple Minds all have a pop[*].

German TV shows were worth their weight in gold, as the band usually went on after the eighty-year-old bloke who tap-danced on top of a grand piano while hypnotizing budgies. And that's the highbrow end. They loved to build sets that in some indefinable way pertained to the song you were performing, so when we went there to promote our next single 'Street Café', you can imagine what the set was like. No, not a street café, rather a more evocative Turkish bath with a swimming pool full of cellophane, which also contained several dancers with Christmas trees on their heads. *Natürlich!*

At one show the make-up girl didn't have any make-up for black skin, but rather than telling Andy Qunta, our black keyboard player, this, she simply made him up as if he were white, which meant he did the show looking terribly ill.

'Hey Little Girl' was the single we released and it hit number 47 in the UK after Radio 1 playlisted it, which was very exciting, although none of us had any illusions about it going any further. Chrysalis in England weren't particularly supportive as the band was an American signing. Steve Dagger, Spandau Ballet's manager, later told me he had the same problem in reverse whenever they went to the States. So when Ray turned up at a TV show in Germany and announced that it had dived out of the chart, none of us were too upset. 'Just kidding, its number seventeen and we're booked for *Top of the Pops*.' *Top of the Pops*!

We rushed back to London for the show and I managed to smuggle a few friends into the studio, including the rather lovely Yvette, who was lodging at my house. Just as we were about to perform, the wardrobe

[*]   Occasionally you'd hear that so and so who plays for such and such had moved to Cologne, Malmo or Oporto, which I always took to mean they'd gone and married the local record company rep.

hamper she was sitting on collapsed, and that week's chart-toppers, Kajagoogoo, gallantly rushed to pull her out by the legs – or at least get a hold of her legs, which were very, very long. All except Limahl, of course.*

Back then you recorded TOTP on Wednesday and it went it out the next evening, so you put on the same clothes, found a pub with a telly and went and stood under it. Not really . . . There was a Musicians' Union ruling at the time, which meant you were supposed to re-record your song especially for the show. It was an open secret that nobody actually did. This was the eighties after all, when production and cutting-edge recording technology was king. Pop singles were mini sonic masterpieces, crafted in ludicrously expensive studios, often on several different continents, and months and fortunes were spent honing and perfecting them. The idea that you could just go into a studio and bang it out again in a couple of hours was plainly ludicrous.

Instead, you went into a recording studio, set up, ran through it a couple of times, then your manager would take the Musicians' Union rep to the pub, returning to find the song miraculously recorded and mixed to the exact same pristine standard as the record. Amazing! The only time I remember there being a hiccup was once doing a 'recording' for Stephen Duffy when the MU bloke said, 'I don't think you've recorded it at all!'

We did our fake recording at the Townhouse, then establishing itself as one of the world's premier studios. It was situated on Goldhawk Road in Shepherd's Bush, and by a happy coincidence Emma was flat-sitting for a friend who lived directly opposite. I still managed to be late, though, and the only excuse I could come up with was, 'The traffic was against me . . .'

After that it was up to Manchester for some kids' show, but all I can remember about that is that Tom Robinson was on, and Bob doled out a load of Valium, which meant we spent the evening crawling around the hotel bar in hysterics.

Next we went to Newcastle to do *The Tube*, which was a live rather

---

* In the bar afterwards I met Paul Gambaccini, who was extremely friendly and charming. After talking for about five minutes, I noticed a fuming Limahl, sulking petulantly behind him.

than mimed performance. (My granny told me later, 'You sounded much better on *Top of the Pops*.') Before we went on, we were told that wunderkind producer Trevor Horn would be watching, as he was interested in perhaps producing our next record. I don't think he ever got in touch, maybe because there was an unsigned band from Liverpool on the same show called Frankie Goes to Hollywood. So I guess we *do* know he was watching.

An incredibly enthusiastic elfin creature called Nick Laird Clowes introduced us and his intro went, 'They're double platinum in Australia, and you know how many records that means they've sold!' I had no idea what sales garnered you an Australian platinum award and I was in the band, so quite how *The Tube*'s audience were supposed to know I have no idea. He was not to be a TV presenter for very long.

Nick travelled back to London on the same train as us, and we established that we'd met at the Language Lab (I also remembered seeing him in a Beatle suit backstage at Earls Court when Pink Floyd performed *The Wall*). His band, Dream Academy, were still going and he asked if I'd be interested in doing some gigs with them. I said yes, unaware that this would have huge ramifications later on.

*

Next stop was Belgium, for a telly in Brussels, after which we went to the most glamorous party I'd ever been to. It was some EU bigwig's daughter's twenty-first, and we were told it was pretty smart, but for some reason none of us had packed suits, so Iva lent us each one of his Johnson's numbers – infuriating when you've got an Antony Price in the wardrobe at home – and spent the evening shepherding us around with the cry, 'Come on suits!' After that humiliation, even if I'm going to darkest Peru, nowadays I always pack a whistle.

The party was in an enormous hall, full of dry ice and lasers, thronged with beautiful, bright young things, girls sprayed silver and gold head to toe, and they were handing out *bottles* of pretty much everything at the bar. John lost his wallet outside the party, so Bob tried to get him to retrace his steps, saying, 'So where have you been?' John wandered along the pavement, pointing at various pools of vomit, saying, 'Well I've been here . . . and here . . . and here . . .'

John Lloyd and myself – 'The Suits'

The evening ended with Andy, John, Bob and myself, drunk out of our minds, breaking into the Atomeum. We climbed to the top, and after we'd had the obligatory aerobatic piss, I found a sign I thought was so incredibly amusing I had to own it. I tried to wrench it off using both my legs for leverage, until someone pointed out that were I to succeed I would promptly fall the 300 or so feet to the ground.

The band went home, or in Bob and John's case went on to Italy for a holiday, while I was asked to accompany Iva to Norway for some interviews. I was happy to do this as I was in no hurry to get back to my comparatively low temperature life in Queen's Park. Plus, with the band out of the way, things were ratcheted up a gear. It was business class flights, a limo at the airport and I got my own room at the Grand Hotel in Oslo, which I immediately took advantage of by pulling the label's press girl. Tacky I know, but I was only twenty, for God's sake.

We were interviewed by the state radio station, and despite our perception of Norway as all mixed saunas and porn, their remit was so strict that they could only play pop music for three hours a week, and music with drums was only allowed on Monday. No wonder Ibsen wrote like he did.

It was also nice to have some quiet time with Iva, as while we'd all been mucking about on tour, he was actually under a lot of pressure. Admittedly he was the one making the real money, too, but we were having a hell of a lot of fun off his back.

The joy of cocaine

Things went from good to better as we were asked to support David Bowie on his upcoming *Serious Moonlight* tour, which was the dog's bollocks, as he'd just released the most brilliant record and was quite rightfully towering, colossus-like, over the music world. I think the first time I heard 'Let's Dance' was the last time I experienced that full-on euphoric rush of childish pop fandom, with the possible exception of New Order's 'Regret'. It was just perfect. What was especially great was that it married all the things I loved – Chic, New York and epic production – with all the things Icehouse loved – Bowie, New York and arty, oblique lyrics.

As the new Icehouse album had been such a huge success down under, the band was asked to appear at the Countdown Music Awards in Melbourne. Iva very nobly said he wouldn't do it on his own, so I was flown 12,000 miles to mime one three-minute song, my condition being that they put me up in Sydney for a week afterwards – it was a long way, after all.

After the awards ceremony, we went out for dinner, then on to a club with none other than Mr Countdown himself, Molly Meldrum, who, it seemed to me, was a bit like Australia's Jonathan King – more than a bit, if you catch my drift. We were all invited back to his place, but I was the

The road

only one in his Rolls-Royce when it left the club at high speed. After an hour of nervously keeping my distance in Molly's Lawrence of Arabia-inspired shag palace, I practically burst into tears when the rest of the band finally showed up.

After all this excitement, I went home to London with nothing to do but twiddle my thumbs, excitedly awaiting the Bowie jaunt.

By the time the band returned to London, my home life had changed beyond all recognition as I'd split up with Emma and had to vacate Queen's Park. I then bumped into Tamsin de Roemer, a girl I'd met once when I was fourteen and was now infatuated with. She was living in a palatial apartment in Knightsbridge with two other models and an old friend of mine, Michael Weston. The first time I went to visit, everyone was lounging around drinking champagne and I naively asked what they were celebrating. Everyone just looked puzzled.

One of the girls was away modelling in Japan, leaving a room spare for a few months, and I was asked if I'd like to move in. I think my answer was more of a splutter than an actual yes. The flat was pure James Bond. No really, George Lazenby had actually lived there while making On Her Majesty's Secret Service. The steady stream of decadent and beautiful people traipsing in and out meant there was never a dull moment.

Whenever my friends came to visit, they'd ask what we were celebrating.

I, however, was still utterly dedicated to, and insecure about, my ability to play my instrument. I spent hours every day practising on my new ludicrously expensive hi-tech Steinberger bass, which I'd spunked my grandmother's modest inheritance on. A little headless stick made of carbon graphite, the Steinberger was to be my right arm for the next four years.

On the girl front, I was getting nowhere with Tamsin, and when Kate Dowson returned from modelling in Japan sooner than expected, within a couple of weeks I found myself cohabiting with her.

A regular visitor to the flat was Scott Crolla, who actually was getting somewhere with Tamsin. He was an up-and-coming fashion designer, who had an unbelievably groovy shop on Dover Street in Mayfair, with prices to match. We became firm friends, and my wardrobe exploded in a welter of chintz, silks and brocades, either for free or at mate's rates.

In less than six months I'd gone from being a Queen's Park pot-smoking second-hand-clothes-wearing slacker muso on the dole, to globe-trotting model-girlfriended Crolla-suited Knightsbridge-dwelling ponce in a hit band. I must have been unbearable.

*

Icehouse were only due to do a few dates with Bowie, so to make the trip up from Oz feasible, we were booked on to a huge travelling German festival called A Midsummer Night's Dream. It comprised the sort of line-up that only a German promoter could think up. By that I mean, whatever your taste in music, there was something for everyone . . . to hate. There was us, a couple of German heavy metal bands, Robert Palmer, Peter Tosh, John McLaughlin with Al Di Meola and Paco De Lucia, Mike Oldfield, all topped off by those monsters of rock, Crosby Stills and Nash. As we were to find out pretty much straight away, David Crosby was indeed a monster of rock, albeit of a more chemical nature.

We reconvened in London in May for brief rehearsals of our new, shortened festival/support set, before heading off for the German festivals. The band was sounding great by this point, and in retrospect I realize what a great place it was for me as a player. Iva gave me free rein to embellish as I wished, and if there's one thing a young bass player

wants, it's to embellish. This is how I came to develop the sort of mish-mash rock/disco style that served me so well later on.

It was thrilling arriving at our first festival; I'd been backstage at such things before, but never in a foreign country and never with a laminate – the access-all-areas pass you wear around your neck with the pathetic swagger of a prefect. Everywhere you looked there were bands, crew, photographers, girls, liggers and record-company types, and I'd never seen so many . . . mullets.

The backstage area was a maze of Winnebagos and Portacabins, and it was with mounting excitement that we were led to our dressing room, which turned out to be the smallest caravan I'd ever seen. So small, in fact, that we had to get changed two at a time very carefully since everything we touched seemed to be a folding bed. Humble as it was, our caravan did have one distinct advantage over the other supposedly more luxuriously appointed dressing rooms in that it was the only one with a fully functioning gas hob. David Crosby's crew were all over us like a cheap suit. In return for various perks, we got changed as fast as we could, vacating the caravan so Crosby could be led in with his enormous sack of cocaine and Merit chemistry set to do whatever it was he needed to do.

My overriding memory of the first show is standing at the side of the stage, listening in awe as Robert Palmer and his amazing band pumped out the most lean, muscular, tight electro-funk set I'd ever heard. Robert's shows were very serious affairs, with all sorts of segues (when you go straight from one song into another) and complex time changes to keep the band on their toes. It was about twenty minutes in before there was enough of a gap for him to even say hello to the audience. No one, with the possible exception of Prince, worked a band as hard as Bob. Apparently, if there was ever a day off on tour, he'd have them set up and play the hotel bar. Dude.

I can remember very little about our actual set. This is something of a recurring problem for me, as unless something out of the ordinary happens, I tend to recall little about time spent onstage. This may be because it's the one time I'm taking something seriously and concentrating, or perhaps it just doesn't register. Hopefully it's the former. I do recall that it was quite daunting playing to so many people, but a little disheartening being on in broad daylight. In fact, it was so early in the day that only the out-and-out nutters were stoned or drunk enough to abandon themselves to the music. I'm not saying that sober people can't make a good audience, they just tend to be quieter.

Another of the great revelations of festival life was catering: an enormous tent full of food that is free. My usual lunch would consist of, say, schnitzel, bratwurst – we were in Germany, remember – steak, curry, fish, lasagne, a couple of vegetarian options and three types of salad, nicely topped off with both of the soups. At our third show I'd just eaten all that and was on my way back for all the puddings when I noticed something of a commotion at the entrance. There was a big scrum and flashbulbs going off, and then I saw the cause. DAVID BLOODY BOWIE HAD JUST WALKED IN! And he was only with TONY BLOODY THOMPSON, his drummer, previously of Chic, and his bass player CARMINE ROJAS – who I'd never heard of, to be honest. I dropped my trifle in shock, though I managed to hold on to the roly poly, and stood there dumbstruck. For some unknown reason, Bowie noticed me, reached out and grabbed me, saying, 'I think you should be in this.' The cameras popped, and I still have the photo of me with Bowie, Tony and Carmine as it appeared in several German newspapers the next day. I'm wearing an incredibly bemused 'Who me?' expression, and unfortunately, as it was 1983, my girlfriend's bloody kimono.*

We were about halfway through our set when I got the second shock of the day. Turning round, I saw what appeared to be Robert Palmer at the side of the stage, checking me out. My heart jumped and I immediately got my head down and started paying proper attention to my instrument.

That night in the hotel bar there was a tap on my shoulder. I turned to find one Robert Palmer poking his head through the hotel bar fauna. 'You're the guy with the stick bass. You've got something going on; we need to talk.'

With that he was off, over to the restaurant where he was dining with David Bowie. I was gobsmacked, not least by his thick Yorkshire accent. I don't know how I thought he'd sound – Roger Mooreish perhaps – but certainly not like that. Having a great vantage point, I spent the next two hours pretending to chat up the girl from our record company while desperately trying to lip-read their conversation.

After dinner, he came to join me and I went into a complete panic. I'd never met one of my heroes in anything other than a fan/star situation before, and now one actually wanted to talk to me. A pretty drunk and chatty one at that. What do you say? Couldn't I have someone like Simon Le Bon to practise on for half an hour?

I, of course, did the only sensible thing and got into an argument with him.

Robert was thrilled to be on the same bill as David Crosby, and was greatly looking forward to meeting him, as being a singer he admired him, which was fair enough, but as for meeting him, well, seeing how long he'd been spending in our caravan, I didn't think he'd make particularly sparkling company. When I pointed this out to Robert, he took offence and started denouncing me as a young punk with no respect,

---

* Twenty-three years later, when Bowie made a guest appearance with Gilmour at the Albert Hall, I asked if he'd mind having his picture taken with me, in an attempt to recreate that shot. When I pulled the same face he said, 'I remember that photo.'

    'No you don't,' I laughed.

    'Yes, it was in Germany, 1983. I was wearing this scarf.'

    I was stunned, as I did seem to recall him wearing a scarf, so I went and dug out the picture, and d'you know what, he wasn't.

blah, blah. I tried to explain it was nothing of the sort, and that I loved *Déjà vu* as much as the next man, I just knew what sort of shape he was in. Robert was having none of it, though, and stormed off to bed, while I wallowed in a pit of misery, convinced I'd totally blown it with him.

Redemption was soon coming, though. The next morning, Robert was on his way to breakfast, suited and booted and no doubt with a spring in his step – he was impervious to hangovers – when who should he encounter, coming the other way on hands and knees in his underpants, but one David Crosby.

'Good morning!' said Robert.

Crosby looked up slowly and replied, 'Uh, mornin', man.'

During the next show, Robert pulled me to one side and said, 'Sorry, I see what you mean.'

Jeff 'The Buzzard' Aldridge, the Chrysalis's A&R heavyweight from New York who'd got Icehouse their worldwide deal, showed up in Germany at some point. One night, I ended up in a basement nightclub with him, completely legless, and he asked – though he wasn't making much sense by this point – if I could get him back to his hotel. I said of course, carried him upstairs, found a taxi, put him in it, took all the money out of his wallet and told the driver to take him to the airport.

He somehow sorted himself out, and next day asked me what the hell had happened. When I told him, he sportingly forgave me, although the next time I went out with him, which was in New York, I had to jump out of the cab and make a run for it, as he'd upset someone on the street so much they smashed the cab windows with an umbrella.

In 1983, you had to drive through a corridor of East Germany to reach beleaguered Berlin. We were travelling in three cars, and John Woodruffe, one of our managers, decided to make the border crossing that little bit more interesting by leaving his passport in one of the other cars. He was in the lead car, so his passport was at the other end of no man's land when he discovered it was missing. Remonstrating with an armed and twitchy adolescent East German border guard to let you get out of the car and walk back through the mines and tank traps is probably one of the least rewarding and profitable ways ever to spend time, especially with a hangover. With Michael Hoste helpfully shouting in English, 'Try to understand!' at the seventeen-year-old conscript whose knowledge of English began and ended with 'Papers!', things started to look less funny. Then, with enormous bravado, John simply got out of the car and, with God knows how many machine guns trained on him while threats were barked, walked back to West Germany, opened the boot of our car, rifled around a bit, got the offending document and walked back into the Soviet Bloc without being shot once. All front, these border guards.

The show was in a wood outside Berlin, in a hidden amphitheatre Hitler had built so he could go and listen to Wagner with 15,000 of his closest Nazi Party friends.

It was invisible until you were practically on top of it, half underground and full of spooky echoey tunnels. The CSN road crew took great delight in finding hiding places where they could sneak up and whisper 'Daaaavid' to freak out the narcotically paranoid Crosby.

That night in the hotel bar there was a commotion at about 11.45 as word spread of an enormous Heath Robinson-type clock made of glass tubes and balls that worked on displacement of water and was situated in a shopping centre round the corner – apparently midnight was really something as the whole thing emptied and reset itself. Various band members and crew made a frantic dash to find this wonder, and we all arrived just in time to see it do its thing. As I stood in rapt wonder, watching the bizarre contraption, I noticed I was standing next to Graham Nash.

'Christ,' he said. 'It looks like Crosby's hotel room!'

Later on, in a nightclub called the Zoo, Robert Palmer invited me to come out to his house in Nassau after the tour. Gulp.

*

No trip to Berlin was complete without crossing over Checkpoint Charlie into the dark, bleak East. We tried to go in by car, but the TV in soundman Andy Hilton's Range Rover was so obviously a CIA listening device/missile-guidance system that we were turned back and had to return on foot. You had to change money, the lowest limit being £12, before crossing over, which meant there were an awful lot of people changing exactly that amount, something border control was obviously used to as they had piles of bags filled with the equivalent in Ostmarks.

There was precious little to buy with them once you got into the East, except Communist flags and apparently excellent quality orchestral scores. We went to a restaurant and I recognized nothing on the menu, so relied on my old standby 'When in doubt, order the most expensive thing' – obviously this doesn't apply in places like Tokyo or Zermatt – which turned out to be a sausage and a piece of bread.

You weren't allowed to take money back into the West, so I gave it away to the children who hung around the border for that very reason. You were searched thoroughly to make sure you weren't smuggling any incredibly small East Germans out of the country – I can't think what else they could've been looking for – although one of the Simms brothers, Bowie's backing singers, got into a spot of bother with linguistics.

He'd bought a load of Communist posters, which were pulled out of his bag, and the official demanded to know what he intended to do with them. Having majored in German at college, he confidently replied, in German, 'I'm going to hang them on the wall!' meaning his den, bedroom, or perhaps fire station, as I seem to recall that they were also firemen, only instead of saying, 'Die Wand' (interior wall), he said, 'Die Mauer', which means outside wall, though within a hundred miles of Berlin its meaning was reserved for one wall in particular. Oops.

Our first show with Bowie was at Feyenoord Stadium in Rotterdam. It was enormous, although as we were the first of two support acts, UB40 being the other, it was far from full when we played.

When I returned five years later with Floyd, having played dozens of stadia by that time, I had the classic experience of someone revisiting a childhood haunt. 'Gosh, it all seemed so much bigger then . . .'

Having a top-ten single at the time meant we garnered polite applause for at least one song, but you're never really going to win over a crowd who are there for someone as iconic as Bowie, especially when it's still daylight and the main act's crew are making damn sure you're only a third as loud as the headliner. As a sort of revenge, when we played the Milton Keynes Bowl, we did 'Let's Dance' as our soundcheck number, so the audience that were there early enough had already heard it by the time Bowie went on. That's why I liked the fact that Pink Floyd dispensed with using a support band, even though it's nice to have the company.

Later that night, in the hotel bar, I somehow ended up sitting with

Tony Thompson, and probably annoyed him no end by desperately try-ing to winkle Chic stories out of him. I was surprised to learn that his hero was John Bonham – I shouldn't have been really as most drummers worship him – and he was much happier talking about Led Zeppelin than his time with the gods of disco. Then Bowie showed up and asked me how I'd found playing my first stadium – I nearly got into an argu-ment with him as we disagreed over the best way to play to huge crowds. What was with me? Give me an icon and I'll give you an argument! I never start arguments with ordinary people. Then, to top it all off, Carmine Rojas and Carlos Alomar, Bowie's wonderful guitarist, joined us and invited me out to a nightclub with them. Bloody hell!

When we arrived at a huge club somewhere in the city centre, all hell broke loose as we made our way to the roped-off table, as people des-perately clamoured to get a sight, or hold, of Bowie. Someone even got their hands around his throat and nearly throttled him at one point. I'd never experienced anything like it before and completely lost my rag, shouting, 'Leave him alone! Fuck off!' The rest of the band were far more relaxed, this seeming pretty much the norm. We finally made it to the table and a slightly ruffled David decided to leave anyway, having some-how located a companion for the evening during the scrum. Carlos laconically remarked, 'Going out with David is fine; you just gotta let him leave, then you can have a good time,' as if this was all in a day's work, though I found out years later that it was in fact anything but, and was still talked about in Bowie's circle as a one-time horrific experience.

*

Onwards to Edinburgh's Murrayfield Stadium, and as this was the first gig to be held there, and Icehouse were the opening act, we have the dis-tinction of being the first band ever to play live at Murrayfield. Admittedly the Thompson Twins went on about twenty minutes after us, but their stuff was practically all taped. We were pretty unimpressed with them in general; they seemed a bit divaish, getting a van to take them the fifty yards to the stage because of the very slight drizzle, while being massaged all the way.

I knew that the phrase 'See you, Jimmy' was a popular one locally, although I had no idea what it meant, assuming it was an innocuous greeting or 'Why aye, man'-type affirmation, which is why I bellowed it out to the crowd as we left the stage, blissfully unaware that I'd just asked 50,000 people outside for a fight. Luckily, no one took me up on it.

The hotel we were staying in had one of those old-fashioned Italian restaurants, complete with red-shirted waiters wielding enormous pepper grinders and a dessert trolley ('Would sir care for something off the trolley?' 'Yes please, I'll have the wheels.').

We convened for dinner, hooking up with some of Bowie's band on the way. John Woodruffe came down, and we asked if he'd care to join us, too, but he declined, rather smugly informing us that he was meeting Coco Schwab, Bowie's legendary PA/manager/general factotum.

The guys from Bowie's band were pretty sure that Coco had already gone out, so I decided to have a bit of fun. I called over one of the ancient waiters, and asked if he could do me a favour. Indicating John, sat on his own on the far side of the restaurant, I asked if he could take a note to him, without telling him whom it was from, and wait for the reply. I slipped him a tenner and he was off, bowing and scraping as he went.

The waiter got to John's table, handed him the note and dutifully stood waiting for the reply.

John, a bit puzzled, took the note and read it. It said, 'I am a lonely old Italian waiter. What are you doing when you've finished your meal?'

John looked from the note to the waiter and back again. Unfortunately we gave the game away a bit by collapsing in a convulsing heap of hysterics. Sure enough, John sent the waiter back with a reply: 'CUNT!' Lacking in nuance perhaps, but I got the general idea.

Playing Milton Keynes was a source of great pride, being the first major venue I ever played in England, even if we were on ludicrously early. The Tube did a special on it, in which they went around interviewing members of the audience. Out of 400,000 they spoke to about ten, including two girls who said, 'We're not here for Bowie at all, we're Icehouse fans!' What were the chances of that?

It was also the first of many shows I played that were promoted by the legendary Harvey Goldsmith. Every day at exactly the same time, before Bowie came on, he would go onstage and ask the crowd to stop pushing those at the front, relax and maybe even sit down. As a result, we went around doctoring the call sheets so they said:

      4.30: ICEHOUSE
      6.00: THE BEAT
      7.35: HARVEY
      8.00: DAVID BOWIE

I had one of those nice moments backstage when I was standing chatting to my mum, and a limo pulled up right next to us. The door opened and out got Bowie, with me practically barring his way. 'Hi, how are you?' He beamed, shook my hand, then introduced himself to my mum.

As usual, I can remember little about being onstage, except that on the first show, while playing 'Street Café' John kept shouting at me and trying to draw my attention to something. I thought I was doing something wrong, like speeding up, but that sounded wrong so I tried slowing down, again wrong, while John got more exasperated with me by the second. By now my tempo fluctuations had come to Iva's attention and he started giving me dirty looks. Christ! Eventually I realized John was just trying to point out that my girlfriend and flatmates were standing right in front of me, trying to catch my eye.

That was the end of our touring until after the next album *Sidewalk*, the first proper album I ever played bass on, although it could have been very different. In the course of researching this book I have discovered that Iva turned down support slots on both Bowie and Peter Gabriel's subsequent US tours so that he could write the score for Russell Mulcahy's first movie *Razorback*, which admittedly I did get to play on.

WHAT?! IVA! Why you . . . I oughta . . .

In the light of this discovery, I now feel much better about leaving the band to play for Bryan Ferry, but I do have an ARIA Hall of Fame award for my time with them, and they will always have a special place in my heart as being my first professional band and putting me on planes on a regular basis.

8

'I'm cultivating faulty syntax, I intend to be a legend'
Robert Palmer

After the Icehouse/Bowie tour, I called Robert to find out if he'd meant it when he'd invited me out to Nassau, and indeed if he'd given me his real phone number. It took some doing, as an American operator kept telling me that the country I was calling was unavailable. I'd never known a whole country be engaged before.

Eventually I got through, and Robert was as erudite and charming as I remembered, reiterating his invitation. I was in a complete flap, not knowing what you did or were expected to do when you visited a rock star, especially in such an intimidatingly glamorous location. I got out all the money I had in the world, which was a couple of grand, for the trip, as I had no idea what largesse would be expected. None, as it turned out.

Just before I left London, Robert's manager David Harper dropped off a load of Robert's favourite toiletries – Redken (cue terrible gags about London's mayor, then and now). It appeared that the downside of living in the Bahamas was the unavailability of European and American luxury goods, and decent dairy produce. I subsequently elected to take him a wheel of brie, some lime pickle and a bottle of Metaxa. Why, I don't know, but consumption of the latter sealed our friendship and resulted in a very dangerous midnight climb down his back wall to the rocky shore beneath.

The plan had been for me to stay in the new extension to his house, but builders are builders wherever you go, and when I arrived he and his family were living in a sea of concrete dust. Their house was right opposite Compass Point Studios so I was put up in one of the studio apartments and told not to worry about it. We then spent three weeks mucking about in his home studio. I'd never been to the Caribbean before, but we may as well have been in Slough for all the beach I got to see.

Robert and Sue Palmer's house was lovely, although surprisingly modest, being essentially the same size and layout as a London terraced house, except rather than having the usual 40-foot garden backing onto another garden or a railway line, it had a marble terrace backing onto the Caribbean Sea.

We'd get up around eleven, have brunch, then start working, and usually drinking. The Palmers' social life was bizarre, revolving mainly around gatherings associated with his kids' school at nearby ludicrously exclusive Lyford Cay, a community so up its own arse that they'd recently turned down Sean Connery's bid for a house, as he was a mere actor, rather than the dull super-rich banker-type they preferred.

One of his friends was a very sweet local musician, who'd gone to London a few years back to try his luck, but couldn't cope with autumn: the site of all the trees 'dying' making him so depressed he had to return. Emil Schult, from Kraftwerk, was another mate. He'd gone from one extreme of super hi-tech industrial music and design in Germany to living in the most remote practically uninhabited island of the Bahamas, and had only returned to the relative civilization of Nassau because his daughter had fallen ill. On the few occasions when Robert let me out of the studio, Emil would take me on tours of the island. I was so urban and naive that I was terrified walking through the lush rainforest, thinking venomous death lurked around every corner. The day Robert's son James casually brought a tarantula back from school I nearly had a heart attack.

Robert's enthusiasm for and sheer love of making music was astounding, and I was really moved by the fact that such an established older artist – he was thirty-three to my twenty – with a direct line to the finest players in the world still had an eye open for what he called 'a kid with a riff'.

He had a fancy schmancy new Sony two-track digital recorder, which as well as buttons saying 'Record', 'Play' and 'Stop' had all sorts of weird new commands like 'Go to Zero' 'Swing Search' and 'Item Delete'. One stoned evening we decided it would be fun to write a song called 'Go To Zero' and release it under the name 'Swing Search', i.e., a band looking for its swing and forced to forever start again.

As the evening wore on and we got more inebriated and easily amused at our own nonsensical creation, we got into a deep conversation – you know the sort – on the very nature of writing lyrics and what purpose they served. I mentioned that I loved personal lyrics of the type Pete Townshend wrote at the time, acknowledging that unless they contained some universal truth they were of no use to anyone who didn't have a specific interest in the person writing them. 'I for one,' I said, 'would be interested to hear Pete

Robert's home studio

say "I do this and I do that, and when it's cold I wear a hat" but that doesn't apply to the majority of listeners does it?'

Robert thought for a minute, then started giggling softly as he scribbled, and so the chorus of 'Go To Zero' was born:

> 'I do this an\d I do that, and when it's cold I wear a hat,
> It's mostly cold.
> It pays to advertise they say, I'll keep my hat on anyway,
> Or so I'm told.'

At one point in the song we needed an 'oo' rhyme and couldn't think of anything, until Robert suggested 'Adrian Belew', then lifted a guitar solo of his from an old demo and put it in. When The Power Station recorded the song, obviously they weren't going to use an Adrian Belew guitar solo, so Robert suggested they change the lyric to 'Andy Tayleroo'. Sadly they bottled it, and on the record it's 'Red, white, black and blue'.

By the time my stay was up, we had about ten hours of music, which Robert painstakingly edited down to five, then three, then one and a half, exactly a cassette full for me to take home, which of course I've lost.

Compass Point Studio was having a new mixing desk put in one of the studios, and the day before I was due to leave Robert was asked if he had anything he fancied recording, to help them check it out and make sure everything worked. We had 'Go To Zero', so he suggested I stick around for a couple more days so that we could go in and put it down. I'd had fairly limited recording experience at that time, so the prospect of going into the then legendary Compass Point with Robert was beyond exciting. Unfortunately we were in the land of 'Soon come' and three days later it was apparent that I was going to have to wait until Christmas before they'd figured out how to even plug the bloody thing in.

Sensing my disappointment, Robert booked – and paid for, I just didn't have that sort of money – one of the other studios, and in we went. There was a certain irony to the fact that if the Palmers needed a pint of milk, loaf of bread, etc., it was five miles to the nearest shop, however, if you needed to make a record, you only had to fall out of the front door. The song came out great, and a couple of months later, when Robert was asked to be involved in the Power Station project, he submitted it and on it went. He even snuck me over to New York to ghost the bass on the record, as he thought it had to be played 'just so'.

If mucking about with Robert Palmer had been intimidating, it had nothing on being summoned to the high temple of music that was The Power Station to play for my absolute god of the bass, Bernard Edwards. Especially as I was there to play the bass instead of the bloke in the band, interplanetary superstar John Taylor, or at least provide a colour-by-numbers track for him to copy.

As is customary for any majorly important, potentially life-changing experience, I went out of my way to make it as difficult as possible. In this instance it meant slamming a bathroom door on my right hand the night before I left for New York. My first and index fingers swelled up and playing was agony, but I wasn't going to tell them that, was I?

I arrived at the studio and was shown straight into the control room, to be greeted by the sight of my hero, Bernard, and engineer Jason Corsaro deep in concentration as a thunderous track boomed out of the speakers. Looking through the window into the studio, I saw Robert singing his heart out, surrounded by Fonzi Thornton and other members of the legendary 'Chic choir'.

The track stopped and Bernard pressed the talkback button to give instruction. I was agog, before he could say anything, Robert saw me, held up his tie and said, 'Hey! Guess where I got this?'

I had many things racing through my mind at that moment, but where Robert had obtained his tie, and indeed that he was wearing one at all, was not one of them.The fact that Robert had interrupted Bernard, forcing him to look at me in a 'who are you?' sort of way, was.

I shrugged.

'Crolla!' he shouted back.

Before I'd left for the Bahamas, I'd suggested to my mate, designer Scott Crolla, that if he were to furnish me with a few of his fabulous, and far from cheap, shirts, it might inspire Robert to visit his swanky Dover Street shop and furnish himself with Scott's wares on his next trip to London. It appeared the ruse had been a partial success. In exchange for my hundreds of pounds worth of Scott's finery, Robert had indeed gone to the shop – and bought a tie.

My memories of that trip to New York are a blur, as Robert dragged me from bar to club to movie premiere – Talking Heads 'Stop Making Sense' – to bar to party to restaurant to bar, with The Power Station at the epicentre. I remember ending up in some swanky uptown apartment with John Taylor as dawn broke, but I don't remember spilling my drink on the pile of coke on the table, a fact that John embarrassed me with in front of Pink Floyd some years later.

I do remember going in to do the bass track for 'Go To Zero', with Robert, Bernard and Jason present, and being pretty much paralysed with fear. I plugged in, and as Jason worked on getting a sound, I did my normal warm-up routine, which consisted of playing Chic bass lines – something I wouldn't have done had I thought about who was in the room.

'Shuddup, motherfucker, you makin' me feel old!' said Bernard, though luckily he was joking.

After the success of The Power Station album – amazingly, Robert claimed to have been unaware of who Bernard was before working with him – Robert engaged Bernard and Jason's services to produce the next Robert Palmer effort. Rather than use Robert's band, Bernard went to Compass Point with his shit-hot New York players in tow, Tony Thompson, Eddie Martinez (guitar) and Jeff Bova (keyboards). Obviously he didn't have any need for a bass player, so imagine my surprise when I got a call from Robert saying Bernard wanted me to come out and play on the record. Apparently he'd said, 'That English kid of yours, he's got a vibe, get him down.'

I asked Robert if I could speak to Bernard, as I was still very new to this level of recording and wanted to ask what I should bring with me, in terms of basses etc.

'Don't bring nothin',' he replied.

'Sorry?'

'Don't bring nothin', I'll take care o' you, OK?'

So I set off for Nassau with, well, nothing.

I arrived and went straight to the studio, to be greeted by the somewhat intimidating site of this very expensive band thrashing out 'I Didn't Mean To Turn You On'. Blimey.

I didn't start work till the next day, and luckily for my nerves it was just Robert, Bernard, Jason and I in the studio. I told Bernard that, per his instructions, I didn't have a bass to play, and perhaps he had a suggestion. He walked over to a bass case in the corner and opened it.

'I thought you might like to play this.'

He handed me a Musicman Stingray Bass.

'This isn't the one that . . . ?'

'Yup.'

It was the very bass that had given me goose bumps when I'd heard 'Everybody Dance', 'We Are Family', 'Good Times', etc.

Just being around Bernard was a constant masterclass. He used to take me off to the dining room and give me little lessons, showing me those magical Chic bass lines. He was full of great little tips like, 'Play whatever you want, go anywhere the fuck you want, just make sure you're back in time for 1!'

I'd recently bought, and loved, his solo album *Glad To Be Here* which I found quite by chance lurking unannounced in my local record shop. When I mentioned it, he got quite upset, telling me that despite selling untold millions of records for Atlantic, they had begrudgingly put it out without any promotion whatsoever. Record companies, doncha just love them.

Julio Iglesias came to record in one of the other studios for a few days, and we had great fun trying to persuade Robert to do a duet with him, my choice being 'The Girl Is Mine', but sadly it wasn't to be, partly because any room Julio was in was locked. Paranoid pillock.

If I'm honest it wasn't the greatest of times overall, though, as I didn't play particularly well and the other players hardly made me feel welcome. Which is fair enough, as you shouldn't really be in that sort of company unless you're really something special or at least have earned your stripes, which I hadn't. Admittedly, I did keep my head down and paid attention to everything that was going on. Just wanting to learn and get good enough to work at that level of brilliance, but I was only ever going to be 'the English kid' on that outing. For years afterwards I felt terribly insecure about sessions, which was only compounded by the fact that I'm usually in and out so quickly. When a producer or artist told me after only a few runs at a tune, 'Yup, that's it, we got it.' I always assumed that as soon as I walked out the door they were on the phone going, 'Hello, Pino, can you get down here . . .'[*]

Still, I got paid more than I ever had in my life up until then, and although I only ended up on one song on the album, 'Riptide', the credits do read, 'Bass: Bernard Edwards and Guy Pratt'. I've yet to beat that one.

On my twenty-first birthday I was at home in London with Kate, the rest of the gang and Karin, my sister, in the Knightsbridge flat. My birthday is traditionally a bit of a downer – at least when I used to spend it in London – as it's just after New Year, and everyone's always skint and partied out by then. The girls had baked me a cake and we cracked open our one bottle of champagne, then the doorbell rang, so I went down to see who it could be.

I opened the door to find Robert, Sue, their two children Jim and Jane, photographer Graham Hughes, and a couple of their friends bearing cases of wine. Robert then burst into a full-on Billie Holliday-style rendition of 'Happy Birthday' on the doorstep. It remains one of the most touching and brilliant moments of my life.

The last time I went to Nassau I had to dash around the world to make it in time for New Year's Eve. I was in Japan and Robert said to come over as Chris Blackwell was having a big party at his house up the road. Come to Chris Blackwell's New Year's Eve party in Nassau? Not half! I can't remember why, but I had to stop off in LA and New York en route, and it was a trying journey. I'd also made it my mission to take a kadomatsu, a Japanese New Year decoration consisting of bamboo and pine branches, to Nassau for them. I finally got there, and burst through

---

[*]   Pino Palladino, ludicrously brilliant bassist, currently playing for The Who.

the front door in a complete state, clutching the by-now-battered kadomatsu. Robert took it and gave me what appeared to be a full tumbler of water. I was parched and gratefully took a huge slug of . . . tequila, most of which ended up on the wall.

I had a bath, calmed down and we went up to the party. Blackwell's place was as impressive as you'd imagine, although there wasn't much of a party going on. It was basically a load of New York music lawyers, and Talking Heads' manager Gary Kurfirst. After an hour or so, we admitted the party was actually a bore, and by midnight we were back at Bob's watching *Scarface*. It was the first time I'd seen it, made all the more thrilling by the fact that Miami was only about thirty miles away.

I didn't work with Robert again for several years, by which time he'd had enormous hits, moved halfway up a mountain in Switzerland and got divorced.

Since he'd moved, Robert would record in Milan, and so in 1990 I spent April billeted in an extraordinary prisoner village-type development near the airport called Milano Due. It was also home to a major TV studio, where they filmed bizarre game shows that all seemed to involve housewives stripping, and was the property and brainchild of one Silvio Berlusconi.

It was just off the motorway, on the other side of which was a huge field that at night would fill with transvestite hookers. Enormous trucks used to veer hazardously off the road, causing hordes of strumpets to tramp as fast as they could through the mud in their heels, flashing their wares in the headlights. It was like *Carry On* meets *Mad Max*, and an endless source of entertainment.

We recorded at nearby Logic Studios, a wonderful state-of-the-art facility in the middle of an industrial estate, which as well as being fabulously designed and kitted out, featured a snack bar which did a killer panini and an espresso to knock your head off. Remember, this is in the pre-Starbucks world, when, pizza, curry and Nescafé was all you could expect in most English studios.

The album was *Don't Explain* and was a double effort, being half Robert's usual heavy rock, calypso, sophisticated funk and pop, mixed in with a few classic ballads, which is why I think it was produced by Teo Macero who, although being a legendary jazz producer and pioneer of electronic effects, was probably at a bit of a loss with the metal tunes.

Robert had a great fondness for good malt whisky, so I'd brought him a particularly fine vintage Macallun, although I didn't expect him to tear into it as soon as I got to the studio, which kind of made a mess of the session. Robert got so enthusiastic about the track we were cutting that he kept demanding to listen to the intro again, exhorting us with how great we all were, but preventing us from getting the rest of the song down.

Towards the end of the evening, he'd stopped making any sense at all and actually tried to describe the vocal effect he was after by saying, 'Nineties' bananas have a more intelligent kiss.' The frightening thing is I sort of knew what he meant.

We had a wonderful engineer, Pino Pischetola, who being Italian was without a doubt the best-dressed engineer I've ever worked with, although that's hardly a fiercely contested title. He had a fabulous way with English, 'The door, she is closing,' being one of my favourites. On one occasion he was doing a rough mix of a track, and in order to balance it properly he was listening incredibly quietly on the small speakers, forcing him and us to pay proper attention.

Suddenly Mary burst in, arms full of tequila, limes, and a blender.

'Whoa! Mary's margarita time!' exclaimed Robert excitedly. Delighted as we all were at the prospect of her fabulous cocktails, poor Pino nearly lost his mind as Mary set up her blender on the desk, right next to the speakers, while he strained to pick up every subtle nuance of the mix, accompanied by,'GGGGWWWWRRRMMMMMWWWWR-RRGGGHHHHMMMMMMWWWWWMMMMAAAAGGGG-WWWWWHHHHHHHSKLASHSKLOSHFFFFDDDDRRRPPPPPPPPP!'

My girlfriend at the time, Susie Newall, came out when I'd finished recording, which was nice as it meant I got invited to dinner with Robert again. You didn't get asked out without a date, as he said he didn't like the way men behaved when unaccompanied. I know what he meant, but it was a bit sad being stuck in that godforsaken future-world complex on the outskirts of town for weeks on end with just the other musicians for company, lovely though they were.

Robert could be very critical of my girlfriends, which I took to be paternal concern, although it could just have been rudeness, so when Gala and I set up shop a couple of years later, I really wanted her to meet him. We went to Lugano for a long weekend, and at about six o'clock on the first morning, with the girls tucked up in bed, Bob and I sat amongst

Gala and Robert – 'Luxury Siege'

the debris of his kitchen table. We'd all been trying to invent cocktails for the last few hours, and the last efforts had all turned out dark grey or black. I asked him what he thought of Gala, and he laughed and said, 'Oh man, she's supersonic!'

We would go and stay with him and Mary, his unceasingly attentive girlfriend. These were fabulously debauched times, although they were never keen on you leaving the house, figuring they had all the gourmet food, cocktail ingredients, narcotics, firearms, films and musical equipment anyone could ever wish for. This was true, but the area around Lugano is stunningly beautiful and one did occasionally hanker for a peek. It was a situation Gala and I referred to as 'luxury siege'.

I used to get sporadic calls from Robert over the next few years, as he usually asked me to be in the band if he had a TV show to do in England. On one occasion we did *Wogan* while it was being guest presented by Gloria Hunniford, as Wogan was out getting his wig fixed or something. After we'd performed our song, she gave the final address of the show, saying who was appearing next time, blah, blah, and I noticed that I was plainly visible behind her left shoulder. I took to mouthing her autocue, copying everything she said, but a second or so before she said it, thus blowing the illusion that she was ad libbing. Afterwards, I was severely chastised by the floor manager, which Robert thoroughly enjoyed. The next time I did *Wogan* was with Kirsty MacColl, and I actually went one better, as Roland Rivron and I managed to get ourselves banned from the green room for life, for doing something involving Giles Brandreth's jumper, although we were both so pissed that neither of us can remember what it was. Luckily for us, the BBC shortly moved out of the Shepherd's Bush Theatre, as the ban only applied to that building.

Robert was an absolute one-off, and for all his apparent preoccupation with style, it was just that, style.

Because he always lived off the circuit, Robert was never co-opted by fashion, either sartorially or musically, and he took everything at face value. He once described his love of all things Italian to me as, 'They compare themselves to nobody, whether it's making a pair of shoes or a Bloody Mary. They just do their best.' Which always struck me as a pretty fair description of him. Robert wasn't interested in whatever styles or players were fashionable at the time, he just did what he wanted with whoever he wanted, whenever he felt like it. When he hooked up with Gary Numan in 1980, I'm sure he didn't have to join a very long queue. He was working with Lee 'Scratch' Perry long before everyone else got on the plane to Kingston and was experimenting with African forms when Peter Gabriel was still writing about Burgermeisters.

He was a total dude, and I miss him.

9

DREAM ACADEMY

My first rehearsals with Dream Academy were in Nick Laird-Clowes's bedroom in his parents' house in genteel Campden Hill Road. This was infinitely preferable to the sweaty fleapits most fledgling bands worked in, if quite comically cramped.

I loved Nick's songs; they were wistful, occasionally protesty and full of sixties idealism, not to mention very nice tunes. He knew David Gilmour, who'd produced some demos for them, although sadly none that I got to play on. The other members were Gilbert Gabriel on keyboards and the beautiful Kate St John on oboe, sax, etc., who went on to become first Nick's and then my girlfriend years later. She never came to these early rehearsals, which was probably just as well, as there would have been nowhere for her to sit. There were various other girl singers, cellists and what have you who came and went, so I was never quite sure who was actually in the band early on.

We did a few gigs at the Titanic, the posh trendy hip-hop club off Berkeley Square that was a continuation of the old Language Lab, which was handy as I was usually there with my bass anyway, as I used to go and play along with the DJs. The things you do to avoid queuing and paying, honestly. At one of them, a welding mask-clad Tom Dixon banged car parts on 'Life In A Northern Town' and cellist Adam Peters was snapped up to score 'Ocean Rain' for Echo & The Bunnymen. It was all go down there. I drafted in my mate the sadly no more Jake Le Mesurier to play drums. He was one of the funniest people ever to draw breath and a brilliant drummer; legend has it he taught Stewart Copeland how to play reggae.

On 30 April 1984, Nick called to tell me he'd been asked to support David Gilmour at the Birmingham Odeon. The booked support band, TV Personalities, had been amusing David by doing 'Arnold Layne' in their set, but when they played 'I Know Where Syd Barrett Lives' it was understandably a bit much, so they were sent home. I was thrilled at the news, until Nick told me that we weren't doing it as none of the girls were available, or fancied it, or were doing their hair or something. It was a good job he called, because after five minutes of me shouting at him, we were doing it.

We had to meet at the Kensington Hilton at 2 p.m. the next afternoon, to travel up with David's band on their tour bus. Cool! I invited Tamsin de Roemer to come with me, and maybe take some pics, as she was quite a keen photographer. In that wonderfully considerate way girls have, she said she'd love to and perhaps I could meet her at 1 p.m. for lunch at the RAC Club first? But of course!

As soon as I put the phone down, I realized we'd have about sixteen seconds to have lunch before tearing all the way across town to be at the hotel in time. Not only that, but if I was going to the RAC Club I'd have to wear a fucking tie. Not perhaps as rock'n'roll as I'd envisioned. Naturally she'd gone out and was uncontactable for the rest of the day, so there was no chance of suggesting we meet instead at the pub next to the hotel at opening time, to make absolutely, positively, definitely sure we weren't late. We made it to the bus – just – after I suggested that perhaps lunch was absolutely out of the question.

The drive up was uneventful, as David, and indeed his rhythm guitarist Mick Ralphs from Bad Company, weren't on board, having for some bizarre reason decided to do the trip in David's Ferrari.

David's band couldn't have been more helpful, which was just as well as we'd come with hardly any equipment and were having to perform without drums, let alone oboes or cellos. If they hadn't let us use their amps we'd have been really stuck. The gig hadn't sold particularly well, and was practically empty when we played. One song, 'Moving On', had a couple of very pronounced bass plucks in the chorus, and every time I did one, what little audience there was would cheer sarcastically – although Nick swears it was my brilliance, dear man.

When we came off, Nick grabbed me and said, 'David is just dying to meet you!' He'd heard my playing on some demos and had apparently commented to Nick that he thought I was quite good. The ever-effusive Nick had of course translated this as, 'God, he thinks you're just incredible!' Nick then proudly presented me to David and left us to chat. I couldn't muster a single word, and we just stood there until it became so unbearable one of us had to walk away.

The demos I played on ended up being used on the album, which manager Tarquin Gotch sneakily tried to get out of paying me for, even though we'd become friends. Managers, eh?

After the success of 'Life In A Northern Town' everything changed. Nick even moved out of his parents' house. When it was time to make the second album, Hugh Padgham was enlisted to produce it. Then, as now, he's one of the top producers in the world.[*] I was thrilled about working with him, until I was informed that, actually, he was going to use Peter Gabriel's band: Jerry Marotta on drums, Larry Fast on keyboards and Tony Levin on bass. Tony Levin! Christ! I couldn't compete with that, he was an absolute god. It would have been absurd for me to suggest that, though puny and unknown in comparison, not to mention nowhere near as good, I deserved to play on the record because of the time and dedication I'd put into the band. So I did just that, and amazingly Nick agreed, due partly to the support I got from Emma Dixon, now Kamen, who worked in Tarquin's office. We'd never even met, but had developed something of a phone relationship and she remains one of my bestest friends.

Lo and behold I got my gig back at the expense of Tony Levin. Not that I feel bad about that, as I'm sure he just took one of the seventy-nine other jobs he doubtless had on offer at the time. Ironically, a few years later I would get a shot at the Pink Floyd chair simply because he wasn't available. Where would I be without him? Cheers, Tony!

[*] The last number one I played on was a McFly song that he produced.

10

BUDAPEST

On my last tour of Europe with Icehouse, we played our first head-lining stadium gig! In Budapest! Except we didn't, because we weren't actually headlining, we were co-headlining, and we weren't actually playing, we were miming. To over 10,000 paying people. Not good. We didn't discover any of this until we got there, which understandably caused a bit of a stir with our management, not to mention our co-headliners, Spandau Ballet.

We got in the day before, probably from somewhere in Germany, as that was where we did most of our touring – we were actually rather large there.

Hungary was, of course, a grey, bleak Communist country at the time. Even the immigration form demanded, if arriving by car, that you tick what colour the car was, one option being 'drab'.

The Inter-Continental Hotel, where we were billeted, was a glittering island of western European decadence slap bang in the middle of all that grey. I was sharing a room with John – if you *are* headlining a stadium, you really shouldn't still be sharing rooms – and we were at first amused, then a bit put out, and eventually exasperated by the amount of attention we got. Pop groups, especially Australian ones, were a pretty rare commodity in Budapest back then, which meant the hotel staff were quite keen to get a look at us. This meant that a chambermaid brought us towels, even though we had them already, then another changed our already changed beds, while another checked the minibar, and so on. Then *two* of them came in to give us some paprika. It was the local speciality, granted, but its uses in a hotel room are severely limited. Then someone came to check the towels and give us some more paprika, next up was paprika and an ashtray, then paprika and slippers, until eventually we had to leave the room with half the hotel staff still in it.

The first thing that struck me about Budapest was how old it all seemed. Being a Londoner, I am of course used to being around what our American cousins like to call 'old shit' but this was old, old. Like really old, spooky old, vampire-Gothic gargoyles-coming-to-life old. There were very few cars, and toothless old hags swept the vast ancient boulevards with fucking broomsticks. I kid you not.

I also got to see a side of the place I could've really done without, as I got a proper, head-splitting, I-want-to-die earache. This was probably the direct result of our terrifying Malev Air flight; the only plane I've ever been on that was full of flies and flown so badly it felt like the pilot had an accelerator pedal.

Usually a doctor would come to your room, but this being Hungary they just didn't have that kind of infrastructure. Besides, he wouldn't have been able to do much squeezed in amongst the hundred or so cleaning staff currently in residence.

I was therefore given the address of a hospital and set off in the terrifying old jalopy that passed for a cab. The drive was at breakneck speed, for no reason I can think of other than that it was quite possibly Budapest's only taxi and he had other jobs to do.

The hospital I arrived at seemed more like a mental institution from a movie set in the Victorian age than somewhere for the treatment of simple earache. It was nestled amongst beautiful though decrepit gardens, where starched white nurses led dressing-gowned people in various states of madness past the neglected flowerbeds. I was taken down possibly the longest corridor I have ever walked in my life, past rooms full of implements that wouldn't have been out of place in the *Saw* films.

The doctor sat in an unnecessarily huge room, as if things weren't Kafkaesque enough, and helpfully didn't speak a word of English. After much burning of sage, three exorcisms and a botched attempt at sawing my leg off, I finally convinced him to look in my ear. He gave it a cursory glance, wrote out a prescription and sent me on my way. I was more than happy to leave, especially once they'd got the leeches off.

I wandered the streets, still in agony mind, asking directions from the dead-eyed zombies that populated the place, who would point vaguely and shuffle off to continue nursing their broken dreams. I eventually found the pharmacy, a shop, again pointlessly huge, with a wooden wall with a slit in it, through which you handed your prescription. When my drugs came, someone actually had to come through the door at the side, as I had so many pills they wouldn't fit through the slit. It was a veritable mountain of pharmacopoeia, at least fifty each of four different medications, all with helpful use and dosage instructions in Hungarian. I figured this must be how they kept the populace so docile: whatever your ailment, they just got you completely out of it. God knows what they would've given me if I'd been *seriously* ill.

I went back to the hotel and took two of each, which seemed the most reasonable thing to do. My earache certainly went, but a lot of other things went with it.

Spandau were coming in from Hong Kong – of course! – where they'd been filming their latest video epic, which naturally involved flying around in helicopters, meeting local dignitaries and miming their new single in an empty nightclub. Quite why they couldn't have done it in Basildon is a mystery.

I was quite excited at the prospect of meeting them all. I already knew Jon Keeble a bit through connections that are of no interest to you, dear reader, but I was particularly looking forwards to meeting their manager, Steve Dagger. He'd managed to garner a reputation as a bit of a maverick mastermind, in the Loog Oldham/Kit Lambert mould, and seemed at least as glamorous and interesting as his charges. He didn't disappoint, being one of the finest music-biz storytellers I've ever met, the funniest thing being that half his stories were about *his* band.

Spandau had become a big-time pop group since I'd last looked, which was a bit of a disappointment, to be honest. I was expecting a bunch of Baudelaire-quoting, Gitane-wafting, smoking-jacket-wearing aesthetes, with jewel-encrusted tortoises that followed wherever they went. What I got was a bunch of norf London lads who'd had a 'right result, as it goes!'. That's because I'd been reading interviews with Gary, who was, and thankfully still is, closer to the former.

After we'd dealt with the tiresome matter of miming to our somewhat underwhelmed audience – they were expecting a gig, not a TV show – it was time to get on with the more serious task of getting to know each other, through the medium of drink. The one good thing about Communist countries was that, as satellites of Moscow, they all had plentiful supplies of terrifyingly strong vodka.

There was some sort of gala reception happening at the hotel, which was being addressed by Christopher Reeve. We didn't realize we were invited until it was pretty much over, although I seem to remember going and heckling the speeches with someone, perhaps Gary.

I thought the best way to make friends would be to hand out my various painkillers, tranquillizers and mind-control drugs. I was certainly never going to get through them on my own, and this seemed like a good way to find out what they *really* did. As everyone had had a few drinks by this point, they were more than willing to take part in my experiment, which soon had John Keeble throwing up in an ashtray while trying to get into the lift. Marvellous!

Tony Hadley confided that he was concerned about his weight to myself and a member of our road crew, who claimed to be a fully trained doctor. This guy convinced Tony that he should spend a week eating nothing but hard-boiled eggs, adding that he'd definitely shed an awful lot of pounds, but he 'might have a bit of trouble walking up stairs' by the end. Whether Tony took him up on it I'll never know.

The evening ended up with Andy Qunta and I in a room with Gary and Martin Kemp, who along with Tony Hadley were trying to comfort their recently spurned wardrobe guy. There was much sobbing and consoling going on, and I was feeling distinctly strange by this stage. I asked the brothers about Hong Kong, and Gary immediately started expounding on the exciting cultural aspects of the place. He told me how you could see right into people's apartments when you fly in and out. Martin joined in with, 'Yeah, and they're filthy.'

The conversation then went something like this:

'But, Mart, you gotta understand that these people have been forced into what is a completely unnatural way of life for them.'

'Yeah, but those flats, they're just dirty.'

'Yeah, but these people come from a tradition and a culture that's all about land and ancestry and the village, so this is all totally alien to them.'

'No, Gary, those places were just filthy.'

'No, but Mart, these people are torn away from everything they know, and forced to work in sweatshops in a completely unnatural capitalist society, and besides, they haven't got any money!'

This was too much for Martin: 'Our Aunt Lil never 'ad any money, but at least she kept her curtains clean!'

A few years ago, Gary married the delightful Lauren, and Gala and I attended the wedding. It was a lovely day, with lots of old faces. I hadn't seen Martin for a good while, and when I spotted him chatting to a kind-looking older lady, I went over to say hello.

'All right, Guy, have you met my Aunt Lil?' Martin asked.

I nearly fainted. She was real. Flesh and blood. I'd spent years wondering if I'd heard him right, or if, under the influence of severe Hungarian medication, I'd just made the whole thing up. The poor dear was probably very confused as to why I was so utterly and totally genuinely thrilled to meet her, but believe me, I was.

11

THE SHOW MUST GO ON

Although there are *way* too many chemical/alcohol/narcotics-related stories in this book for my liking – not to mention my poor mum. Sorry, Mum, I know you did your best – there is one that needs telling for the sheer primal professionalism it reveals.

At the time of my last Australian tour with Icehouse, the sheen had worn off a bit and I was frankly very unhappy. I don't want to lay the blame for this at Iva's door, as there were personal reasons as well, although I can't recall what they were.

We were playing in northern New South Wales, near to Mullumbimby, which is a very hippified part of the world where they grow a mind-bendingly strong strain of grass called Mullumbimby Madness and everyone lives in eco domes and swaps wives every three years. Well, maybe not everyone, but you get my drift. The point being that most people you encounter, befriend or just strike up a conversation with are certifiably insane.

After our show, I was drowning my gloom in tequila at a nightclub when a nice enough-seeming girl engaged me in conversation. It turned out that she was a nurse, which is usually the sign of a good-hearted and compassionate soul. Not quite, as this being Mullumbimby she was of course mad, having become a nurse for the sole purpose of getting the keys to the pill cupboard, an objective she had fulfilled. She sensed I was a little on edge, and on opening her handbag, which was a veritable treasure trove of pills, she produced something she was sure would make me feel better. Having had more than my fair share of Mexico's finest, I thanked her and took a couple. Two minutes later nothing had happened, so I took a couple more, and then a couple more. I ended up taking a potentially lethal dose of twelve tablets of an unbelievably strong barbiturate used for the treatment of seriously withdrawing heroin addicts. I didn't know this at the time, but they seemed to have little effect until I passed out cold.

As I wasn't turning blue, it was thought best just to get me back to the hotel and let me sleep it off. The next morning I was still sleeping it off when it was time to leave, so my bags were packed for me and I was carried onto the bus. When we arrived at the next hotel I was still sleeping it off, so I was carried to my room. When it was time to go to the gig for a soundcheck, I was still sleeping it off, so I was carried onto the bus again, then carried into the gig and laid out in the dressing room. I was still sleeping it off about forty minutes before we were due onstage, by which time the band were becoming a tad concerned. Apparently I suddenly sat bolt upright, got up and changed into my stage gear. We did the gig, which by all accounts was a stormer, and at the end I walked offstage and stood in the wings, just out of sight of the audience, until the band came back on for the encore. We did an encore, apparently very good, and walked off. As soon as I was out of sight of the audience I went down like a sack of King Edwards and continued sleeping it off for another nine hours. When I came down for breakfast all bright and breezy the next morning, I was somewhat puzzled as to why everyone was shaking their heads and tutting – and why we seemed to have skipped a town on our itinerary.

12

EIGHTIES VIDEO

Ah, the eighties video. What fond memories I have of those oeuvre-defining mini-masterpieces, those artistic gems of subtle nuance and inner meaning, those untrammelled steaming great heaps of pointless self-aggrandizing arse. They presented a magical world where people turn sharply towards rapidly opened Venetian blinds, gaggles of fifties news photographers pop flashbulbs at nothing, insurrectionists hand out pamphlets, camels sway across deserts as winged demons attack people who carry on bravely, er, miming a pop song.

Granted, there were a few good ones, say about twenty out of maybe 17,000.

I was in a fair few myself, doing ridiculous things like pretending to play the cello in 'Windswept' by Bryan Ferry or being a short-sighted fantasizing schoolboy in 'School's Out' by Krokus – only because the producer was a friend, honest – and running around London dressed as a giant mobile phone, which I'm embarrassed to say was as recent as 1999. I even got to do the moody sitting-around-a-table-in-suits, turn-to-look-menacingly-at-the-drummer-then-stand-up-and-slam-your-fist-on-the-table role, a classic eighties textbook job for Icehouse's 'I Don't Believe Anymore'.

As it was about the end of a relationship, it naturally featured Iva singing the song in a surreal kitchen while a model screamed at him, causing the taps to blow off, the walls to collapse, the fridge and cooker to explode and, of course, the crockery to fly through the air. Because if it didn't, you see, the audience might not have realized they were

having a row. Genius! The funny thing was, as these pretentious little vignettes were primarily to be shown on children's television, there were strict rules governing what you could show. So rather than the terrifying *Carrie*-style tableau the director had in mind, the crockery had to move slowly through the air so as not to appear too violent. This meant that rather than looking earnest in the middle of a supernatural maelstrom, poor old Iva was sat at the table while cups and saucers slowly wobbled past him on bits of string, like an Ed Wood movie.

The call time on videos was always a real pisser as well. Apart from the odd flight, it was pretty much the only aspect of my work that required me to be anywhere at 8 a.m.

It's fine getting up early if your plane is leaving at 10 a.m. – there's an undisputable logic to that – but when experience has taught you, repeatedly, constantly, continually, time after time after time that there is absolutely no way that you'll be required to do anything until 4 p.m., it becomes a tad tiresome.

When you start recording an album, the band, apart from the

drummer, aren't usually expected to arrive until sometime in the afternoon of the first day, as setting up the drums and getting the drum sounds right will take a good few hours. Video production people, however, despite evidence to the contrary, will always insist you get there early, promising that you absolutely, definitely will be needed at call time. This has never happened. Once. Ever. You muppets.

I once bet an assistant director £50,000 that I would be languishing in the dressing room for at least three hours before being required to go and shuffle around a bit holding a bass, and guess what, she wouldn't take it. Amazing!

Sorry, I think I'd better calm down a bit. It's just that the money that was thrown at these things was staggering, money that some poor fledgling band would spend the rest of their careers paying off, just because of some jumped-up hairdresser's 'vision'.

Something which I always thought must've been a common occurrence at an eighties' video shoot:

'OK, everyone, we're going from the second chorus. Neil, you look great. Chris, love the hat . . . On standby, confetti . . . on standby, the horse . . . Action!'

After a few seconds . . .

'Cut!'

'What is it?'

'Terribly sorry, Russell, but there seem to be two men fencing in the back of the shot.'

'Fencing? Well, I haven't got anything about that. What about you, Saskia? Have you got anything? No? How about, Pandora? Has she got anything? No? Best just let them get on with it, I suppose. OK, first positions!'

Because no matter what the style of song, for a period of time it seemed that no video was complete without two blokes with rapiers giving it the old 'touché!'. I reckon it was two guys who started fencing in Elstree in 1980, fenced all the way up past Pinewood, Shepperton, Borehamwood, up over Hampstead Heath, through Richmond, then Leighton House, finally ending up at Three Mills Studios in the East End five years later, having appeared in 14,000 videos along the way.

The American equivalent, of course, was the fourteen-year-old black kid break-dancing for no apparent reason in the background of any song, no matter how far removed the music from hip-hop.

The girl in the video went through a strange transformation as the decade progressed, too. In 1980–82 she was either a ballerina doing endless pliés in a deserted theatre, a weirdly painted sylph-like creature darting in and out of shot, or just a girl sitting on a bed crying. By 1985 she had regressed to about twelve years old and was running around in a leotard with a long ribbon on a pole doing gymnastics. By 1990 she was five years old, dressed as a fairy, living in a trailer park in the Midwest being shot on hand-held Super 8. Quite what she'd done to deserve this downward spiral is anyone's guess.

I once did a video for Daryl Hall where we had to spend fourteen hours doing it again and again because one of the dancers couldn't dance, but kept insisting he could, and everyone believed him. Christ on a bike.

Second only to the joys of video-making must be . . . The promo tour!! What could be more fun? Swanning around Europe miming new single from (artist's name here) atop the dizzying heights of those pantheons of thrusting twentieth-century culture, the European daytime TV show!

Oh, dear reader, if you've never drunk from that flagon of pure Bacchanalian bliss, how to convey to you the otherworldly pleasures of this, surely the most noble of all earthly assignments?

Actually, not quite. It's sort of fun the first couple of times, but it gets very old, very quickly.

We've already touched on this area with Icehouse, but there were a host of artistes with whom this was the only performing I knew. Chester Kamen and I used to refer to it as 'catalogue work' as it was essentially modelling, there being a very fine line between us and the girls in the 'Addicted To Love' video. That line being that we could, if push came to shove, actually play our instruments.

In 1999 I did a little euro TV jaunt with Electronic. Bernard Sumner, Johnny Marr, Ged Lynch (drums) and Phil Cunningham (guitar). Sadly that's all we did, as it was the greatest band that never was. Whenever I see Ged, we always share a little sigh of regret, shake our heads and look glumly at our pints.

We went to Stockholm for a TV show and had twenty-four hours of non-stop laughter. When you turned on the TV in the hotel room, it went straight to full-on industrial-strength porn. No mucking about, just noisy, weird, unsettling, juggling pinkness. When you changed channels you went through three more porn stations before you got to the familiar ennui of CNN. We were appearing on Sweden's equivalent of *Richard & Judy*, where we mimed a song, then Johnny and Bernard went to join the wholesome host couple on the sofa for a chat.

The theme of their show for that week was love, and the studio was dressed up with hearts and arrows. The first and pretty much unanswerable question to the lads was, 'So, Bernard, Johnny, what is love to you?'

Bernard thought for a second and said, 'Well, it's not what was on my hotel room telly last night.'

13

WOMACK AND WOMACK

'm not quite sure how I got the Womack and Womack gig back in 1986, but I was thrilled when I did. It was the first time I'd been asked to play for a proper American soul act, let alone one with such a distinguished heritage.

The band comprised of Cecil and Linda Womack; he brother of legend Bobby, who was the writer of 'It's All Over Now' among other things, and she daughter of Sam Cooke. There were innumerable brothers, sisters, cousins and children on board, and as a family they'd all either been married to, toured with, made an album with, robbed banks with, murdered, or been to jail with pretty much everyone in the history of soul music.

Linda appeared to be in a state of permanent gestation, and when I turned up they had a three-month-old baby of indeterminate gender, called simply, Womack Womack, as I think they'd pretty much run out of names by then. One of the brothers was even called Friendly Womack – I never met Hostile, but I'm sure he was around . . .

It was a very odd band for me to be in as the other players were all proper circuit musos. They included Trevor Morrell, a fantastic drummer and Barbadian giant of a man who, despite his fearsome appearance, had the voice and demeanour of a choirboy, and Tommy Ayres, a legendary keyboard player from Sheffield – which for some reason is a breeding ground for British musicians – who is still the only man I have ever encountered who would get proper pub-car-park-fighting drunk before going to work.

I remember once sitting in a bar with him before a gig, and he came back from the bar bearing a load of triple tequila and pineapples for the band. I politely declined as back then, perhaps surprisingly, I didn't like to drink before gigs. A little during, and invariably afterwards, but not before. Obviously it didn't count if you were still drinking from the previous gig. He remonstrated, explaining that after three of these, Trevor and I would be the best rhythm section in the world. The funny thing is, he was absolutely right, although not in the way I'd envisaged, for no sooner had we downed the last of the three than Tommy had his arms around Trevor and myself, bellowing, 'You're the besht rhythm section in the world!'

One of the more memorable shows we did was 'The Womack Family Reunion!'. This was basically a con whereby the public thought that Bobby Womack was going to join the several hundred other Womacks on stage and would sell out the Albert Hall.

It's also the only gig where I've been required to wear a tux. It was about then that I realized I was basically in a local pick-up band for a cabaret outfit. It was tremendous fun, belting out various R&B classics as a procession of well-known and bit players from the history of soul trotted out their wares.

The biggest shock of the evening came when Friendly suddenly announced, 'Ladies and gentlemen . . . give it up for the great Mary Wells!' Fuck! We had no idea she was scheduled to appear and started busking 'My Guy' as well as could be expected. It turns out she'd once been married to Cecil, and was now apparently married to I don't know, Louché Womack perhaps? And she came running on with the obligatory Womack accessory, a baby.

Mary had had a few – not babies, although I wouldn't know – and as she approached the front of the stage, she tripped and fell on the baby. We were aghast, but kept our heads down and played on. She then stood up, picked up the baby, who rather worryingly wasn't crying, and threw it to a member of the road crew, who, luckily, was looking that way at the time. She then carried on to the front of the stage, singing away as if nothing had happened. Unfortunately for her, the audience had in fact clocked *exactly* what had happened and sat there dumbstruck, rather like the audience from 'Springtime for Hitler'.

One of the last shows I did with them was *The Tube*, that legendary, never-bettered, cutting-edge Tyne Tees masterpiece. On the same show was a successful actor who'd just had a hit single, and apparently could really sing. Malcolm, the show's producer, suggested to Cecil that it would be no bad thing if he were to let said actor join them onstage for a song. Cecil agreed, but had real trouble remembering the actor's name.

We were doing a song called 'Soul Man' – not the Sam and Dave classic, but a more inclusive ditty, where the family would explain how every man, woman and child present was in fact a soul man, whether they liked it or not. We got to the inevitable breakdown section of the song, where it goes down to a basic beat and the crowd are exhorted to join in, and Cecil tried to apply the mnemonic he'd come up with to introduce the actor. It should be pointed out that this next exchange took place between the brothers and was very much in the style of a southern baptist revivalist meeting.

'We got a man here!'

'We got a man here?'

'Yeah we got a man here!'

'Lord have mercy!'

'We got a man here so hard.'

'So hard?'

'*Sooo* hard!'

'Sanctify me!'

'So hard they call this man the hammer!'

'They call him the hammer?'

'They call him the hammer!'

'Mercy on my soul!'

'They call him the hammer because . . . '

'*Loooooord* have mercy!'

'Because every time he picks up a hammer . . . '

'He picks up a hammer?'

As you can imagine, this went from being highly engaging and amusing to really rather tedious quite quickly.

'Every time he picks up a hammer . . . he puts a *nail* in someone's coffin!'

'Sanctify me!'

'Ladeez an' gennlemen . . . please welcome . . . Mr Jimmy Nail!'

It then came to pass that an incredibly humble and sheepish-looking Jimmy Nail shuffled onstage. Bear in my mind that all the time this was going on, the rest of the family were still chanting, 'I'm a soul man, you're a soul man, she's a soul man, they're a soul man' etc.

Jimmy went to the mic, and although what he meant to say was how honoured and privileged he felt to be sharing a stage with such esteemed company, thanks to the wonders of Geordie pronunciation, what he actually said reflected how I was starting to feel about the gig – it came out as, 'These people . . . arsehole people!'

I sidled up to him and asked if I could buy him a drink.

14

BRYAN FERRY

The second album I made with Icehouse was *Measure for Measure* in 1985. Conveniently for me it was recorded in England, due to the choice of producers.The first half was overseen by David Lord in Bath, who had recently produced Peter Gabriel's fourth album, and the second batch was to be steered by none other than the legendary Rhett Davies, Bryan Ferry and Roxy Music's producer, who also had an amazing history of engineering for Brian Eno, Robert Palmer, early Genesis and on and on. Bryan Ferry had recently released *Boys and Girls*, which I adored, so I was thrilled to bits to be working with Rhett.

I thought there was an obvious reasons for hiring Rhett, seeing as Iva had a tendency to sound a bit like Bryan Ferry, sometimes to the point of parody (an Icehouse B side called 'Dance On' had six Roxy Music song titles in the lyrics). Getting in his producer, therefore, would ensure he either did it properly, or was told, 'Oh come off it,' if he strayed too close.

We were working at EG's – Bryan's record and management company – studio in Old Church Street, just off the King's Road in Chelsea. Brian Eno was living in the basement for some reason and even ended up on the record. I encountered him in the courtyard one afternoon, stripped to the waist and tinkering with a rather battered-looking old bicycle. 'Look at this, isn't it great?' he said. 'I got it for £30!'

I mumbled agreement, although it didn't look *that* great, and seeing as he'd recently produced U2's *The Unforgettable Fire* you'd think he could afford to splash out on a newish bicycle.

I had worked with quite a few other people by now, including Dream Academy and Stephen 'Tin Tin' Duffy amongst others, and was getting a pretty good reputation as a player, as well as seeing my Robert Palmer co-write, 'Go To Zero', appear on The Power Station album. This had garnered me a publishing advance that was more money than I'd ever seen, and I was even contemplating buying a flat (I didn't, of course, choosing to have a couple of years high on the hog instead. D'oh!). As much as I enjoyed playing on the Icehouse record, being bossed about by Iva was beginning to get to me, and I was thinking of looking for pastures new.

One day, while Iva was in the loo, Rhett conspiratorially said, 'You know, you'd be perfect for Bryan.' Before I could say anything, Iva was back and Rhett gave me a 'shhh' signal. Did he mean *Bryan Ferry*? I wondered. Blimey, now we're talking. That would certainly be moving up a gear, back into the world of big-name players, which I'd had a brush with through Robert Palmer. I spent the rest of the day numbly putting down my parts, unable to think about anything apart from what Rhett had said. Much as you do when you're freshly in love. Not that I was in love with Bryan Ferry, you understand.

As luck would have it, Bryan had a job come in while we were recording, writing a song for the film *Legend*. Whenever Rhett had any spare time, he would work on the track, a leftover from *Avalon*, with Bryan. As the deadline approached, Bryan still hadn't written any lyrics, and in order to put a rocket up his arse, so to speak, Rhett suggested that Iva should have a run at it. Iva was delighted. At last! A chance to actually *be* Bryan Ferry! The plan worked, Iva supplied a perfect facsimile of a Bryan Ferry song, including vocals, which spurred Bryan on to finish the song within days. Rhett then suggested that perhaps I'd like to come down one evening and put a bass on it, as a sort of audition for Bryan. Gulp.

I'd finished my work on the album by then, and on the day in question I had a session with Dr Calculus, a Stephen Duffy project. Seeing as I'd had a bit of a late night, and the part I had to play was an endlessly repetitive dub-type riff, I asked Stephen if it would be OK if I had a doze while I played it. I could literally do it in my sleep, and wanted to be rested for my big date later.

I even agonized over what to wear for the session with Bryan, settling on a very fogeyish mustard-coloured corduroy suit, offset by a psychedelic African-print Crolla shirt. I used to make a point of wearing a suit to sessions. No one else did, except for a couple of bonkers old horn players, and it probably just made people think I was a pretentious twat, which I expect I was. What a dreary old queen, honestly . . .

I walked into the familiar control room to find Rhett and Bryan sitting at the mixing desk. Bryan immediately got up and proffered a hand. 'Hullo, I'm Bryan!' I love it when famous people do that. 'Really? Bryan who?' Although, of course, it would be terribly arrogant not to. I was immediately impressed by the fact that he was actually as tall as you'd think.

The song was pretty much finished and already had a bass on it, so this was just to see if Bryan liked what I did. He did, and I actually ended up on the record, for the end of the song at least, although EG rather meanly tried to play the 'audition' card as an excuse for not paying me.

The next time they called me in was to have a crack at a song called 'Kiss and Tell'. After a few minutes floundering around with a misguided and overly funky slap idea, I suddenly locked into what is, to this day, probably the finest bass part I've ever come up with. That was it, I was in. For the next year or so I would be sequestered in first the EG, and then AIR Studios on Oxford Circus with Chester Kamen, his other young hot-shot gunslinger. Chester was the most fantastic guitar player and a very witty companion, although he's also the author of some of the worst puns in Christendom.

Rhett had been looking to put together a group of core players, so that Bryan didn't have to go to New York and run up huge studio and musician bills every time he had an idea. Just as well really, as once Chester and I had settled in, Rhett jumped ship, deciding to leave the music business and play golf instead. I'm happy to say that twenty years later he's back, and looking very well rested.

As part of this economy drive, Chester and I were told to record over old tapes, half of which seemed to be back-ups or slave reels of songs from *Boys and Girls*. It was great being able to see how painstakingly the tracks had been put together, with little bits of white editing tape coming up every couple of feet on some reels. One guitar solo seemed to be glued together out of bits of Mark Knopfler, David Gilmour, Chester and someone else – I forget who – which was tricky, not to mention expensive.

I was really into Trevor Horn's masterpiece, *Slave to the Rhythm*, the Grace Jones album, and Scritti Politti at the time, so being locked in a studio with drum machines and synthesizers that could go 'Bong', 'Shplanng!', 'Digidigidigit', 'Bbbbbbbrr!' 'Fffffyyyyuuuuuuuwwhhh rruuupppTANG!' was pure bliss.

After my disastrous first introduction to David Gilmour with Dream Academy, I met him again when Bryan shot the video for 'Is Your Love Strong Enough?', which both David and I were to appear in. I found myself stuck in the dressing room with him, quietly noodling on a handsome white Stratocaster. 'That's a nice-looking Strat, David,' I ventured. 'Is it very old?'

'There aren't any older than this.' he deadpanned, flipping it over to reveal the 0001 serial number.

I have seldom enquired about the age of a guitar since.

The first time I ever went to Italy was with Bryan, to do some glitzy TV awards thing in Milan. I can remember very little about the show – I think we were miming 'Is Your Love Strong Enough?' – and there were a host of European pop acts appearing. One of them was HSH Princess Stéphanie of Monaco, trying her hand at pop music – on the days she wasn't busy getting knocked up by her staff – and she was being all matey backstage.

Chester didn't realize who she was, thinking she was just some French chanteuse, so he steamed in there. I must say, I did enjoy watching him put his foot in it.

'So are all your family French, then?'

'My muzzeair was Americain.'

'Oh yeah. What? War bride?'

This was at the time that the American Catholic Church was seriously lobbying to have Princess Grace canonized.

There was a lavish gala dinner afterwards, full of the stars and leading lights of Italian television, whoever they are. At the table next to us was some fat, old, sweaty, big-shot TV producer, who apparently had the hots for me. I was admittedly looking rather fey, in a crushed-velvet Crolla nehru suit with a bobbed pageboy haircut. When I refused his overtures to join their table, he sent a companion of his to play femme fatale and lure me over. She was quite the most stunningly gorgeous blonde creature I had ever seen, although it was a long dinner and I'd had a few by then. She asked for a light and said she'd like to talk to me, so I made my excuses and went over to her. She was leaning back against a pillar and being most seductive, with her incredibly smoky, husky, deep voice. And I mean *really* deep voice.

I was a little unsettled, but utterly bewitched.

Someone walking past stopped to talk to her, and halfway through babbling in Italian, they turned to me and said, 'You know she is a man, yes?'

'Course,' I spluttered, not knowing what to do with myself.

The champagne was flowing freely, and after a while I actually thought, Sod it, I don't care if she *is* a man. Luckily I was rescued by my compadres and dragged away from what could have been a life-changing experience. Or not.

15

THE SMITHS

When The Smiths exploded in 1983 in a blaze of outsized Evans floral-print shirts, jangling Rickenbackers and gladioli, I for one didn't take that much notice. I mentally bookmarked Morrissey in the same place as Jim Morrison, i.e., yes he is a genius, but I don't really need him round my gaff. It's a view I've subsequently revised.

For me rock'n'roll was pretty much over, with the notable exception of U2, and along with most people I knew, I was consumed by hip hop, and in my case all things suave and funky – or slick, epic and pretentious, depending on your view. The idea that England still had a great rock group to give the world seemed ridiculous, and this was still pretty much my view when I went in to bat for Bryan Ferry.

One day in the spring of 1986, Chester Kamen and I were mucking about as usual in AIR Studios, playing around with bits of tunes, as we were wont to do in our accepted roles as apprentices to Mr Ferry's sorcerer. On this particular morning, Bryan came dashing in, all Dunhill smoke and Commes des Garçons, as he'd had an idea.

'Listen to this!' he commanded, so we did.

It was a Smiths B side, an instrumental called 'Money Changes Everything', and it was just gorgeous. I'd never paid much attention to The Smiths backing tracks before, as I just assumed it was all about Mozza, in much the same way as I'd never really listened to The Doors, though that was mainly because of that fucking awful organ.

'We're going to record it, and I'm going to write a song over it!' he exclaimed, which was actually a pretty smart idea. The Smiths sold an awful lot of records, and Bryan might just have found a way into those lonely tear-stained bedsits . . .

We set about this new challenge with our usual *A Team* zeal, and within hours we had the basics of the track down, including one of my customary smug and busy bass lines. We continued to toil for a couple of days, and then came up against a brick wall. Chester, brilliant guitarist that he is both technically and emotionally, just couldn't cop the intro. He could play it all right, he just couldn't *play* it. He knew it, Bryan knew it and I was staying well out of it.

There was only one thing for it. We had to get the bloke who had played it: Johnny Marr.

Two days later he arrived, with his vintage amps and vintage guitars, and I remember being distinctly frosty, nodding a cursory hello before burying my head back in the paper.

We were all pretty lithe back then, but he was proper rock'n'roll skinny, wearing white jeans and a rugby shirt (a *rugby* shirt?). He got himself plugged in and tuned up, and was asked if he'd like the track 'upstairs' (on the big speakers).

'Uh, yeah, man, why not, rock out,' he replied meekly.

I tutted and probably ruffled my *Guardian*.

Then something happened: he played the guitar. I was on my feet in a second, bounding across the room to get a look at his hands, to try and figure out how the fuck he was playing what sounded like three parts at once. I wasn't alone, we were all jostling for position, as if we were ten-year-olds and Johnny had the porn mag.

After that the atmosphere changed and I became charm itself. Johnny had heard about me through his producer Stephen Street and we found we had a lot of common ground. At the end of the first day, Johnny asked me if I 'liked to party'. I replied in the affirmative and he gave me his phone number. For a second I had a sneaking suspicion he was gay, but this turned out not to be true.

He and his wife Angie were staying in Kirsty MacColl's flat in Olympia, and over the next few weeks I staggered out into many a dawn from their flat, him lending me innumerable pairs of shades.

Johnny personified the type of English rock star I'd thought had long since vanished. When he got his first big cheque, he bought his girlfriend a ring. With his second he bought his mum a business. Next he bought a flat in Chelsea. Proper. Although apparently it was me who taught him that you *always* carry your passport, which was a classic case of all mouth and no trousers, my reasoning being that you could just get on a plane and *go* at any time, though looking back, I rarely if ever did.

Johnny is one of the most brilliant people I've ever met. He had a fantastically invigorating effect on the sessions, and ended up playing on loads of the tracks, his unique thumb-picking style either inspiring or intimidating Chester to get picking lessons. All this coincided with the release of *The Queen is Dead*, arguably The Smiths' best album, and things suddenly got very hectic for Johnny, as they rode the crest of a critical and commercial tsunami.

However, all was not well in Rusholme. Smiths' bassist Andy Rourke got busted for smack, and his future with the band looked somewhat uncertain, not least the upcoming American tour. It's tricky getting a visa with any drug convictions, but with a fresh one, it's almost impossible. Thus it was that one afternoon I got a call from Mr Marr. 'Guy, how do you fancy coming to the States to play punk rock and fall over?'

Wahey! It was one of those once-in-a-lifetime calls. Admittedly it was somewhat odd being a stand-in, but let's face it, how many people would be bothered, as long as Mozza and Johnny were up there. We were hardly talking Roger Waters, and Oasis fans didn't exactly leave in droves on Bonehead's departure. Although I must confess that in the court case years later, Morrissey's assertion that Andy and Mike were 'as interchangeable as the parts in a lawnmower' was, I thought, a mite harsh.

The band was rehearsing at Stanbridge Farm in Sussex. A lovely old farmhouse with a cottage attached and a converted barn for rehearsals, set in lush countryside near Gatwick Airport. When I arrived, there was something of a siege mentality as news of Andy's bust had got to the press and various redtop hacks had been lurking about the place. At the same time Boy George was being hounded just because the tabloids *suspected* him of doing drugs – though at the time people did seem to have a habit of walking into his house and dropping dead from a heroin overdose – so he sent a message of support.

Rehearsals themselves were a tad strange, as Andy taught me his surprisingly sophisticated parts, without seeming to be too bothered about the whole thing, although that might just have been the heroin.

My girlfriend and I had been considering going veggie for some time, and if I was to be in the employ of one of the most militant vegetarians in the world, now seemed as good a time as any to take the plunge. I also had very long hair, though not a ponytail, as Mr Rourke has suggested, that I'd been meaning to lop off for a while. Then Johnny's mate Andrew Berry turned up and gave the band some of the best haircuts I'd ever seen. This seemed to be my cue to go from what Johnny has since described as 'futuristic surfie bob' to 'post-modern Billy Fury'. On the other hand, maybe I just cut my hair off and went veggie in a craven attempt to gain acceptance, I can't remember, to be honest.

It was the first time I'd hung out with real-life proper northerners, and they *were* different, moaning about things like even the water being soft down south. I got along fine with Andy and Mike – hired guitarist Craig Gannon was a sweet but simple lad who would later freak out on the road – and I hardly ever saw Morrissey. I don't think he liked the look of me from the start, and never seriously entertained the idea of me touring with them. Whatever.

However, Johnny was my mate, and we had a ball.

It may surprise you – it certainly surprised me – to find that The Smiths drink of choice was a champagne cocktail, consisting of cognac and champagne with a lump of sugar in it. Lethal. Especially when combined with any of Andy's enormous store of prescription medications.

In the evenings we used to play something that could loosely be described as a game. We'd sit around in the cottage and someone – usually Johnny or me – would sneak out into the rehearsal room, pick up a guitar and play the opening riff of 'Voodoo Chile' unbelievably loudly. Upon hearing this, everyone else would jump up, run out and join in. We'd do this all night. It doesn't sound that funny, I know, but if you were there, mate, it was fucking hysterical.

It was on one such night that I made my big mistake. Phil, Johnny's tech and old mate, had driven all the way up to London to meet someone outside a phone box in Notting Hill. The meeting had been a success and we were coked up to the gills. According to Johnny, there was also some acid involved, and a game of football where I was both referee and manager.

At about 9 a.m. we decided we'd had enough and went to bed, but after staring at the ceiling for about half an hour, I realized I hadn't finished.

Deciding that Johnny must feel the same way, I headed up to what I thought was his room to resume activities. I banged on the door. 'Come on, Johnny, I know there's some left!' I implored. Silence. Bastard! He couldn't possibly have got to sleep that fast. How unfair. So I kept up my banging and shouting for about ten minutes before sloping off, muttering curses about my so-called mate.

Morrissey had probably been terrified when some lunatic started shouting and hammering on his door at 9.30 in the morning. He got up half an hour or so later and got the train to London. If he hadn't wanted me in the band before, he certainly didn't now.

After that things got really interesting. Caroline, my girlfriend, came down for the last couple of days, as there was precious little work going on by then. As I was supposedly going to America for a few months, we decided to have a romantic weekend in Brighton. The Grand Hotel was full, so we got a suite at the Ship, and everything was fine, or so we thought.

On our return to London, we got a visit from a pair of Anti-Terrorist Squad detectives, who were rather keen to know if I intended to assassinate the president of Tanzania. I didn't, but they rather thought I did, and it was then that life became somewhat Kafkaesque.

It had only been a couple of years since the infamous Brighton bombing, when the IRA blew up the Conservative Party conference at the Grand, almost nailing Thatcher, and the security forces down there were still somewhat jumpy. Our visit coincided with the Commonwealth Games in Edinburgh, from which thirty-two African and Caribbean nations had withdrawn in protest at Britain's refusal to impose sanctions on South Africa – good old Maggie! Not plucky little Tanzania, though, they knew a chance for gold when they saw one, and the president, no less, had been staying in the suite beneath us at the Ship.

I'd had my Steinberger bass with me, which, being a hi-tech little stick thing made of carbon graphite, was carried in a padded shoulder bag that looked very much like a gun bag. Too much, as it turned out.

A maid had been cleaning our room and come across the bag, and she'd told the management, who in turn informed the police. The hotel had Caroline's credit-card imprint – OK, so she paid for the room –

which the police had run a check on. It wouldn't have taken them long to discover she was the daughter of a high-street fashion magnate, thus giving the whole episode a bit of Patty Hearst *frisson*.

I was duly interviewed by the police, showed them my bass and a video of me playing it on TOTP, but despite this, and the fact that I didn't have a criminal record or links with any organizations, political or otherwise – unless you counted my membership of the Musicians' Union and subscription to *Private Eye* – they still weren't happy.

What made it worse was that, as well as the Anti-Terrorist Squad, the Brighton Constabulary had decided they wanted a bit of the action, so there were now two agencies competing for my head. I was staying in Caroline's flat, and she had a lodger, who was interviewed by Brighton police. At its conclusion, when she had emphatically pointed out that neither of us was weird or unstable, she had asked the copper, 'So that's it, then? Guy's in the clear?'

'Oh yes,' he replied. 'As long as nothing happens to the president.'

I can think of no other time in my life that I've been so concerned about the wellbeing of a politician.

Soon after our return to London and subsequent hounding, I was informed that Andy's court case wouldn't be for some time, so he was free to tour with The Smiths. It had always seemed too good to be true – me playing with them, not Andy going to court. Even though I did lend him a nice Crolla suit for his appearance, which I never saw again. Moreover, after the coke-fuelled alarm-call incident I knew deep down that there was no way Mozza would have me on the team.

Mojo did a big piece on that period a while back, in which I was described as 'the unlikely Guy Pratt'. I was naturally incensed at the time, but thinking about it, it's pretty fair comment.

The US tour was a huge success, which I got to see for myself, as Johnny, sweetheart that he is, flew Caroline and me out to LA to hang with them for a week, to coincide with Caroline's twenty-first birthday.

From then on things began to go awry for the band. They'd fallen out very badly with their label and felt like they'd been ripped off, 'Frankly, Mr Shankly' having been written about Jeff Travis (the boss). Morrissey was never happy with whoever tried to manage them, and this meant that Johnny would have to write, arrange and mix records, while also dealing with van hire and other day-to-day nonsense. I don't want to get into too much detail, because if you're a Smiths fan you probably know it all better than me, and if you're not then you probably don't care. Either way, Morrissey will doubtless pronounce me a foul and putrescent liar if this is ever published. Whatever. Anyway, by the time they'd finished *Strangeways, Here We Come*, it was clear that something had to give.

Johnny and I had been spending a lot of time together after the tour, including the most fantastic surprise birthday.

Caroline and I had gone up to Manchester to spend New Year's Eve with Johnny, Angie and their two terrifying Alsatians. Heaven help anyone who needed to go to the loo during the night. We stayed for a couple of days, only leaving the house once to go into town and buy some records – for some reason I insisted that Johnny buy Duran Duran's 'Notorious' 12-inch, but I had to take it to the counter, for reasons of local credibility. On the morning of 3 January, my twenty-fifth birthday, I was amazed and infuriated when Caroline woke me up at 7.30 a.m., on the grounds that we had to get the plane back to London. I could think of no reason why we had to leave so early, or at all, let alone fly, until Caroline explained that Johnny and Angie had to get the plane down so we were going with them. The idea of Johnny doing anything before lunchtime was absurd, especially after a late night, so I was rendered speechless when he came into the room, dressed and sort of awake.

I had a God-awful hangover and was spitting daggers at everyone all the way to the airport, on to the plane, then all the way to London. Once at Heathrow, Johnny and I went to get a bite while the girls got the luggage. 'Wait a minute,' I said to Johnny. 'Why are we eating here when we could just wait till we're in town and get something decent?'

'Yeah, you're right,' replied Johnny, proceeding to order a full hangover breakfast – well, full for a veggie anyway – so I did the same.

The girls came and got us, and after a couple of minutes of me screaming, 'This isn't the way to the fucking cabs!' we were at passport control, and then on our flight to Rome.

It was a fantastic and beautifully orchestrated surprise, and I felt truly awful for having been so vile to everyone.

We had the most wonderful day, and ended up in some great restaurant where, after we'd eaten, I thought I'd introduce Johnny to the delights of grappa. Not that there are any really, it's foul stuff. We let the waiter know we wanted large ones, to which he obviously thought, 'All right you smart-arse English peasants, you want large? I give you large.'

The measures he brought were fucking enormous, and obviously pride demanded we finish them. It was downhill from then on.

We went in search of a club, and found ourselves in one of the most bizarre nightclubs I've ever visited. Gay clubs are usually a safe bet for a good time: the clientele are uninhibited, up for it, and there's usually a ton of action of one sort or another. Not this one, though. We found possibly the only closet-gay club in the world. Almost everyone was obviously gay, uncomfortable about the fact and avoiding everyone else.

I can remember very little except Johnny dropping and breaking his glass, yet somehow holding onto the bizarrely intact middle of it. He also made me ask the DJ to play 'Blue Monday' in the style of Peter O'Toole. Apparently I then attacked the taxi that took us back to the hotel, but it was once we got back there that things really started to go wrong.

We'd just about made it to the lift when I fell over, half in, half out, and for some unknown reason, I decided I liked it there, and so remained, prostrate, the lift doors opening and closing on my waist. The party tried to persuade me to get up, but I was having none of it. Unsurprisingly, it wasn't long before the staff became aware of the ruckus and a manager was summoned.

He shouted and gesticulated, demanding to know what was wrong with me. At this, Johnny took umbrage and leaped into the fray. 'What's wrong with him? Eh, well, what's wrong with you, pal!' Apparently the only thing I came up with to justify my situation was, 'Me and Sid had a bad lunch.' I dunno, you tell me.

In the end, Caroline went to the desk and managed to soothe some ruffled feathers, and I was persuaded to return to our room. After that it's all a blank.

I woke up the next morning with the classic Withnail 'bastard behind the eyes' headache. I knew I'd been very, very drunk and probably awful, but I was in my bed, and so was Caroline, so it couldn't have been that bad. One thing was bothering me, though, it was a reasonably nice hotel we were in, nothing flash or grand, but nice, so it seemed odd that half the wallpaper was missing from one wall, as if they were in the middle of redecorating. It's the sort of thing you notice when you check in to a room after all.

Roman hotel wallpaper

But wait; there was the missing wallpaper. It was on the floor. In pieces. Oh dear.

It transpires that on returning to our room, after making Caroline throw the TV aerial out of the window to prove her folk rebel status – as opposed to rock rebel, which would obviously have involved the TV itself – Johnny, mischief-maker that he is, had brought to my attention how easily removed the wallpaper was. He chipped away at a bit of it, but I wanted it all. Apparently I started ripping it off in sheets and wrapping it around my compadres, who then tried to restrain me and forced me onto the bed. The only evidence of this is a picture that Angie took, which shows Johnny and Caroline trying to hold me down. The look on my face is that of a gleeful one-year-old.

When I was finally subdued, the girls breathed a sigh of relief and headed for bed. Johnny, though, thought otherwise. Apparently, as Angie led him from the room, he turned and shouted at me, 'Guy, man, I can't believe you're wimping out on me like this!' Prompting me to stand up on the bed, stark naked, by now, for some reason, and declare 'Whaddya mean! I'm ready! Let's go!'

Quite where a naked, insane bassist and stupendously drunk guitar legend had to go in Rome at that time of night is anyone's guess. Luckily, we ran out of steam almost immediately and were herded to bed.

The next morning, as everyone surfaced, we realized we had a real problem on our hands. It's not that we hadn't been in this sort of situation before. We had. What was different was that this was a holiday, we weren't on tour and there was no tour manager, promoter or record company to make it go away. We were going to have to deal with it ourselves, so Caroline and I, armed with no Italian language skills whatsoever, went in search of a DIY shop. With great difficulty, we purchased a bucket, brushes and wallpaper paste, smuggled them back to the hotel and set about trying to reattach the wallpaper. This we did, albeit with one strip upside down and done to such a standard that we probably had half an hour to make good our escape before it came down again. We concocted some family trauma as an excuse for cutting our trip short and hastily checked into another hotel. Amazingly, we got away with it, and I've never touched a drop of grappa since.

My relationship with Johnny wasn't just about mucking about, though. Johnny had foisted me on Kirsty MacColl, insisting that I played bass when Kirsty covered The Smiths' 'You Just Haven't Earned It Yet, Baby'. On the same session we cut 'Days', and I'm eternally grateful to Johnny for that introduction, as not only did I have some great times with Kirsty and her then husband Steve Lillywhite, I also ended up playing on some great records as a result.

Johnny and I had an unspoken agreement that we were going to start a band with David Palmer on drums when The Smiths boat crashed. Mark Fenwick, Mr Ferry's manager, had noticed this, and was thus being extremely nice, asking me if I had any bills that needed paying – unheard of! – because obviously if that was going to happen, he wanted in.

When The Smiths did finally go tits up, Johnny just vanished. I was desperate to speak to him, to see if there was any hope of the band happening, and I needed to know quickly because something had come up.

If he'd returned my calls, who knows, maybe I would have said, 'Thanks, David, but I've got something on.'

What he did end up doing was going on tour with The Pretenders, which was probably the best thing for him at the time: playing wonderful guitar and being loved for it, without having to deal with all the other arse.

What I ended up doing is another story altogether.

16

I n Thailand in February 1987, I rediscovered Pink Floyd. I was on holiday with Caroline, who'd given me a Sony Pro Walkman for Christmas. CDs were still in the domain of the audiophile, and the Pro was the dog's bollocks as far as portable audio was concerned. I still have it, eighties design at its best. When I wasn't pointlessly recording our Tuk-Tuk or elephant rides, I was scouring the markets for interesting cassettes.

In Chiang Mai, amongst the Buddhist temple choirs and androgynous Korean pop singers – it would appear that it was them, rather than Bryan Ferry, that David Sylvian was aping – was a bootleg tape of *The Wall*. I'd been to pretty much every performance of it at Earls Court, even managing to get backstage on the night of the party, and it remains the best show I have ever seen, but I hadn't *listened* to it in years.

Although I'd always carried a flame for them, in these days of classic rock reverence it's hard to describe just how unfashionable Floyd were amongst my generation in pre-Ecstasy eighties London.

I became obsessed with this cassette, especially the guitar playing, which I still think ranks as David's finest hour. I seemed to remember there being more songs, and I was right, the bootlegger having decided to omit most of sides two and three as the integrity of Roger's grand concept took second place to getting the whole thing onto one tape.

When I got back to London, I was amazed and horrified to find several messages from Mr Gilmour himself on my answer machine. He'd been putting a band together for an Amnesty International show, and

David

thought I might be a suitable bassist. The moment had passed, he'd got someone else and I was gutted, as I assumed this was probably my one chance to play with him.

After missing out on the Amnesty gig, I started to bump into David more and more – I was obviously getting invited to better parties – and he'd always remind me what a great show I'd missed, twigging straight away that I'm an easy wind-up.

The newly founded Q magazine ran a news item on Pink Floyd reforming *sans* Roger Waters, recording an album and touring, but I gave it little thought. Until David called me from LA. He asked me if I'd heard about the Floyd thing and I said yes. He explained that they were finishing the album and then going on the road for a year.

'So, two questions, Guy, are you interested? And are you available?'

I spluttered something about probably being able to muster some sort of interest and it being just about feasible that I could find the time.

'So you're not busy then?' he asked.

Musicians, like actors, hate to be seen to be 'resting', although it's never really bothered me, so I pretended I was juggling loads of alternative offers, when the only *real* competition was starting my dream band with Johnny Marr, which I knew deep down wasn't going to happen.

He laughed and said he'd be back in touch in a few days.

True to his word, he duly called the next week to arrange an audition. He said it would be an idea for me to learn the vocals to 'Comfortably Numb' and 'Run Like Hell', which was exciting news indeed. That Friday, I bumped into him at Island Record's twenty-fifth-anniversary bash, and being somewhat relaxed, tried to impress him with a drunken rendition of the harmony part to 'Comfortably Numb'. It's pretty high, so I did it in the style of an asphyxiating cat.

He politely informed me that my services were only required for the half-spoken verses, and removed his fingers from his ears.

The audition was the following Tuesday, and Caroline left for Ibiza on Saturday, so I had a few days alone at home to swot up. I'd put it about amongst my more debauched mates that I was to be left well and truly alone, as I wanted to be on top form for the audition.

So it was that at about 10.30 p.m. on Monday night, I was sat at home with a mug of cocoa – maybe – ready to turn in and get a good solid, sober night's sleep, so as to be bright-eyed and bushy-tailed for Mr Gilmour. I was just turning the telly off when there was a tap, tap, tap at the window – we lived on the ground floor – I went to look and was confronted with a very demented-looking Tim Cansfield, a fine guitarist and friend I used to work with a lot.

I let him in. He was raving, 'Payback time, man!' revealing the substantial bag of nose in his hand. 'It's my turn, commeonnnn!' All this delivered in a thick Trinidad accent, I should point out. I explained that tomorrow was my big day, and I was trying really hard to be good. He looked crestfallen but understanding, but it was too late, the seed had been planted.

'Oh fuck it, you can't fight fate!' I yelled, motioning him to sit down as I went to fetch a bottle of brandy.

At six o'clock the next morning I showed Tim the door, the pair of us having well and truly put the world to rights. I staggered to bed to lie in state for a few hours, secure in the knowledge that I'd completely blown the best gig I was ever likely to get.

I got up about half nine, had a shower and left for the studio, gibbering with fatigue and resigned to failure.

It was a dismal drive down the A316 to David's beautifully appointed houseboat studio in Hampton. Walking along the path, through the opulently manicured gardens, I thought ruefully how nice it would have been to be involved in this sumptuous world.

To make things worse, when I walked in, one of my competitors, Graham Edwards, was there. I always used to be able to gauge how well I was doing by who the opposition was for gigs, Graham being sort of mid-range, but you never bumped into them in situ.[*] It was an awkward moment, which David seemed to enjoy. I asked Graham what he was up to, and like a true pro he reeled off an impossible list of albums, tours, writing gigs, productions, record labels, publishers and needy countries that were all begging for his attention. I didn't hear a word, I didn't care, my main concern being to breathe downwards and try to keep the smell of brandy hidden. Then it was his turn, 'And what are you up to, Guy?' I just couldn't be arsed with the game. 'Nothing,' I said, catching David smiling.

Graham left and I got my bass out with all the enthusiasm of a condemned man picking his own axe. 'Don't bother with that,' said David, 'I'm sure you can play the parts, I just want to see if you can sing "Run Like Hell".'

What? This changed everything. 'Run Like Hell' needs to be performed as the ranting of a truly deranged man with nothing left to lose, and just then I was that man. I went into the live room, put on the cans and David ran a recording of the song from his solo tour, the idea being that I would sing every alternate line. I put every ounce of my battered being into yelling it out, in the style of the late lamented Joe Strummer performing at Glastonbury without the aid of a microphone.

David was visibly surprised by my performance, and said he didn't have 'Comfortably Numb' set up, so perhaps I could come back in a day or two to try that.

I left with a spring in my step. Once again Jah had smiled down and I was still in with a shot.

I needed to pull myself together and be ready for my next appointment. Or get a gram and more brandy.

Two days later I returned, without the encumbrance of a bass, all ready to do battle with 'Comfortably Numb'. David asked if I could sing

---

[*]   Having said that, I should point out that Graham moved to LA and became a successful songwriter, probably earning more money than I could ever dream of.

'Run Like Hell' again, as he thought my previous effort was so on the money it must have been a fluke. It was genuine puzzlement rather than cockiness that led me to say, 'Why? I've already done it.'

David just said, 'All right, I suppose you'd better speak to my manager, then.'

It took me a second to realize the significance of what he'd said.

'Um, what? You mean I've got the gig?'

'Yup.'

'I now play bass for Pink Floyd?'

'Yup.'

I sat down, not quite sure what to do. I certainly wasn't about to call his manager, the legendary and fear-inspiring Steve O'Rourke.

Realizing that I wasn't going to say anything, or leave, David suggested we listen to some of the new album. I nodded enthusiastically, and out of the speakers came a big lumbering groove, with a rather lovely little guitar figure in it, and the unmistakable earthy rumble of the exquisite Tony Levin on bass. I can do this, I thought, this is going to be fun. Then another voice kicked in: of course you can't. You're going to get fired immediately, you idiot.

There was a dreamy Gilmour vocal about voids, distance and ribbons, suitably bleak Floyd fare, and then a chorus line about the circling sky, which I assumed was the title. I had a sneaking, and correct, suspicion that the song was actually about learning to fly, which tainted it a bit, as although things like flying and sailing are hard to beat in terms of metaphysical allusion, I have a slight problem with songs about rich men's hobbies, although I'd be very impressed if anyone came up with a moving tune about the eternal struggle that is polo. It turned out the song was indeed called 'Learning To fly', and I still reckon my title is better.

Nick Mason popped in. Fuck me, I thought, he looks just like Nick Mason.

Apart from David, who it must be said, got out a bit, I'd never seen a member of Pink Floyd anywhere, except at a Pink Floyd gig, and assumed that all rock stars of that stature never left Switzerland, or wherever it was they lived in their solid-gold ski lodges atop mountains of caviar and foie gras, surrounded by waterfalls of Dom Perignon . . . you get the picture. I'd seen Clapton and Page here and there, and even had dinner with Rod Stewart once, but the usual form for the real behemoth rock legends was that you'd suddenly see them out and about at every gig and club going for a couple of months, then read that they'd been checked into rehab. (Like back in 1981, when for a while you couldn't *move* for Pete Townshend.)

I eventually summoned up the courage to speak to Steve O'Rourke the next day, and surprised both him and myself by asking for and getting more money than he was offering.

Mine was the last place to be filled, and of course I was only even considered because

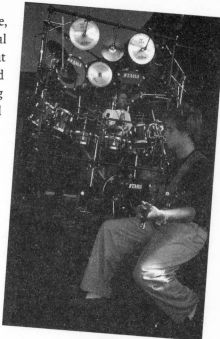

Soundcheck with Gary Wallis

the great Tony Levin wasn't available, so I was intrigued to know who my brothers in arms would be.

Gary Wallis was the percussionist/drummer, a man I'd learned to dislike from afar. Partly because he played for Nik Kershaw in a huge flash cage, in a huge flash manner, but mostly because I knew he'd snogged Caroline before I met her, and hated the way she'd go 'Ooh look, there's Gary,' whenever he was on TV. We were all on the telly quite a lot back then. In fact, some months I earned more money miming bass than playing the bloody thing. Obviously that all changed once we went on the road and became brothers in arms.

On guitar was the well-travelled and respected Tim Renwick, who had played for the likes of Clapton and Elton, and who I'd met once on a TOTP recording for Nick Heywood. And there were two backing singers, one of whom, Rachel Fury, had played my father's daughter in a TV *Play for Today*, as well as touring with me in *The Lover Speaks*. On the night of our last show supporting the Eurythmics in Brighton, on 23 December, I had somehow persuaded her to come swimming with me in the absolutely freezing sea at about three in the morning. It was very game of her, although she did get a nasty case of pneumonia as reward. She was great fun and I was glad I knew at least someone in the band.

Over the next few weeks I studied the Floyd back catalogue, which was illuminating. (Unlike most musicians, I'd never made a point of learning other people's songs, daft really.) There were occasional calls from the office regarding what I should be revising, as David was still working out a set. I was told one day to have a look at 'Echoes', and I remember thinking, That's on side two of *Meddle* isn't it? So I had a look and, sure enough, there it was, although it wasn't so much *on* side two, it *was* side two. Just another twenty-six minutes of music to learn, then.

There was an informal band meeting at David's studio for everyone to say hello and discuss the coming tour, and for some reason or other I didn't go. I can't remember why not, as it probably looked really bad, but I suspect I was probably just asleep.

I had also set about getting my affairs in order. The tour was structured so that we could all take a tax year out, something I declined to do for several reasons. Being something of a bleeding-heart leftie, unlike U2 and the Stones, I think you *should* actually contribute towards hospitals, streetlights, etc., although preferably not cluster bombs and illegal invasions. Besides, two-thirds of the tour would be in the States, where you had to pay withholding tax anyway. More to the point, I was convinced I would be found wanting and sent home within the first couple of weeks.

I had a farewell party at the pop-star nightclub *du jour* Brown's, where I got so smashed and behaved so appallingly that Caroline stormed out, along with most of my friends. The ever-dependable Andy Caine[*] stayed to look after me, and tried to stop me throwing empty champagne bottles at the wall, saying, 'Guy, you can't do that!' To which I apparently replied, 'I can do whatever I want. I play for Pink Floyd!' Twat.

The big day arrived and I set off for Heathrow in the cab I'd booked. Until 1994, Pink Floyd never once supplied transport to or from home or the airport, a staggering feat of meanness in an otherwise generousish operation. At Terminal 4 I spotted none other than Rick Wright getting out of the car in front of me. I rushed over to introduce myself, but

---

[*] Ubiquitous backing singer and songwriter – the true voice of practically every boy band ever.

he had absolutely no idea or interest in who I was.

Inside, I finally got to meet my compadres. Along with Tim, Gary and Rachel was Jane Sen, who would be in charge of press, and assistant tour manager Mal Craggs. I'd met Mal a few years before, and was praying he wouldn't remember.

Sometime in 1984, I was having dinner with Andy Qunta and my friend Andy Hilton, Icehouse's soundman. He'd made a fortune with his company Hilton Sound, who rented outboard-effect equipment to tours. During the meal he got a call on his enormous new mobile phone. There was a crisis on the Phil Collins tour, which was then in France. One of the Lexicon Reverb units had gone down, and they needed a replacement before tomorrow night's gig in Bordeaux. None of Andy's staff was available. I offered – insisted more like – to carry out the daunting task. I'd been to Bordeaux on holiday that summer, which I kept telling Andy made me uniquely qualified, though Mr Qunta pointed out that I didn't actually have to fly the plane.

Andy reluctantly agreed, and the next afternoon I was Bordeaux bound. I got to the gig, dropped off the Lexicon, enjoyed the show and backstage hospitality afterwards, then was taken back to the hotel, along with the stricken unit, on Mr Collins's tour bus. I should point out that Phil was very charming and personable, certainly more than he needed to be, seeing as I was just the delivery boy from the hire company.

I then sat up in the bar with the crew until seven in the morning, missed both my wake-up call and flight, and lost my wallet. Andy in London and Mal in Bordeaux then spent a nightmare few hours trying to get me and the stricken Lexicon home, both probably wishing me dead. So when Mal asked, 'Haven't we met before?' I was emphatic in my denial.

I was sat next to Tim Renwick in business class, as we were both smokers, and within about five minutes we had each other in hysterics, thus beginning a lifelong friendship.

My favourite pastime back then was video dubbing, which I did with my mate David Malin, who Tim knew. What you did was tape *Dynasty* or some other soap or documentary, then plug in a mic and do your own dialogue, the rule being that you couldn't have seen the programme before, so it had to be completely off the cuff. I explained this to Tim and he loved the idea, so we watched the in-flight movie without headphones, substituting our own plot and dialogue. I can't remember much, other than that the film featured Raymond Burr and at least one nun, and Tim had some riff about dry-cleaning bills, which cracked me up. You had to be there, really, but you weren't. Unless you're that stewardess who asked us to keep it down at one point, in which case, sorry.

Tim came from Cambridge and had known the Floyd lads since time began. David later told me how he and Syd Barrett used to go into the local music shop every Saturday to have a go on the one hopelessly unaffordable Stratocaster in town, along with every other wannabe rock star. One day they walked in and there was some snotty little tyke in shorts already twanging away on it, and to their shock and dismay he was better than them! This was Tim Renwick.

On arrival in Toronto, everyone had to wait for me as my superdooper MIDI Programmable Bass Amp seemed to have got lost. Good start. Luckily it was found and we made our way to the waiting limos. Limos!

Our route to the hotel took us along a flyover that offered a great view of the city, and someone pointed out the colossal CNE Stadium, which was to be one of our first shows. I gulped. Fuck. This really is it. I am definitely getting sent home before we get there.

Home for the next six weeks was the Four Seasons Hotel, a place I would grow to know and love. I really like staying in the same hotel for long periods, the relationships you build up with the staff, little quirks and what have you. For instance, every night I would call the operator to book a wake-up call, for nine the next morning, and every morning the operator would duly call and say, 'Good morning, Mr Pratt, it's nine a.m., and twenty-three degrees Celsius.' Or whatever the temperature was that day. So eventually, when booking my alarm call I'd say, 'Just call me when it gets to twenty-two.'

It was in the Four Seasons that I developed a bizarre condition that would afflict me on the road for several years: whenever I walked out of my room, I would automatically turn left. This meant I had a 50:50 chance of hitting the lift. I would walk entire corridors before realizing that the lift was only fifteen feet on the other side of my room.

We all convened for our first dinner at a smart Japanese restaurant around the corner, which suited me fine. Japanese was very much a minority cuisine in England in the eighties, and I was delighted to find that Tim shared my passion for sushi. There were no fewer than seven good Japanese restaurants within walking distance of the hotel, so we would feast practically every night we were in Toronto.

Nick Mason was at the head of the table and I took to him immediately. He's a very dry and funny chap who wasn't so much like the drummer in a legendary rock group as that nice man your parents know who collects cars. He's probably going to hate me for that. I can't remember Rick being there, but I guess he was, and I also met the American contingent. Margaret Taylor, the other singer, who was Japanese American; Scott Page, the saxophonist and full-on LA muso, complete with ludicrous über mullet; and hip young New York keyboard player Jon Carin, who would become my closest friend in the band. We would also be augmented later by Laurelei and Durga McBroom on backing vocals.

Then there was our tour manager – Mal was actually assistant tour manager at this point – who was the biggest chancer I have ever met. He must have got the gig through blowing smoke up David's arse, as he was a serious piece of work. His sole objective was not to aid the smooth running and organization of the band, but to blag and cajole any and everything he could get his hands on by using and abusing the band's name. He would be gone by the first gig.

Initial rehearsals were in some godforsaken warehouse and were pretty shambolic, as David wasn't joining us for a while. Rick was waiting for the band to buy him a stereo so he could remember the songs, while Nick could barely play and seemed far more interested in the logistics of the show than actually playing the drums in it, which was fair enough as it was a pretty enormous undertaking.

Whenever anyone asked if we needed anything from the music shop, Nick would say, 'Oh, you're not going to the stationer's are you?' He doesn't feature much from here on in, I'm afraid, as being accompanied by Nettie, he tended to be off doing other things, and had a much more highly developed sense of bedtime than most of us. Besides, he's written his own book.

Gary and Jon were deep in what they called 'Midi Hell', i.e., endless programming for the countless electronic keyboard and percussion sounds required. I was more than happy pottering about with my new mega bass rig and the vast array of effects I would be called on to use. If the bass playing itself wasn't particularly demanding, most of the songs being pretty straightforward down the bottom end, there was at least a whole world of strange and original sounds that were part of the Floyd canon. I would have to reproduce wind, ticking clocks, and various BBC Radiophonic Workshop-type textures as well as the old 'Dong ding-ga-donk, dong dong daah!' that the world knew and loved.

I also had my own tech, or roadie in old-school parlance, for the first time, and after a few days of cringing embarrassment at asking for new strings or what have you, Jon Carin pointed out that he had his pride, too, and did actually expect to be asked to do things. His name was Syd Price, and he was a fully paid-up member of the Tony Hancock appreciation society, so we were going to get along just fine. Hancock fans will appreciate the joy of having a Hancock fan called Syd to shout at: 'Syd, Syd for heaven's sake, man, look at the state of this pedal board! I bet Dame Clara Butt never had to put up with this!'

Lunch was purchased from one of those stainless-steel food trucks you get outside American factories, like the one where Eminem lambastes his homophobic workmate in 8 Mile, and whilst being a pretty cool piece of Americana, it was somewhat lacking in the variety department. It was a typical example of our tour manager's craft: having spent most of the day blagging himself the best tables in the city's finest eateries, he didn't have time to arrange food for something as unimportant as the band.

It was Tim, veteran of premier-league touring and therefore automatic shop steward, who brought our attention to the catering's shortcomings, and by the following day a sumptuous array of film location-style foods where brought in. I was duly impressed.

On about day two or three, we went out to see where the actual stage was being built, and where we would be doing production rehearsals, in a hangar at Toronto Airport. The venue was pretty mind-blowing, not to mention the stage, and the fact that we all had to have security clearance IDs to get in. There was some sort of angle on it being a bonded area, meaning none of the gear had to clear customs, as it wasn't actually in the country, which had various tax advantages, blah, blah, but that's for another far more tedious book . . .

It was then we discovered that in constructing the most state-of-the-art sexy and hi-tech stage imaginable, the designers had overlooked one teensy little thing: the band.

While great care had gone into allocating space for the various lighting droids, laser points, pyro clusters and other essentials of a psychedelic stadium extravaganza, there was practically no room designated for musicians, and certainly not for their troublesome amps and speakers.

Without wishing to appear ungrateful, I pointed out this omission, and after much disgruntled huffing and tutting, a compromise was reached whereby I could have a rack tucked up against Rick's keyboards, so I could at least access my settings, while my speaker cabinets had to be slung underneath the stage, which was made of iron grillework so smoke could be pumped through it. The only problem with this arrangement was that my speakers – mighty Ureii JBL 18-inch jobbies, beloved of dubheads and reggae practitioners around the world – while sending out the most gloriously rich bass tones imaginable, are basically inaudible until you're at least 20 feet away. This meant the follow-spot operators up in the rigging would enjoy the most beautiful bass experience while I was left wading in sonic mud on the stage below.

The thing that really stunned me was that rather than being buried at the back like most hired hands, I was allocated Roger's old stage-left spot, with a mic at the front, level with David, though I was still convinced that once David arrived and things got going properly, I would be found out and despatched back to London, tail between my legs.

There was a drinks party at Nick's house one night – out of the band proper only Rick was staying at the hotel – and I remember sitting at a table with Rick, Nick, and Steve O'Rourke, as they discussed their various leisure pursuits: Nick his cars, Rick his yacht, Steve his broken leg, and how he intended to be back on skis that winter. I was amazed at how little they seemed to know about each other; as if they'd only just met at a conference.[*]

Toronto was a lovely place to be in late summer, as we settled into our routine and got to know each other. Tim and I were inseparable, and spent our evenings drinking and eating in the Japanese restaurants and

---

[*] This lack of personal interest is rife in music. Years later, when I was working with legendary production team Langer and Winstanley, I was appalled to discover that Clive Langer wasn't sure where his partner of over twenty years, Alan Winstanley, lived! Blur, likewise, seemed to have precious little knowledge of each other's lives and loves.

bars of Yorkville, the trendy area our hotel was located in. For some reason Toronto seems to have more clairvoyants per capita than anywhere on earth, and Bloor Street, behind the hotel, was lined with hundreds of them. They would wander up like zombies, drably enquiring if you wanted your future told. I developed a stock response of 'I don't know, you tell me.'

At the end of the first week, Mr Gilmour arrived. I'd been quietly dreading this moment, as I was still blatantly terrified of him, and sure that once he got involved I'd quickly become unstuck. We arrived at rehearsals to find him already there, regally cooling himself with a miniature electric fan one of his daughters had given him.

Alarmingly, things didn't hot up in the manner I was expecting, as this was David's first outing as bandleader, a task he didn't attack with particular verve or gusto. The axis of the band's live show had been David's insistence on music first, versus Roger's conceptual and theatrical mores, both of which were integral to achieving the incredibly high standards set in the past. In the end, Bob Ezrin, who'd produced the record, was drafted in to produce the show. I'm not sure exactly what that meant, but it certainly entailed a lot of pointing, shouting and grand theatrical gesturing, which is very much Bob's forte.

Whatever it was, it worked, or helped anyway, because suddenly, about two days before our first gig, we had a show. Nick became 'Nick Mason-Boy Drummer' just like Bob said he would, Rick had his parts down, David had taken charge and everyone was in their respective grooves. The rest, as they say, is geography. Or is that history? Don't change the subject!

17

My first show with Pink Floyd was at Lansdown Park, Ottawa, Canada, on 9 September 1987. It was probably the most terrifying gig of my life. I say probably because, as I've stated before, I can remember precious little about the show itself. We were a bit fingers and thumbs, and struggled with 'Echoes', which was only to stay in the set for another few shows. There seems to be much documentary evidence that we played it as many as eleven times, but we're all certain it was only twice, or three times max. It was retired until David got it out of the cupboard and dusted it down for his 2006 tour, where it was polished up and restored to its former glory.

The problem was that David wasn't happy with the somewhat hippyish lyrics, thinking they were a little out of step with the times. In addition to that we didn't really know each other well enough to be comfortable with such a loose, sprawling epic track, with the 'wind' section, where the band just fade out of the 'space jam' section into nothing, coming back in after a 'felt' rather than specified amount of time. Some of the younger players – mentioning no names – had trouble with the piece not being a counted number of bars, and David complained to me that 'Modern musicians just don't know how to disintegrate.'

When I reminded him of this a couple of years later he quipped, 'Well, you certainly spent the next thirteen months proving me wrong.'

Touring with Pink Floyd was different to anything I'd known before or since. Instead of buses, people carriers, cars, the odd ferry and commercial flights, with Floyd you never even got to see an airport terminal, as you were whisked straight to the plane on the tarmac. The first plane we had on the 1987 tour was a prop job that belonged to Charley Pride, who was that rarest of things, a black country singer. It was festooned with photos of him playing golf with upstanding Republican Bob Hope types, and was pretty ropey all round.

I suffered from a quite pronounced fear of flying at the time and needed a couple of Bloody Marys just to keep calm, which probably made me look even more of an alcoholic than I actually was. Thankfully, this flying hall of fame was soon replaced by a preposterously appointed Boeing 727 that belonged to an Arab prince. It came complete with lounge, dining room, bedroom with en suite marble – yes, marble – bathroom, and a pilot who used to fly Colonel Gaddafi, until he got fed up with the CIA pestering him to spy for them.

Rather than folding away tables, putting seat backs upright and fastening seatbelts, we'd have competitions to see who could stay standing the longest on take-off.

Whenever Nick had a go at flying, we'd run up and down the length of the plane in a huddle, thus making it hard to handle and deflating Nick's sense of himself as a pilot. It's still the most expensive bit of childishness I've ever known.

Much to the principal's credit, unlike most bands, rather than driving to the gigs in limos, or rather limos for them and vans for us, we all travelled to and from the gigs in vans. The reason being that it's more fun if you're all together with the dressing-room booze, rather than David, Nick and Rick sitting stiffly in a stretch with the local promoter and whatever girls he's trying to impress.

Immigration and customs were invisibly taken care of most of the time, although occasionally dogs would be run over the luggage to keep us on our toes. Apparently most airport dogs are bomb dogs anyway, and couldn't detect your case if it was made of cocaine, although there was one occasion in 1994 when we arrived in Gothenburg and the dogs went berserk over my bags, causing everyone to be searched and resulting in one (minor) conviction. The thing was, not only was there nothing illegal in my luggage, I wasn't even there! I'd gone to London to see the Plant/Page reunion show, and so missed the whole trying experience. The late lamented Tony Howard, our tour manager from '89 on, memorably told me once that I was the least of his worries, because if I

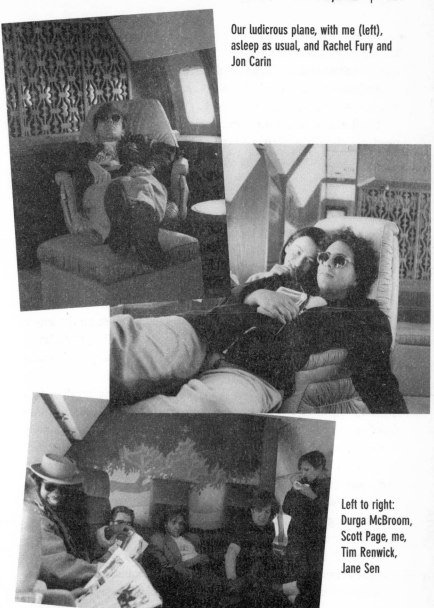

Our ludicrous plane, with me (left), asleep as usual, and Rachel Fury and Jon Carin

Left to right: Durga McBroom, Scott Page, me, Tim Renwick, Jane Sen

ever got my hands on any narcotics, by the time we left the country, 'I know they're long gone, man.'

The only downside to this sort of travel, and believe me, I'm not complaining, is that you don't get to meet any other bands, which is one of the joys of normal touring. Then you're often sharing bills at festivals, supporting or being supported by others, but this wasn't the case with Floyd, as apart from having no support band and never playing festivals, because we needed our own stage, very few big-name bands came within a 500-mile radius of us. If we were playing Dallas, no one else was playing Texas that week, as we'd hoovered up pretty much the entire state's disposable income. Well, apart from Garth Brooks or Dolly Parton. Obviously I'm exaggerating a teensy bit here . . .

We had numbered luggage tags, so your bags were collected from your room and magically reappeared in the next one when you arrived. The usual routine was wake-up call at nine, bags collected at ten, then depart from lobby at eleven. In reality this meant that when the wake-up call came, it was the cue for whatever band members were still drinking and hovering in your room to go back to theirs and start packing. So basically, packing your bag, making it to the lobby, and doing the gig were the only things required of you. Sometimes, though, even that was asking too much.

Once, in Hanover, having been on the road for months, I just couldn't face the heaving mass of clothes, books, CDs and other rubbish piled up in my room, so I went down to the bar and offered anyone in the assembled party $200 to pack my cases. I think Rick offered to take me up on it, but I could hardly accept from him . . .

On another occasion I went too far the other way. I was in my room, unable to sleep and somewhat neurotic and paranoid for some reason – I can't imagine why. It was 8 a.m. and the wake-up call was looming like some dreadful galleon on the horizon; only this time, I'd be ready.

I packed fastidiously, then unpacked, reorganized and packed again. Then again. Then I did what's known as an 'idiot check', where you look under the bed and all the other not-so-obvious places just before you leave the room to make absolutely sure you haven't left your passport in the trouser press. I then repacked and repacked again. So when the wake-up call came – admittedly still nearly giving me a heart attack, despite the fact I'd been preparing for this moment with the devotion of a Shao Lin monk for hours – I knew I was ready. I knew for sure that I had packed everything. There was nothing for it but to sit smugly, finishing off the less desirable liqueurs remaining in the minibar and await the luggage call with confidence. Sure enough, at ten on the dot the knock came at my door. I opened it with relish, proudly indicating my immaculately packed valises. The bellhop took them and I lay back on the bed with a sigh of genuine accomplishment. I now had a full hour in which to wash and get dressed.

Get dressed.

Oh dear.

'I knew for sure that I had packed everything.'

And for once I had.

Packed.

Absolutely.

Everything.

More to the point, the luggage was now halfway to Milwaukee.

Mustering all the self-esteem I could in my altered state, I made my way to the lobby in my dressing gown, purchased a supposedly amusing 'Wisconsins do it better' T-shirt, some ghastly Bermuda shorts, a pair of sub-Green Flash tennis shoes, and had to endure the righteous guffaws of our party for the rest of the day as the self-styled fashion guru of the band came utterly unstuck.

The sheer amount of luggage we all had after a couple of months away was preposterous, and on the 1994 tour, Tony Howard tried valiantly, if in vain, to put a lid on it, telling us all our limit from then on was two suitcases.

We agreed, although obviously suit carriers didn't count. Or holdalls. Or any bags we'd been given by promoters – and there were many. Obviously several of us needed guitars with us, and so we also had a little bag for portable recording set-ups, and of course our sound systems. And maybe another suitcase . . . so it went on.

One of the few times we stooped to travelling by bus was going from Seattle to Vancouver in December '87, doing a runner straight from the gig. Mal Craggs stood up and pointed to a big table in the middle of the bus: 'It's seventy miles to the Canadian border. I want everything on here now.'

There was a bit of mumbling and shuffling, then someone threw a little bag of weed onto the table, and after a slight pause it was followed by another; then a wrap of coke, more weed, a bag of Es, another wrap of coke, some pills, more weed, wrap, Es, pills, coke, and so it went on until there was a mound of mood-altering substances.

Mal continued, 'You've got about an hour. Do it or chuck it.'

Musicians are a contrary bunch, quite happy to waste food, money, time, talent and just about anything except . . .

What followed was monumental, as everyone who imbibed puffed on spliffs while being spoon-fed coke. Es got shoved into mouths along with various other pills, all washed down with copious amounts of champagne, vodka and beer. Within about ten minutes it became the Love Bus, as everyone giggled, hugged, shouted and danced to The Beatles – I remember surveying the scene and thinking it was like a surreal ad for a compilation album: 'People of all ages will just love . . . ' – apart from the more responsible, who just sighed or looked on in horror.

We reached the border at about 1 a.m., and there are few stranger places on earth to be at that time than the Washington State border. It was, and probably still is, pure *Twin Peaks*

Most of us were in no fit state to deal with anything as rooted in external reality as Immigration and Customs, and had filled in our forms with the addition of flowers, dragons and ancient Coptic symbols. I thought it only sensible to adorn mine like my old schoolbooks, with studious copies of The Jam, Clash, and Sex Pistols logos.

Alan Comer, our assistant tour manager, very nearly got into a proper barney with two bizarre-looking characters who didn't seem to understand his barked Scouse instructions to 'Get to de back o'de fockin' queue!' I realized it was a problem of linguistics rather than bolshiness, and suggested Alan substitute the word 'line' for 'queue'. It worked, and the two bearded, lumberjack-shirted weirdos – I think one had an eye patch and the other a chainsaw, but admittedly I was as twatted as a Crosby in a caravan – politely moved aside.

As I stood sweating in line, soothed only by the gentle swaying of the room, Rachel Fury sidled up to me in a bit of a state.

'Guy, what am I going to do?' she begged, practically sobbing.

'What do you mean? You're stamped, you're through, you can go back to the bus.' I reassured her.

'I know that,' she whispered, 'but where's the door?'

She had a point. I had a quick look around and suggested, 'I think it's the wooden thing in the wall.'

Somehow we all made it and the bus continued through the snowy wastes, arriving at the Vancouver Four Seasons Hotel at about 1 a.m. The luggage truck had already got there, but the bags hadn't been sorted and delivered to our rooms as yet.

I've seen many wondrous sights in my life, but nothing had prepared me for the awesome majesty that is . . . the Pink Floyd luggage.

From sea to shining sea it stretched, a glistening, gleaming array, bathed in the dappled light of untold crystals from the assembled chandeliers. Well, not quite, but it was certainly a fuck of a lot of bags taking up the entire vast lobby of the hotel.

David decided he couldn't retire to his suite without something from one of his bags, and set about looking for it. Not an easy task as, despite there being literally hundreds of bags, cases, safari trunks, campaign chests and suit carriers, a surprisingly high number of them looked the same, there being the standard-issue Samsonites, Louis Vuittons – for the wives – Mandarina Ducks, and holdalls with Pink Floyd and the name of a stadium along with a date emblazoned on them given us by various promoters.[*]

As he set about his task, something very strange happened: whenever he came across a bag that looked like his, he'd bend down to inspect the tag, and every time he did this, the bag he was inspecting got wet, causing him to leap back and look up, to see where the liquid was coming from. With every soaking he became more paranoid, and being somewhat tired and emotional, he concluded that there must be some sort of liquid-dispensing satellite following him around the lobby.

What was actually happening was that he had bottles of beer in both pockets of his flying jacket, and every time he bent down, beer flowed up his back, over his shoulders and down the back of his head, thus wetting whatever bag he inspected, not to mention giving him a phenomenal Morrissey-type quiff.

---

[*] Daft really, as they never saw the light of day after the tour. The idea that anyone would want to stand by the carousel at Ibiza or Bangkok Airport waiting for a bag proclaiming the name of their band or anyone else's is patently ludicrous.

On another rare drive, this time from New York to Hartford Connecticut, Mal cocked up and the bus didn't show. The gig was that day, so something needed to be sorted sharpish, but the only wheeled transport available in Manhattan to take a party of twenty-two turned out to be a preposterously long limo. It was done up inside like a Turkish brothel, and you had to shout to be heard from one end to the other. We drove round and round the city, as there were only certain corners it could take, which severely limited our options for getting off the island. Eventually we did, and once we were on the freeway, someone had the bright idea of going to McDonald's. Everyone agreed, and we turned off at the next one, the only snag being that the limo wouldn't fit in either the drive-thru lane or the car park.

Amongst the crew was an 'ambience coordinator' – I should point out that he wasn't actually hired by the band. I think they found him in one of the flight cases left over from the Genesis tour the year before and let him tag along as a sort of necessary evil. He had two jobs essentially. One was to obtain cocaine for anyone in the band or crew party who felt they needed it, and the other was to look after our parents whenever they came out on the road, both of which he did fantastically well.

He used to do merchandising for Frank Sinatra and had quite the driest and potentially offensive New York wit imaginable. Once I asked him how far the equipment trucks had to drive that night, and he thought for a second before replying, 'About a hundred dollars.'

Much as all this sounds like a drug-crazed, childish rampage, I should point out that most people were pretty restrained, several didn't indulge in much more than the odd sherry and half the time that Jon and I stayed up all night getting high, rather than careering around nightclubs, we were usually in one of our rooms, listening to gig tapes to see how we could make the show better. But there aren't many funny stories in that.

David and I played on a Peter Cetera album for producer Pat Leonard when Floyd first hit LA. That experience taught me that one should never hire musicians in the middle of a tour, especially one as huge and out of control as the Floyd's. Our playing, and my behaviour, was, well, enormous.

Peter Cetera had been the lead singer with Chicago, famed for such saccharine anthems as 'If You Leave Me Now'. Pat must have thought his songs could do with a bit of English meatiness, so he asked us to play on one of his ditties, a playful romp about teenage suicide called 'You Never Listen To Me', which is just the sort of adolescent petulance that applied to my performance.

By the time I got to the studio I'd been up for three days and was missing a lavish star-studded Hollywood party being thrown for the band by Beverly Hills socialite Wendy Stark. I was neither rational nor in a good mood. Throughout the session I kept calling David to get updates on who was chatting up whom and just how much Gary Wallis was annoying Quincy Jones.

My playing on the song was a prelude to what I'd do for Madonna later, although listening to it now it's absolutely ridiculous, as I'm plainly out of orbit and have no regard for what the bass should be doing. At one point during a take, Pat helpfully pointed out that the next section was the solo, which in my enormity I assumed meant mine, so I played one, oblivious to the fact that there was already a more than adequate Gilmour effort happening at the same time.

Having laid waste to the song, I finally got to the party, after waiting nearly two hours for a cab – the concept simply doesn't exist in LA; I should've ordered a limo. It was pretty much over by then, everyone having left except for a couple of handsome young men whose names escape me and who were much too friendly, Don Henley and the exquisite Joni Mitchell.

I spent one of the most enchanting hours of my life talking to her about bassists she had known and loved. She told me that on the day Charlie Mingus died aged fifty-six, fifty-six whales beached themselves at a town called Mingus in Mexico.

It's only now, eighteen years later, that I've actually looked it up and found out there is no town called Mingus in Mexico. Although he did *die* in Mexico, so maybe she meant the town, Cuernavaca, where he'd lived, but I've just looked *that* up and it's nowhere near the sea. Oh well, it was extremely late, and a wonderful story from a wonderful woman. But what do I say if I ever meet her again?

*

In June 1988 we got taken on a VIP tour of the White House, where, of course, everyone had to first hand in their cameras. Somehow I managed to keep hold of my camcorder, though God knows how as it was enormous. As a result, I managed to get footage of Ronald Reagan's dog Rex, frolicking on the lawn under the watchful eye of his two – yes, two – secret service agents.

As home to the most powerful man in the world – or one of the two back then – I found it rather underwhelming, appallingly decorated and full of old tat. The portraits of presidents past were fascinating, though; JFK has his head bowed, while all the others look straight out at the viewer. Gerald Ford's looks as if a ten-year-old did it using colour by numbers.

We had a guide in front and two secret service goons behind, who every now and then commanded us to stop and stand still. This is because whenever the president is moving from one room to another, all movement in the building must cease. I tried to make a joke of it to the guide, saying it must be impossible to get anything done if Ron's had a curry the night before, but it didn't get a laugh, more of a steely stare.

At one point we were told to be completely silent, as we were about to walk past the office where the president was working. Jane Sen hurried over, grabbed my arm and held out a cupped hand, ready to smother me in case I tried anything. She was right to, as I was seriously thinking of shouting 'Sandinista!' as we reached the door.

We also got the VIP tour of Disney World in Florida – amazing to find that if you take queuing out of the equation, you can do the whole place in half an hour.

When we arrived in Pittsburgh, we had to stay on the plane for about an hour before disembarking, so it was a rather grumpy, petulant band party that checked into the Pittsburgh Four Seasons. Not for long, though, as the hotel was also playing host to the contestants in the World Blind Bowling Championship finals! I kid you not. There were literally hundreds of blind bowlers careering around the hotel.

Bowling seems an odd sport for the blind, as surely most of the gratification is visual.

'Did I get a strike?'

'Er, no, we're still in the hotel and you just caused five thousand dollars' worth of damage.'

As we checked in, people were entering the automatic revolving doors, going all the way round, coming back into the lobby and yelling, 'Taxi!'

Quite why they chose Pittsburgh is anyone's guess, and I rather cruelly suggested they'd all been told they were in Vegas.

Tim and I made our way to the lift and got in just as a load of blind bowlers shuffled in around us until the lift was absolutely rammed. Then up we went, stopping at the third floor.

'Is that you, Maisy? Come on in, there's plenty of room.'

And so another blind bowler squeezed in.

Up to the fourth.

'Is that you, Frank? Come on in, there's plenty of room.'

And so it went on.

I spent the evening quietly reading in my room – as I did more often than you'd think – but it was hard to concentrate with the endless banging of people against walls, onto floors and falling out of lifts.

The gig the next day was great fun as usual and everyone loved it, until we played 'Money'.

Just as David was about to sing, 'Think I'll buy me a football team,' he happened to look at me, and I mouthed, 'Think I'll buy me a blind bowling team.'

It's the only time I've ever known David lose it; he was laughing so much he couldn't sing the line. The girls noticed something was up and, cottoning on impressively quickly, rather than singing, 'Money!', the next time it came round, in perfect unison, they sang, 'Bowling!'

*

A classic tour syndrome is to get back to your room in the wee small hours and clock the room service breakfast form hanging on your door. 'Ah, breakfast, what a good idea,' you think, drunkenly ticking all the boxes and collapsing into bed.

Three hours later you're rudely awoken by an enormous trolley of food that you couldn't contemplate looking at, let alone eating.

In Amsterdam, we all had the same idea, only the guy delivering breakfast was having none of it. He burst into the room, threw open the curtains and started pouring coffee, while exhorting, 'Look, it's a lovely day! You must get up! You are so stupid! You will eat!'

Jon Carin was at the far end of the corridor, and told me he lay there dreading the impending intrusion, which he could track by the choruses of 'WILL YOU JUST FUCK OFF!' Which got louder with each room the guy disturbed.

In Atlanta, I was once woken from a very pissed slumber at about 5 a.m. by a rather seductive female voice on the phone asking if I'd like breakfast at some point. I said yes, put the phone down and thought no more of it.

I nearly had a heart attack when I awoke several hours later to find someone had let themselves into my room, leaving a breakfast trolley at the end of my bed, presided over by a 6-foot inflatable Godzilla. I'm still none the wiser as to who was behind it, so if you're out there, please let me know.

When my lawyer was negotiating my contract for the last Floyd tour, one of the things he requested was complimentary breakfasts in America.

'Fine,' said Steve O'Rourke.

'Guy Pratt hasn't had breakfast in his life.'

That's not strictly true, of course, and hotels are far more enlightened these days, serving breakfast until eleven or even twelve, except in

(left) Speedball's classic post-punk pose. Me, Dave Dyke, Rob Buelo

(below) Icehouse in 1982, back row: Andy Qunta, Michael Hoste, John Lloyd, Bob Kretschmer. Front row: me, Iva Davies

(below) Icehouse's first video

Bowie (without scarf), me (in girlfriend's kimono), Carmine Rojas, Tony Thompson

Trying to recreate it in 2006

What happened? Wembley Stadium, 6 August 1988

Me and the great Pagey, Budokan 1993

More wedding day shots: Rick Wright and
Barry Knight

Gala and her dad

The exquisite Johnny Marr, with Bryan Ferry, at my wedding

Floyd live

Rick, me, Jon Carin, Chiddingford Serviceman's Club

Working out the intro to 'Shine On' as originally played. Munich 2006

Getting down with Andys Newmark and McKay. Roxy Music, 2006

Abbey Road with David Gilmour, Steve Di Stanislao on drums

Britain, where they traditionally serve breakfast between 6 a.m. and five past.

A classic hangover breakfast mistake I often made was ordering the biggest cooked breakfast available, two glasses of orange juice, coffee, a Bloody Mary and a glass of milk. I'd swiftly down one orange juice, followed by the milk, and then realize I was completely full.

By the last month of the seemingly endless 1987/88 tour I had gone onto autopilot. I'd split up with Caroline and had nothing to go home to. I knew the set so well I could do it in my – or more relevantly without – sleep, and that's often exactly what I did.

The tour kept getting extended by just one more show, mainly in order to get it filmed properly, and by the last one, I was finished. I'd been out all night, at God knows what party at God knows whose apartment, and was slinking back to our hotel, the UN Plaza, still drinking a can of beer. Suddenly out came a very chipper Nick and Nettie Mason, off for a spot of lunch or some grown-up, worthwhile activity. I managed to slide the beer up my sleeve, but couldn't escape undetected. 'Good morning, Guy!' said Nick. 'Been out for breakfast?' knowing full well I hadn't, but trying to help, bless him.

'Mmm, brechfes . . . yuh . . . thash right . . . brekfush . . . '

'Well, I expect you want to go back to your room.'

'Mmm . . . rrom, yeh . . . thash right . . . rrmm.'

'Well, off you go, then.' Nick told me they watched in amazement as I walked through the revolving doors and into the bank next door, where I apparently stayed for about five minutes. What was I doing? 'Um . . . five three four, pleesh.'

'Certainly, sir, what currency?'

But that wasn't the end of my troubles. I got back to my room, where I decided a Valium would be in order to help me get a few hours' kip before lobby call at 4 p.m. Bad idea, as I still couldn't sleep and spent the next two hours trying to write Tony Levin's phone number into my address book, having bumped into him the night before. I literally couldn't write the letter 'T'. I finally gave up, and for some unknown reason I double-locked the door and put the chain on. Then I went to sleep. Utterly. Out. Dead.

I was woken by our delightful security man Barry Knight and Alan Comer standing over me, looking not best pleased. I also noticed that my door appeared to have been taken off its hinges and was now leaning up against the wall. Oh dear. Oh dear, oh dear. This wasn't good.

It was gone 5 p.m., and the band had all left for the gig – by helicopter. That meant an extra helicopter had to be laid on just for me.

I quickly threw on the nearest clothes to hand, which was unfortunate. The night before, the rigging company had presented us with blue jumpsuits, emblazoned with the Pink Floyd logo – ideal for painting or scaffolding work. When we'd played Manchester recently I'd admired Johnny Marr's then terribly acid house fashionable Timberland boots and had bought myself some in New York. I arrived at the gig after my private chopper ride looking like a zombie member of Village People. As it was the last show, and it was being filmed, I seem to remember being let off the hook, apart from the odd dig. Amazingly enough, that's the show featured in *Delicate Sound of Thunder*, and d'you know what? I don't look too bad, and I even played rather well. What's truly amazing, though, is that they asked me back for the next tour.

*

After the concert, I stayed on in New York for a few days, first at the hotel with a female companion, then at Jon Carin's apartment in Brooklyn, as we'd started writing songs together and were thinking about starting a band. I was in such a mess that it didn't even occur to me that now might be a good time to go on holiday. Everyone else had, and even Jon was about to, but I couldn't see the point of going to stay at yet another luxury hotel, I just wanted to go home, whatever that was. Carlos Alomar had told me years before that the golden rule for the end of any long tour was, 'Don't go home, go on vacation first, or you're no good to anyone.'

Excellent advice, promptly forgotten.

Jon and I had one last night out clubbing, as a sort of farewell to the life we'd known. Funnily enough, at a club we bumped into our ambience coordinator. I offered to buy him a drink, and when I handed the waitress a $100 bill he exclaimed, 'I thought I got all those!'

We got to bed some time the next afternoon, which was far from ideal, as it meant I woke up at three o'clock. the next morning absolutely ly ravenous. I couldn't find my wallet, but I had my $10,000 cash payment for the up-coming live album. This was a classic bit of Steve

O'Rourke management; the musicians were led to believe that the payment was a tour bonus, which you'd expect for such a long and hugely successful tour, but I knew from the way he'd said it that it was for the album and we were being stitched up.

I took $100 and headed out into the Brooklyn night in search of food. I walked for almost a mile down Court Street – Jon informs me that it's now terribly trendy, but back then it was seriously frontier living – which was deserted and very scary, especially in my fragile state. Eventually I came to a deli, where a load of dodgy types were hanging around outside. I felt all was not right, and even went so far as to take off my Rolex – a gift from Caroline – and slip it in my pocket. There was a help-yourself buffet-style food bar, which I went around filling up a container, then I bought a Coke and a load of vitamins. It came to about $9, so I handed over my $100 bill. The guy behind the counter took it, and then in a loud pantomime voice counted out my change: 'TEN! TWENNY! FORDY! SISTY! EIGHTY! A HUUUUNDRED! YOU'RE ALL SET!'

Everyone in the store was now looking at me. Great. I went outside, desperate to eat. There were a load of surly-looking black dudes hanging around on the steps, so I thought it best to get away. Wrong. I walked a couple of hundred yards up the road, found a bench, sat down and started wolfing down my noodles. I didn't even notice the guy come and sit down next to me. What I did notice however was the tip of a knife pressing into my back. I was amazed at how calm I felt. I'm such a total coward I always assumed that should I ever be mugged or assaulted in any way I'd die on the spot, literally, having no mechanism to cope with such trauma. I was politely informed that I'd been observed in the deli – quelle surprise! – and that my assailant had a pretty exact idea of how much cash I had in my pocket. I put down my food, carefully so as not to push the knife in any further than was absolutely necessary, reached into my pocket and got out my cash, again carefully, so as not to pull the Rolex out with it.

At first the guy thought I had more money, so I had to give him a basic maths lesson. Then, to add insult to injury, he started giving me his life story, telling me how his granny was ill and that he wasn't really a mugger, he was just mugging me, and that I should feel sorry for him. As he was still brandishing the knife, it seemed best to lend a sympathetic ear. He then offered the most extraordinary summary of my predicament as, having noticed that I was English, he suggested, 'See, what wid de Queen, an de fog, an' all dat shit, iss OK fo you.'

I'd never really thought about it before but, dammit, what with the Queen and the fog and all that shit, I suppose it really was all OK for me. I felt a surge of patriotic pride and a new-found sense of purpose. Not really, but I did get up enough nerve to ask him if he could at least give me back my cab fare home. He thought about it, and said he'd give it to 'his man down the road', who'd give it to me. I was hardly going to go up to every dodgy type on the street and ask if he had my cab fare, but I thanked him anyway.

He then sped off on his bike, towards an estate I'd read about in *The New York Times* only the day before, which had been described as 'Crack City'. Ill granny my arse.

I finished eating, lit a fag, got up and started walking home, then realized I felt incredibly liberated. I'd been mugged! I had no money! I was unmuggable! Apart from the Rolex, of course, which by now was down my trousers. I was practically skipping, until I happened upon an enormous bloke carrying an equally enormous pile of newspapers.

'Hey, you wanna buy a paper?' he asked.

'I can't, I've been mugged!' I replied.

'I only wanna dime.'

'No, I have no money, I've been mugged!'

'You bin mugged?'

'That's right, had all my money taken.'

'How many guys?'

'How many . . . ? Well . . . One.'

'One! That sucks.'

I suddenly went from feeling free and unbound to pathetic, and slunk the rest of the way home.

*

Pink Floyd were the first band ever to get permission to play at Versailles, as they've always enjoyed something of a special relationship with France, enjoying a reputation as legitimate artists rather than a pop group. France is also pretty much the only country I've ever visited where it's common to find Pink Floyd on jukeboxes.[*]

We were to play in the car park, facing the chateau, with fourteen rather than our usual two laser tables, and the palace lit up in pink.

Despite being nine months into the tour, it was the nearest we'd played to home, meaning all us Brits had our families over, many of whom were seeing the show for the first time. I was chuffed to bits about Mum and Martin finally seeing it, as well as my dear pal Scott Crolla, who came bearing new stage wear for me. Unfortunately, his thing at the time was quite sober shirts with very arty, tasteful little flower motifs sewn into the edges of the collars and cuffs. Great detail for a cocktail party, but pretty hard to detect on a stadium stage.

On the afternoon of the first show, the three principals had a ceremony with the mayor, involving speeches and a rather amusing presentation. In the courtyard at the front of the chateau is a statue of Louis XIV on horseback, heroically wielding a sword. The band was presented with a gold model of it, only instead of brandishing a sword, he's holding aloft a . . . compact disc. Oh dear.

On our first night in town, we headed for the then compulsory nightspot Les Bain Douche, where I'd bizarrely arranged to take my washing. Due to a misunderstanding on the phone, my friend Brigitte Slammer, Bryan Ferry's French stylist, had insisted on doing my laundry. I was with Guillaume, a TV news reporter I'd met on a previous trip, and it took quite a lot of explaining to stop her storming out.

Big Audio Dynamite were in town, and as I'd met them a few times previously, I got to introduce David to Mick Jones, a teen hero of mine. He'd seen The Floyd at Crystal Palace in 1971 and was apparently a big fan – not something he'd have admitted in his Clash days, of course.

Prince Rupert Lowenstein, the Stones manager, threw a huge party for us after our first night at a hotel by the palace, as I think he was keen to get his hands on the band's books. I went with Amanda de Cadenet, who was there because her dad, racing driver Alan, was inevitably a friend of Nick's, and we were literally the only people in attendance who were connected to the band. It was lavish beyond belief, but sparsely populated, so we made our excuses and left.

[*]   Apart from 'Money' and 'Brick'.

18

FLOYD DOWN UNDER

G oing to Australia with Pink Floyd in January 1988 was like a home-coming, harbouring as it did such fond memories from my Icehouse sojourns. It was also still the only place on earth where I'd been chased down the street by screaming girls. Sadly, this wasn't to be repeated.

We started in Auckland, New Zealand, with one massive outdoor show. NZ Musicians' Union regulations stipulated that you had to have a support band comprising local musicians, so we had a string sextet playing chamber music out amongst the audience.

The stay was livened up by the presence of my mate Geordie from Killing Joke, who got completely twatted and climbed the scaffolding at the side of the stage, hotly pursued by security, during our set. The band all watched this spectacle with glee, David turning to me and saying with mock – or perhaps it was real – resignation, 'Your mate, I take it?'

We had a big party after, the music being supplied by two amazing American buskers David had encountered on the street that afternoon. When he asked if they could do a gig that night they said sadly not, as they were going to see Pink Floyd. 'That's OK,' said David. 'So are we!'

In the van, Geordie got into an argument with backing singer Durga McBroom about who had the longest legs, a dispute he felt could only be resolved by him trying on her tights. In reality, the whole thing was just a ruse by Geordie to put on Durga's tights. Oh, Englishmen and drag, what is that?

The latter part of the evening is lost to the ether, but I was rudely awoken the next morning by the phone, which I blearily answered. At the other end was a giggling Geordie, 'Is she still there?' He laughed.

The lady in question was, and as it transpired she was great fun and had a friend with a helicopter who took us on a tour of the North Island. This was followed by lunch at some media magnate's house where about fifteen topless girls were sunbathing around the pool, which was nice.

Australia 1988 still stands as the best fun I for one – and I'd hazard a guess that most of the touring party would agree – ever had on the road with Pink Floyd, and let's face it, there's some pretty stiff competition for that title. It also contained the most important introduction of my life.

We parked up at the legendary and sadly no more Sebel Townhouse. Though hardly as plush as our usual lodgings, it's probably the most perfect touring hotel I've ever stayed in. The staff were friendly and help-ful to the point of insolence, the bar so small that as long as there were four of you it felt like a party, and the rooms and corridors so dark you felt you were being naughty at any hour of the day or night.

Dodgy Bob, a drug dealer I knew from London, turned up on the off-chance, thinking that wherever Pink Floyd stayed for a couple of weeks *had* to be lucrative – he was wrong: we'd been on the road for quite a while and were expert at extracting contraband without paying for it. He took up residence on a rooftop pool sunbed, hiding when the cleaners came in the morning. He was tolerated by the band until he overstepped the mark by gate crashing an official beach outing and commandeering one of the vans.[*]

---

[*] Years later, at my wedding party, when I asked our security guy Barry Knight to go and find Stephen Fry, who was going to introduce the first dance, he asked me what he looked like. I was aghast that anyone wouldn't know what Stephen looked like, so described him as, 'The really tall posh-looking bloke in an orange jacket.'

Ten minutes later, Barry came back saying, 'I got him.' To my horror, rather than Stephen Fry he'd found the uninvited Dodgy Bob, who whilst admittedly wearing an orange jacket, is only about 5 foot 4, far from posh-looking and was gibbering and rolling his eyes after an enormous intake of E, something one wouldn't im-agine Stephen ever doing. It was nice to see him, although when he informed me that he'd just been busted and was about to go to jail, I had to hold my hands up and say, 'Sorry, mate, it's my wedding day, enjoy the party but don't expect me to get involved with your problems, however immense.'

Here's an example of how brilliant the Sebel Townhouse staff were: we were playing twelve nights – twelve nights! – at the Sydney Entertainment Centre, and so had time to fall into a comfy routine. Every night we'd come back to the hotel and gather in the bar – after a quick visit to Dodgy Bob on the roof – to plan the night's mischief. As a matter of course, you'd ask for any messages when you collected your key. On the second night I was told I didn't have any messages, and in mock outrage I shouted at the receptionist, 'Well, make some up then!' The next night I was informed that I'd had a visitor who I'd just missed. She'd left me a perfumed note saying just how much she wanted to meet me. Everyone was in on it; in the lift a bellhop asked me if I'd seen the 'beautiful Sheila' who was looking for me, as did the barman, and pretty much every member of staff I encountered. The next day the same thing happened, and in fact every day, until I was going out of my mind, wondering who this girl was and why I never seemed to be around when she called. The day we left, when I went to settle my bill, I was handed a final perfumed missive from the mystery woman. Inside was a signed photo of all the staff, wishing me the best for the future, and pointing out that I had after all asked them to make up some messages. Brilliant!

It was great hooking up with all the folk I'd got to know from my Icehouse days, but the most consequential meeting was at a dinner quite early on in our tenure. We were all at a Japanese restaurant, and Rick was accompanied by his daughter Gala, who had just turned eighteen, was breathtakingly beautiful and bright as a button. As chance would have it, her teen idol had been one Gordon Sumner, a smart-arsed blonde bass player, if I recall correctly, which funnily enough, was the category I loosely fell into at that time. I am no longer blonde, only occasionally a bass player and although Sting started balding long before me, he seems to have mysteriously stopped, leaving him annoyingly more hirsute . . .

It was one of those great meals full of laughter, and I obviously made an impression on Gala as we have just celebrated our tenth wedding anniversary and unleashed one Stanley Pratt on the world. Luckily she hasn't asked me to take up the lute, though.[*]

---

[*] We sat next to Sting recently at a festival in Belgium and I'm glad to say Gala felt 'the chemistry just wasn't there any more', so that's all right then.

Gala used to come and bang on my door in the middle of the night, demanding to be let in. I was in a complete panic, and didn't know what to do. This was completely outside of my experience, having never been in a band with people (almost) old enough to be my father. I knew to steer clear of fraternizing with management, backing singers and definitely catering, but *children*? I managed to resist her advances for several months, but it was only a matter of time.

There was an early-morning reception on an island out in the harbour where the band were going to be presented with platinum records etc. Apparently it was a bit of a wheeze, complete with the tethered inflatable pig the band took it upon themselves to liberate. I, of course missed it, as unless there was a plane to catch I rarely surfaced before midday, my pathetic rationale being, 'You don't expect a plumber to get up eight hours before he goes to work, do you?'

The England cricket team were in town, getting their arses kicked by Australia, and if their fondness for the bar was anything to go by, it was hardly surprising. Even *we* had a game of cricket, against EMI, and almost succeeded in getting Ian Botham to play for us. Despite barely knowing one end of the bat from the other, I think we acquitted ourselves surprisingly well, probably due in no small part to the fact that no one from EMI would *dare* bowl out or catch David or Nick – Rick was off sailing – which probably left them both with a somewhat unrealistic view of their sporting prowess.

We adopted Round Midnight a jazz club in King's Cross, as our after-hours haunt, and even played there one night.

The Australian gigs were fantastic, Ozzie audiences showing the same joie de vie for a rock spectacle as they do for everything else, even if we weren't playing in a pub this time. The problem with such a vast, well-oiled machine as ours is that individual gigs tend to blur into an indeterminate mush, as unless anything goes wrong you – or at least I – don't remember much about them.

I recall Mal having a tense moment one night, when we got back to the hotel to find that he'd left something behind at the gig: David Gilmour. How we laughed. Not Mal, though. I can think of other acts where that would have been a novel way of handing in your notice.

We discovered a fantastically witty local surfwear label called 100% Mambo, which became the de rigueur uniform for practically everyone.

Months later, when we were in London, I spotted Boy George and his cohorts at a rave all Mamboed up to the nines, and reported back to the band, 'For the first time in about twenty years you're fashion leaders!'

We bid Sydney a fond farewell and headed up to Brisbane for a two-show stint at the BNE Entertainment Centre.

On a day off at the beach, I asked Jon if he fancied going sailing, which wasn't particularly wise as I hadn't troubled my bed the night before and had forgone breakfast in lieu of several Bloody Marys, bullshitting about my vast maritime experience while neglecting to tell him I hadn't actually helmed any sort of nautical craft since the age of fourteen.

We rented a Hobi Cat and, as there was a good wind behind us, we managed to hare out for quite a distance, even encountering a dolphin before becoming completely becalmed. It was really quite pleasant sitting out in the sun, with the gentle lapping of the waves etc., until 20 yards to starboard a huge, battered fin rose out of the water, cruised along for about 10 yards and disappeared. We froze, saying nothing. I started working the rudder, as if that would somehow turn us into the non-existent wind.

Then it surfaced again, in front of us this time. It was circling the boat, which I believe is what sharks do before they . . . Oh Christ. I started to lose it. Jon tried in vain to calm me by saying it was probably just the dolphin, which it could well have been, supposing that in the last half hour it had grown, changed colour and been in several vicious fights. When it came up again, it had nearly done a full circuit, so when it went down the next time . . . I began desperately thrashing the rudder, which of course probably had no effect other than convincing the shark we were in fact a large dying turtle, and therefore an excellent choice for lunch.

Jon kept on with his 'it's the dolphin' riff, and by this point we were a pair of hysterical, useless landlubbers. I actually tried to picture newspaper headlines in an effort to calm myself: PINK FLOYD SHOW CANCELLED AFTER BASSIST AND KEYBOARD PLAYER EATEN BY SHARK. (BLOODY POMMY IDIOTS.)

Surely it was just too unlikely?

The shark went down for the last time, and we sat there terrified for about ten minutes, until suddenly the wind picked up and we headed back in as fast as my shattered nerves and minimal sailing ability would allow. Once safely ashore I grabbed hold of Jon and screamed, 'That was no fucking dolphin!'

'I know!' he came back, practically sobbing. 'But I was losing it, and I was trying to keep you from losing it, because I can't sail, and if we both lost it we would probably have ended up in the fucking water!'

It was a fair and salient point, and I may well owe him my life, not that I'd ever tell him that, of course.

As a postscript, I read the next day that a 22-foot great white was caught about a mile from where we were an hour or so after our encounter. As if it were needed, more proof that God protects children and drunks.

I seem to remember that the BNE Centre was situated in a wood outside Brisbane, which was good news for one Tim Renwick who, as well as being one of Britain's finest guitarists and a generally splendid chap, was also a keen wildlife enthusiast, bird-spotter and authority on all things fungal.

Or so I thought, until I spent an afternoon in Richmond Park picking magic mushrooms with him, only to receive a message late that night warning me not to eat any of the deadly poisonous variety he'd wrongly identified. 'Still, lovely walk!' he concluded chirpily.

An hour or so before showtime, we were all lazing around in the dressing room, doing the usual endless round of cups of coffee, fruit juice, snacks and inordinate amounts of ginseng and Emergen-C – partly to deal with the night before's hangover and partly to get the jump on tomorrow's – when a clearly excited Tim burst into the room.

'I've just seen something amazing!' he exclaimed. 'Come with me, but you have to be very quiet!' We all leaped up and followed him outside to the eerily silent wood, thrilled at the prospect of having something to do.

Being as quiet as we possibly could – which knowing us lot probably wasn't very – we crept through the trees to a clearing with a small pond. Tim held his finger up to his lips and pointed to a fallen tree trunk. On it sat an enormous frog. 'It's a Brazilian cane toad,' he whispered reverently. 'God knows how it got here.'

We all looked and nodded, suitably impressed, until Scott Page piped up, 'Hey! There's another one . . . and another one, and another one, and one there . . . and over there.'

As our eyes became accustomed to the gloom, we realized there were in fact hundreds of the bloody things all over the place, the lack of exclusivity rendering it far less interesting, and the sheer numbers quite frightening. We turned and made our way back inside, not bothering to be quiet this time, and as we walked into the dressing room, on the TV was a golfer taking aim with his driver, but instead of a ball, he was hitting a Brazilian cane toad. Next up was someone driving along a road, deliberately swerving to hit, you guessed it, Brazilian cane toads.

The cane toad, Bufo marinus, was introduced to Australia from South America in 1932 to combat a plague of greyback beetles that were wreaking havoc on the sugar-cane plantations of Queensland. The experiment was a disaster: the toads had little effect on the beetle but they did breed prolifically, eat voraciously and kill predators with a toxin excreted from their neck glands. Now the population of Queensland was being exhorted to kill the rampant little buggers any way they could.

Tim was most crestfallen that he wasn't able to add, 'species discoverer' to his superb if exclusively guitar-based CV.

*

We did one show in Adelaide, about which I can remember little – except an incident involving tour T-shirts and some girl's rather irate brother, which I'm certainly not going to recount here – before settling in for another long run at Melbourne's Tennis Centre, a yawning great arena, which several years later I saw Elvis Costello somehow transform into an intimate nightclub with a brilliantly personal performance. We stayed at the Melbourne Hilton.

Amazingly enough, Icehouse were in town at the same time, and were even staying at the same hotel as us, which was just brilliant. Their new album, Man of Colours, was an enormous hit, spawning two US top ten singles, and they were playing a massive show at Melbourne Showgrounds. Hooray! The last thing I wanted was to come strutting into town to find them down on their luck, which they were a bit when I left the band.

One night they all – except Iva, who'd been a bit precious and tried to blank me in the lift – came out with us to a club where we were due to perform. We – that is, the hired hands, plus David and Rick, depending on how drunk they were – would occasionally go and play in clubs after the show, doing various Stevie Wonder/Aretha Franklin numbers and other assorted muso favourites. I named the band The Fisherman's after an ingenious rhyming-slang language that Peter Cook had invented, which comprised of only one word i.e., 'Fisherman's', so 'Fisherman's strife' = wife, 'Fisherman's wharf' = Dwarf, 'Fisherman's bar' = car, etc. The Americans in the band never really got it and it's a source of constant annoyance that whenever I see references to, or bootlegs of us performing, we are always referred to as The Fisherman. I wouldn't be in a band called that in a million years. To be honest, I didn't much enjoy being in this one, as I've never been one for pat-on-the-back aren't-we-groovy muso-dom. That's why I can't enjoy hearing Stevie Wonder's sublime 'Superstition' any more, having had to endure so many aren't-we-cool-and-soulful session musicians' renditions of it.

Jon was of the same mind, so when we played in Melbourne, the two of us insisted on including Robert Palmer's 'You Are In My System', which was more fun than all the other songs we played put together. In the audience was Jeff 'The Buzzard' Aldridge from Chrysalis Records, New York,[*] who'd signed Icehouse in the States and had in the past been great for stealing money/drinks off, and generally abusing. This night proved no exception, as when we tried to leave him at the club, with the bill, natch, he jumped on the windscreen of one of the Icehouse people carriers, which was being driven, somewhat unwisely, by an extremely drunk Bob Kretschmer. As we sped off, Aldridge unceremoniously slid off the front and was very nearly run over. Bob turned to me and said quietly, 'Icehouse one, Chrysalis nil.'

One night on the way to bed, I heard a familiar guffawing coming from a room and instinctively banged on the door, not really caring if it was someone I knew or not. Luckily the door was opened by Alan Comer, our assistant tour manager, who had an extremely jolly Durga McBroom and Rachel Fury busily spraying obscene messages in shaving foam all over his walls. I thought it best to up the ante and dismantle Alan's bed, especially as he was so pissed he wouldn't notice until he tried to get in it. I studiously unscrewed two of the legs, leaving it hopelessly listing and impossible to sleep on, but being

[*]   See Ice House Europe.

twatted myself, I felt I should go further, and so removed the remaining two legs. Had I an ounce of sense left in me, I would have realized that I'd just undone my whole plan, as although the bed was – like the room's occupants – completely legless, it was now flat on the floor and perfectly comfortable to sleep in.

Occasionally a doctor would come in to give us all Vitamin B12 jabs, which apparently are good for combating stress and all the other bad things that come from having too much fun. I can't say I ever noticed more of a spring in my step, but it would have had to be something pretty enormous to make an impression on my by then locked-down metabolism.

In Melbourne the doctor must either have just taken a dislike to the band or been envious of our devil-may-care louche lifestyle, as he speared us all with the biggest syringe I have ever seen, leaving it in for a full excruciating minute, resulting in a tennis ball-sized bruise that ached for days. God knows what he would've done if any of us were actually ill.

We were sadly deprived of our plane for this leg of the tour, and had to take – shock horror – commercial flights! Imagine! On one of them David managed to persuade the pilot to let him take the controls, not just for a bit, but for the main descent and through two holding patterns, until we were about a mile from the end of the runway. Had anything gone wrong, it would've made for a hell of a headline, and a field day for the insurance company.

Our last stop was Perth, Western Australia, for one show at the East Fremantle Oval. I'd never been to Perth, as it's so far from the rest of Australia it doesn't make sense to play there unless you're either really small and trying to build up a following anywhere you can, or enormous enough to play somewhere huge to justify the trip. Icehouse fell firmly in the middle of those two categories when I was with them, so we never did it.

Perth is Bond country, that is Alan Bond, or at least it was then, until he fell diving with all the grace and élan of a Maxwell, ending up in jail.

Our hotel, Observation City, was a testament to Bond's omniscience, being a twenty-six-storey monstrosity in an area where nothing else was more than four storeys high. You could see it for miles; it was a proper eyesore, with staff to match. One afternoon I had to go up to Nick's penthouse suite to give him something. As he was only three floors up from me, and applying the law of the higher up the hotel you are, the longer the wait for the lift, I elected to go back to my room down the fire escape stairs. Infuriatingly, they were easy enough to gain access to, but impossible to get out of. After much kicking and shouting, I realized that the only way out was to walk down the full twenty-six flights.

I finally emerged, sweating and furious, in the lobby, and started to make my way across to the lift. At this point it's worth mentioning that as I was only going from one room to another within the hotel, I hadn't bothered putting any shoes on.

'Scuse me, mate, I'm gonna have to ask you to leave.'

A huge security guy – not a porter or doorman, this place actually had bouncers – was barring my way.

'But I'm a guest and I haven't done anything.'

'Yez can't come in here without shoes, mate.'

'But I haven't come in here, I was already in here, I'm just trying to get back to my room.'

'You're not listening, yez can't come in here without shoes!'

'Neither are you, I haven't come in here without shoes, I was already in here, and I need to get back to my room.'

'I can't let you do that without shoes.'

'But all my shoes are in my room.'

'Yez can't come in here without shoes.'

'So what do you suggest I do? My wallet is in my room, so I have to go back up there to get it in order to buy shoes, and once I get up there, I'll have access to all my shoes anyway.'

'You can be as clever as you like, mate, but yez can't come in here without shoes. House policy.'

'So you're suggesting I leave the hotel, my possessions and everyone I know here, and just go and live on the street simply because you won't let me go the twenty-odd yards to the lift without shoes?'

'I don't make the rules, mate.'

It still stands as the most impressively bloody-minded jobsworthiness I have ever encountered, and I can't for the life of me remember how I finally persuaded him to let me get to the lift, I can only assume that I did, seeing as I'm not shuffling barefoot around Perth, living out of dumpsters.

On a brighter note, I did meet and have a drink with Robin 'Confessions' Askwith at the hotel, and it turned out he knew my dad and was a splendid fellow. Likewise Graham Fowler, the England batsman, who recounted over dinner how he'd tried to bite Elton John's ear off at his wedding. Splendid!

19

TOKYO HILTON

I didn't want to include any sex-based stories, as by definition they're crude, unfunny and usually self-aggrandizing, but as my wife has insisted, because she thinks it's incredibly funny, and let's face it, who else is there to worry about, this one gets a mention.

We were playing in Tokyo and staying at the Hilton in February 1988 when one morning, because of the ever-present threat of earthquakes and a generally high regard for civic safety, we had to take part in the most comprehensive fire drill I have ever encountered anywhere in the world.

After being roused by the alarm, everyone had to go downstairs, be ticked off and then wait outside. Not content with that, a fire engine then drove up to the hotel and someone was lifted out of a sixth-floor window, strapped into a stretcher, winched down, then put in an ambulance and driven off. These people just don't know where to stop. For all I know, the hapless participant probably underwent twelve hours of surgery, complete with blood transfusions and skin grafts, all for the sake of authenticity.

A girl I knew – in fact, the girl I'd pulled out of the audience in Austin a few months earlier – was in town modelling. She came to see me for a quiet night in and promptly sent me down to the bar, telling me to wait for her call.

I returned when summoned to find a scene redolent of Kubla Khan's pleasure dome. She'd lit about a hundred candles and turned the shower on full with the door open, so the whole room was like a steam bath. She then started to give me the most exquisite massage.

Now – and this is where the fire-drill stuff becomes relevant – being a nation of almost painful discretion, the Japanese would never do anything so vulgar as fit an audible smoke alarm in your room. A smoke alarm yes, probably a dozen, but audible, no.

Instead, the heady combination of steam and aromatherapy candles sounded an alarm in the SMERSH-type control room doubtless concealed deep in the bowels of the hotel. Rather than bothering with trifles such as calling the room to see if there was in fact any sort of problem, the hotel instead despatched a team of security men, fully equipped with extinguishers and breathing equipment, to break down my door with axes.

Fearing something was awry as I heard wood splintering and urgent barked orders coming from the direction of the door, I got up, opened it, and stood there naked and glistening with oil, surrounded by escaping steam and a halo produced by the sultry candlelight, desperately trying to explain that everything was fine, more than fine, in fact. We were ordered to turn off the shower and lose at least half the candles, and I'm sorry to say that the evening never quite recovered.

20

MADONNA

P at Leonard, Madonna's producer, who I'd become friends with while working with Bryan Ferry, turned up at a Floyd show in Washington, DC towards the end of the tour. I had no idea what I was going to do when it ended, and couldn't really imagine a life after this thirteen-month rollercoaster ride. He had a suggestion: 'How would you like to play on Madonna's next album?'

Daft question really. Her last album, *True Blue*, had been a monster, even if not particularly to my taste, as apart from 'Open Your Heart', I found it a bit lightweight for such a supposedly revolutionary artist. But still . . .

In mid-September, Pat called me and asked who I'd like to play drums on the album. Who I'd like to play drums? Unheard of.

I nominated my mate David Palmer, ex-ABC and Paul Young who was then playing for The The, which was loyal but daft for two reasons. 1. I had could have had the pick of all the LA session gods, and 2. A week before we were due to start recording, David blew the gig out, which pissed Madge right off and got me sacked.

I was gobsmacked and pleaded with Pat to speak to her and get me reinstated, because not only did I desperately want to do the gig, more importantly I'd told everyone.

Two days before I'd been due to fly out, I was woken by the phone at about 4 a.m. and a somewhat shrill female voice demanded, 'I hear you're funny, make me laugh!'

I can't remember what I said, but I suspect I didn't tell her the one about the estate agent who cobbled together a few bits of Judaic mysticism, invented some bollocks about 'The Light', and sold it to a load of gullible celebrities looking to paper over the void at the centre of their pampered existences. Whatever I did say, though, I was at Heathrow two days later with my four favourite basses and a spring in my step.

Warner Bros Records pulled a fast one and bought me a one-way ticket. Brilliant! I'm not quite sure what the thinking was, as for starters a single costs pretty much the same as a return, so there's no real savings there, or perhaps they imagined I'd forget they hadn't got me a return and just buy my own? More to the point, no country on earth likes you turning up without a return ticket, especially when you arrive with a load of musical instruments and a tourist visa.

I got pulled by immigration and was given the full going over. I gave the name and address of my mate Tarquin Gotch, who I would be staying with. As I had no cash – why would I? Credit cards had been invented – they rather amusingly asked if she would be funding me during my stay.

My presence was requested at the studio immediately, which I could have done without after a sleepless night, followed by a twelve-hour flight and a grilling at the airport, but I could hardly refuse, and, besides, I was pretty tingly at the prospect of meeting Madge.

They were having dinner when I limped in. Madge was eating a chicken cacciatore, I seem to recall, from which she looked up and said, 'Thanks for coming,' rather sarcastically, I thought. That was all that was required of me, and I was told to present myself again at eleven the next morning to start work.

When I arrived at the studio, I was greeted by the familiar 'Dum, dum, dum, dom, dom, dom, dem, dem, dem,' that is the traditional ritual of getting the drum sound. The most time-consuming, tedious and aurally trying part of setting up a recording session.

I was introduced to the other musicians, most of whose names I knew from Steely Dan records – proper grown-ups who could run with scissors and everything. Gulp.

I was tired and feeling a tad intimidated, but was rudely shocked into full consciousness by a cry of, 'TIME IS MONEY AND THE MONEY IS MINE!' Madonna was in the house, in impatient mood. She did have a point, though, it is and it was.

She was full of wonderful and interesting motivational techniques, for example, after a bass take on 'Till Death Us Do Part', she enquired, 'Was that good?'

'Um, I thought so, yeah. It was OK.'

'Did it make your dick hard?'

Although I can see her logic, it's setting the bar pretty high to expect any degree of tumescence to be the yardstick – excuse the pun – of an acceptable performance.

Another time, the drummer, the exquisite Jonathan 'Sugarfoot' Moffat, asked at which point of the song he should come in, to which she explained, 'You come in when I do this,' and lifted up her blouse.

Madonna was different to most of the female singers I'd worked with in that her demands were feasible and delivered in plain English, so us musos could usually understand and deliver what she wanted.[*]

When we cut 'Oh Father' with Madonna, the band played it through once, with her singing a guide vocal in the control room. At the end, she went round each of us in turn with notes.

'Sugarfoot, none of those double bass drums and don't do that fill till the second chorus; Guy, just whole notes, maybe that one fill right at the end.'

Everything she said made complete sense, we ran tape and it was done, including the vocal. There was a string section and a Chester Kamen guitar overdub later, but practically the whole record was made in the first take, which is the only time I've ever known that happen.

---

[*] When I worked with Tina Turner, for instance, things were much more obtuse. We were played the demo of 'Simply The Best'. It was very straightforward and mainly involved me playing 'pom, pom, pom, pom', or 8s as we call them.

I hate that sort of Pepsi-ad corporate rock, but it didn't require much input from me, which was fine. After a couple of takes, Tina called all the musicians into the control room. She thought we were missing the emotional point of the song and insisted on reading us the lyrics, as if they were some weighty poem. The lyrics weren't really designed for that sort of scrutiny, though, and sounded even more like a Pepsi ad than the music.

She then suggested I should make the bass sound 'more purple'. I said of course I would.

To this day, I still have no idea how to make a song more, or indeed less, 'purple', and I don't think I ended up on the record anyway.

Although I'm sure any LA musos reading this will be going, 'Like, yeah? So? Dude, like that is so . . . ' Sorry, I'm getting silly now.

One day she asked if anyone would like to accompany her to see George Michael performing at the LA Sports Arena that night. He was on about his fifth hit single from Faith and was pretty much the biggest thing on earth at the time. His gig in LA was obviously the ground-zero showbiz event in the world that night, and we'd been given the chance to attend with one of the biggest and most controversial stars on the planet. Fuck me! It's hardly rocket science, is it? The answer is yes.

No one else seemed to think so, though, and Madonna left saying, 'I'll pick you up at eight.'

She did and we had a delightful ride out to the show in a limo, where I found her very different once you got her on her own.

I asked how she was finding life in LA, as she struck me as such a New York sort of person, which was probably down to the shouting and general impatience. Her reply was quite stunningly poignant. She explained that, much as she preferred New York, she found it too upsetting to live there as all her friends were dead. Most of her friends were dancers, and AIDS had torn through the New York artistic community in general.

When we arrived, the driver opened the door for her, and I was thrilled and delighted when she took my arm to walk in through the back door to the gig.

Unfortunately for me, this was probably the one public event Madonna has ever been to since releasing a record where there wasn't a single bloody photographer.

So you'll have to take my word for it.

When I returned to LA the following February, they were just about finished mixing the album, and I was asked if I'd like to pop down and say hello, which was nice.

The studio was full of lava lights, candles and incense, all very vibey, and they were halfway through a song I vaguely remembered. Madonna motioned for me to sit down next to her and listen, which I did.

The song got to the end of a big chorus, and then kicked into a frankly amazing middle 8, with a gospel choir and some of the most absurd over-the-top bass riffing I'd ever heard. I wondered who it was, as I couldn't remember playing it, and couldn't imagine I'd have been *allowed* to play anything that OTT. Even though it did feature an octave pedal, a trick I'd nicked off the great Pino Palladino.

When 'Like A Prayer', ended I turned to Madonna and said, truthfully, 'That is one of the best things I've ever heard, Who played the bass?'

She smiled and said, 'You, dummy!'

I got called in the next year for 'I'm Breathless', when I finally got to play with the great Jeff Porcaro on drums (he offered me a line at 10 a.m., which was a bit full on, even for me). Pat had said I would be needed 'some time in the next few weeks', then the next day changed that to 'tomorrow'. I was in Miami and had to get a flight at about 4 a.m. to be there. Pat joked that the best way to get me to the studio on time seemed to be to have me come 3,000 miles.

One afternoon there was just Pat, Madonna, the engineer and I doing bass in the control room when the Fine Young Cannibals came in for a meeting. They had recently conquered the world with 'She Drives Me Crazy' and had been suggested to do a track on the album. It was one of the most excruciating meetings I've ever witnessed, as they sat there like schoolboys in the headmaster's office, giving barely discernible sulky mumbles like, 'Well, we don't want to do anything if we don't like it,' while spinning in their chairs. To her credit, Madge really, really tried with them. They had dinner scheduled and as they left, Madge rolled her eyes at me. The next morning when she came in, I breezily asked, 'So how was dinner?' And got back, 'YOU FUCKING ENGLISH PEOPLE!' Thanks for flying the flag, guys.

We were once having a heated discussion about some aspect of morality – she was always game for a heated discussion – and she hit me with, 'Yeah, but it's a Catholic thing, you wouldn't understand.' I pointed out that, though not practising, I am actually Catholic, by baptism at least. 'Yeah,' she countered, 'but that's English Catholic, that's different.'

I tried to explain that what she was thinking of was the Church of England, but she was having none of it. As a result, I tend to be slightly sceptical whenever I hear her pontificate about whatever religion she's currently embracing.

Still, happy days.

21

TOY MATINEE

Nineteen eight-nine kicked off with the most extraordinary New Year's Eve party I'd ever been to. I'd flown to Ireland with my mate Olly Daniaud, and we'd been invited to stay at Luggala by our friends Tom Conran and Katrina Boorman.

Luggala had been the home of Lord Oranmore Brown and Oona Guinness, parents of Tara Brown, the swinging sixties character immortalized in 'A Day In The Life' after dying in a car crash. It was quite the most wonderful run-down, ramshackle country pile. It had a wine cellar flooded with a foot or more of water, so we thought it best to salvage and dispose of as many of the untold bottles of Latour '59 and Petrus '61 as we could, which though exhausting proved a most fruitful and rewarding endeavour.

On New Year's Eve itself, we went to Paddy Moloney's house, he of the Chieftains fame, a nice family home out in the countryside, where a hearty Irish knees-up was going on.

The custom at Paddy's is that everyone has to do a turn, so first John Boorman recited a poem he'd written about the Moloneys, then Angelica Huston sang a heart-wrenchingly beautiful old Irish folk song, whose title escapes me. Then it was my turn, and at a loss for something to do, I grabbed an acoustic guitar and started playing a sort of bluesy shuffle. It's just the sort of thing I hate usually, but I was immediately surrounded by the Chieftains, with uillean pipes, tin whistles, fiddles, bodhrans and banjos, though sadly no harp. They transformed my shuffle into a rousing Celtic war cry, and I suddenly felt like a true Son of Erin, striding off to do battle for Queen Maeve, *en route* to Tír na nOg.

Next up was Jack Nicholson, who when asked what he intended to do just drawled, 'Have you *got* five million dollars?'

I believe that was his going rate for a movie at the time, and although it was meant to be funny it just seemed tacky and childish. Why couldn't he just muck in like everyone else? Dammit all, man!

When I got back to dreary London, I was delighted to get a call from Pat Leonard, asking if I'd care to decamp to the sunnier climes of LA to work on a band project with him. The only problem was that I had a court appearance for drunk driving coming up, about which I foolishly asked Olly for advice. He assured me that if you told the police you're leaving the country, as long as you're gone for a while, which I would be, it gets forgotten about. So I did just that.

The night before I left town, Robert Palmer had a party at Brown's, to which I took Gala. When I introduced her to Robert's bass player Frank Blair, he crossed the boundaries of any known school of etiquette by simply announcing, 'I have just *got* to fuck this woman!' Needless to say, he never did. Sorry, digression.

Toy Matinee by Toy Matinee, is pretty much totally unknown in Britain, and indeed practically everywhere except the US, where it has become something of a cult record. I often bump into people in the States who are far more impressed by me being in Toy Matinee than anything else I've done.

It was undoubtedly influential, giving birth to producer Bill Bottrell's Tuesday Night Music Club at his studio in Pasadena, where musos would gather to drink tequila and jam, from which was born Sheryl Crow's landmark first album.

The band consisted of Pat, the incredibly talented Kevin Gilbert, Brian Macleod, a bonkers Bay Area cyber-punk drummer, session ace guitarist Tim Pierce, the mighty Bill Bottrell in the producer's chair, and myself. Although not necessarily in that order.

Most bands sit around kitchen tables or in mouldy fleapit rehearsal studios for at least the first few weeks of their inception, but we had Pat's state-of-the-art amazingly appointed Johnny Yuma studios in Burbank.

The three months I worked on the album were happy days indeed, being creatively sated, utterly carefree, paid and having a great drinking partner in Brian. Pat was also at his best, finally doing what he wanted after years establishing himself as a numero uno pop songsmith/producer.

It was on this album that Bill Bottrell gave me what I still consider the greatest compliment I've ever had, when he pressed stop at the end of a take, turned to me and said, 'As if a bass player would play that!'

We had all sorts of novel guest artists come and go, including Julian Lennon, a Dixieland jazz band and, thrillingly, Burt Ward, who played Robin in the sixties *Batman* TV series. His job was to say, 'Holy rotting donkey carcass, Batman!' in the song 'Turn It On Salvador', which is about, unsurprisingly, Salvador Dali.

Acid house hadn't registered in America, despite originating in Detroit, and Kevin was very keen to know what the music was about. I told him what I knew, which wasn't much, and played him what I had. We went to a couple of underground raves, and came to the conclusion that the best thing to do would be to try and make an acid house record ourselves.

We thought about asking Pat if we could use the studio after hours, but he was so focused on the record that we knew what the answer would be, so instead we decided to sneak in, knock up a dance classic, and go home with no one the wiser.

Everything was going swimmingly and we had a silly little ditty called 'Last Chicken In The Shop', which featured a chorus of Durga McBroom singing 'Put on a happy face tonight, tonight,' alternating with 'Sit on a happy face', etc. Then at about 4 a.m., just as we were finishing the rough mix, Brian spilled an entire bottle of beer into the mixing desk. There was some fizzing and popping, and then . . . nothing. Oh dear.

None of us knew the first thing about getting beer out of mixing desks, especially very posh mixing desks, and this was a very posh one indeed: a souped-up reconditioned Neve that used to reside at Abbey Road, if I remember correctly.

There was nothing for it, we had to call Pat's engineer, Mike, wake him up and hope for the best. Mike was unbelievably sporting and actually came out with his hairdryer, pulled out bits of the console and blow-dried them. It worked. We all felt terribly guilty the next day, and Pat was none the wiser, just wondering why everyone seemed a little more tired than usual.

The song's still quite funny, though.

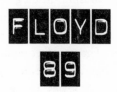

dashed back from LA for our one – yes, one – day's rehearsal for the 1989 tour, but I had other things to attend to first.

Skipping the country and leaving an outstanding drunk-driving charge had seemed like a good idea at the time, until my mum called to tell me that a couple of 'rather charming detectives' had turned up at her house with a warrant for my arrest. Ah.

This had to be dealt with immediately, so I went straight to Kensington police station and handed myself in. I was taken downstairs, where I had my fingerprints and photo taken. Perhaps fortuitously, I had for some unknown reason spent the last three months cultivating a beard. As a result, if my prints ever showed up at a crime scene, the police would be looking for a rather suntanned Captain Haddock.

The young constable who dealt with me seemed inordinately pleased with himself, and when we drove to court I found out why.

'So, er, what exactly were you doing in the police station then, sir?'

Good Lord, so that was it. He thought I'd popped in to report a missing cat or something and he, the ace sleuth, had found and apprehended a wanted felon.

'I came in to deal with my drunk-driving offence, of course.'

The two older coppers in the front sniggered.

As usual for any court appearance – not that I've had many, honest – I was wearing my best nice-boy suit and tie, which worked against me when we arrived at Horseferry Road Magistrates Court. 'That'll be a

Kensington pillock then, right sarge?'

'Right.'

Once released from the burden of my driving licence I had the rest of the day free, but for one more task: the Dream Academy album. There were about seven songs awaiting my attention, Pino Palladino having already done the rest, and today was the only day I had free. So off to the studio I went, where I actually did get them all done, then home to bed. A productive day all round by any standards. Well done, little Johnny short trousers.

The next morning it was off to Docklands Arena where the whole rig had been set up for a run-through. It was exactly the same show as we'd done for the previous two years, so it was more a gentle reminder than a rehearsal.

Months in LA had taken their toll, and the band were quite taken aback by my new bearded, boots-and-jeans, psycho Nam-vet look. I think I was even wearing a 'GOD LOVES YOU' baseball cap, but not for long, once I was back breathing the rarefied air of Planet Floyd.

Although I hadn't been in England much since the end of the last tour, when I had I'd been quite publicly dallying with Gala, I'd even been up to visit her at Oxford, taking her out in my dinky new car, an old Alfa Spyder. Just as well, really, as I wouldn't be driving that again for a while.

This hadn't really endeared me to anyone, certainly not Rick, and certainly not Gala's mother Juliette, who I'd met rather awkwardly with David one night at a bar owned by a friend of theirs.

I wasn't the only member of the party to get embroiled with the band's offspring, though. One of our security guys had apparently been liaising with the delightful Chloe Mason, and I couldn't help but notice his absence. Stupidly, I took this to mean that perhaps my actions weren't so disapproved of after all, and even more stupidly, I thought I'd mention it to David.

'It doesn't take six weeks to rehearse a security man, Guy,' he replied.

It would appear that the only reason I was still in the band was logistical expediency, although David has since assured me he was joking. Ha, ha, good one that.

*

Our first show was at Werchter Park, near Brussels, and if nothing else, it's notable for being the only show I have ever performed with a beard.

When we arrived in Verona the next day, the girls, Durga especially, decided the beard had to go. We had a 'shaving party' in my room, which entailed everyone getting very drunk, and then all mucking in to hack off my beard. Looking back, it probably wasn't the cleverest idea in the world, especially as I think Durga had a cut throat razor.

In Verona, we played in the Arena, which if I recall correctly was built in AD30 on a site that at the time was outside the city walls. The ludii – shows and games – staged there were so famous that spectators came from many other, sometimes very distant, places. The amphitheatre itself could take more than 30,000 spectators.

The round façade was originally in white and pink limestone from Valpolicella, but after a major earthquake in 1117, which almost completely destroyed the outer ring, except the so-called Ala, the Arena was used as a quarry for other buildings. The first interventions to recover its functionality as a theatre were started during the Renaissance.

Thanks to its outstanding acoustics, the building lends itself to musical performances, the practice of which began in 1913. Nowadays, four productions are mounted each year between June and August, although I could be wrong.

Our dressing rooms were originally the holding pens for the Christians before they were fed to the lions, and although cleaned, they looked as if they hadn't been redecorated since.

On our way to the gig, I remember passing a sign for two separate public conveniences, causing Tim to exclaim, 'Look, it's the two gentleman's of Verona!'

*

When we played in Salerno, we had a two-hour drive to the gig, down the most exquisitely breathtaking coast, even passing the island that apparently used to belong to Sophia Loren. We all sat in stunned silence, drinking in the craggy beauty of the mountains, until Jon said quizzically, 'These people move to Brooklyn?'

23

MOMENTARY LAPSE ...
THE SHOW

This chapter is for serious Floydies, so, if you're not one, feel free to skip it. Looking and listening back, I'm in equal parts horrified, amazed, embarrassed and proud of what we – or at least I – did. The eighties were after all about whizz-bang kitchen-sink flashy playing, and seeing as some of us were really quite young, we can perhaps be forgiven some of our trespasses. I, although very conscious of having a 'caretaker' role in the bass department, was still guilty of occasionally overplaying to the point of negligence. Not to mention indulging in completely uncalled for slap bass.

After deciding that 'Echoes' wasn't working as a show opener, we opted for 'Shine On' instead. This usually passed without incident, apart from my gratuitous slapping at the end.

Pink Floyd are one of the few bands who have the luxury of being able to play their *entire* new album before giving the crowd some faves, so that's exactly what we did. *A Momentary Lapse Of Reason* was a somewhat contentious album, being the first post-Rog, and featuring so many outside writers and players. My thoughts are that it doesn't sound particularly like a Pink Floyd record, but that it's a very good album.[*] Admittedly a tad bombastic in parts, but then if you are playing stadiums, why not? As the bass playing on it was all either Tony Levin or David, I didn't feel a great burden of stewardship. Besides, I liked to

---

[*]   As opposed to, say, Roger's *Radio KAOS*, which may have had more Floyd hallmarks, but isn't as enjoyable a listen. IMHO.

think that my style was similar to Tony Levin's – in my dreams anyway.

Most of us were offstage for 'Signs Of Life', the opening instrumental, featuring a film of Langley, the gardener at David's studio, who looked uncannily like Roger.

'Learning To Fly' opened with a big drum and electronic percussion intro, which within a few gigs bore absolutely no resemblance to the record whatsoever. I thought it surprising, though applaudingly egalitarian, that David gave Tim the guitar solo on this, being so early in the set. *

'Yet Another Movie' had an intro of absurdly huge drums being answered by absurdly huge synth sounds. Gary had light sabre-type sticks for this, which was visually stunning for the audience, but hard to take seriously from where I was standing. The song proper had a simple but enormous BOOM! . . . BOOM BOOM! bass drum part, played by both drummers, which I was to augment with Dum . . . Dum Dum. The slight problem was that Gary and Nick have very different ideas of where the beat is, so what I heard was BOOBOOM! . . . BOOBOOBOOBOOM! And had to pick a point somewhere in the middle to stick my notes. When it came to discrepancies such as this, though, I always deferred to Nick.

'A New Machine' was just David belting out some fantastically bleak lyrics through a vocoder, giving me time to run around the back of the stage for the next song.

'Terminal Frost', an instrumental, featured Scott playing soprano sax, for which he needed my mic. This meant that we had to swap places, so I got to be on stage right for this one, having to rely on Scott's monitors to hear myself, which wasn't ideal, especially as I was playing fretless.

After a reprise of 'A New Machine' it was time for 'Sorrow', for which I make no apologies. Everything about this song is absolutely fucking enormous, not least the bass part, which on the album is a synth, but I like to think I made it my own. Well, I would. I even stand by my jump kicks.

---

* Trainspotters note. At my suggestion, at the very end of the song, David and I play the riff from the end of verse two of 'Young Lust'. It's an all time fave of mine, and I was determined to get it into the show somewhere.

'Dogs Of War' was another full-on onslaught, and Jon's big nerve-racking moment. The song started with a film of Alsatians running out of the sea, and the music had to be perfectly in sync, as the film ended with a shot of David mouthing the line 'Dogs of war' as the real David sang the line 'Dogs of war'. In order for that to happen, Jon had to hit 'start' on his sequencer at the exact moment the second dog from the right's back left leg hit the water. No pressure there, then.

It was probably Scott's finest moment of the show.

'On The Turning Away' is a great song and classic stadium fare. It's also the only song I ever seriously cocked up on. I didn't come in till the second verse, so I had a chance for a breather in my backstage cubbyhole. At one show I took the opportunity for a bit of a lie-down, being pretty much exhausted for some reason. I found myself really listening to, and enjoying, the song. After the first verse I remember lying there thinking, I love this bit, this is where I come in. I was listening for the slinky bass intro, and started to get perturbed when I didn't hear it, which was obviously due to the fact that I wasn't playing it. Shit! I jumped up and found Syd standing there, holding my bass – he hadn't wanted to disturb me, bless him! – and I legged it onto the stage so fast I almost went over the front into the pit.

That was the end of part one, and we all headed back to the dressing room, where canapés were served and everyone stuffed themselves with prawns and smoked salmon, and many enjoyed a well-deserved glass of champagne. I know I did, even though I don't really like the stuff.[*] There would be jokes about who'd fluffed what or who'd done something funny, but little in the way of self-congratulation or back-slapping, which is far healthier than, 'Hey, man, you were great, you rock!'

'No, you rock!'

'No, *you* rock!'

But then, we were (mostly) British.

'One Of These Days' was just heaven for me. I'd come on alone, in the dark, hearing the excited hubbub of anticipation rising from the crowd. I could do anything! I'd nervously check and recheck my effects

---

[*] My drinking requirements were: two bottles of water and a bottle of beer for the first half, then white wine spritzers, starting weak and getting stronger, throughout the second. If you're interested.

before starting, even though the song has a built-in fail-safe mechanism, the two 'donk, donk, donk, donk, donk' single hits before the riff starts.

I'd hit one, a spotlight would come up on me and the crowd would go mental. One more and we were off. Jon actually doubled me with a sampled bass after four bars, but who cares, it was my moment. In the middle section I got to play a solo of sorts, as well as the Dr Who theme. This meant I had to actually look at the bass, and so missed the pig doing its inimitable thing over the crowd.

When the drums and everything else came crashing in, I'd be flying by the seat of my pants, as ninety-nine times out of a hundred, in all the excitement, the drummers would speed up madly, something Jon or I couldn't do, as we were playing to a delay. We'd look at each other and shout, 'Whoa there, Steve!'[*]

As it was all bells and whistles by now, Gary and I used to throw in the 'Ba-bang!' chord from 'Waterfront' by Simple Minds, seeing as it was essentially the same riff. Glorious fun.

'On The Run' was all on tape, except for the scream that accompanied the flying bed. We all got to take turns doing it, although I only remember doing it once.

'Time' was my other nerve-racking moment. The 'tick tock' at the beginning is produced by playing the muted two top strings of the bass. It has to be at the right tempo as the guitar is going through about a zillion delays when it comes in. The tempo is set at one beat to one revolution of the spinning clock in the film. This isn't easy, as for a start I was standing practically underneath the screen, and the clock is moving forwards in the film, getting bigger as well as spinning. I never got bored of listening to Nick's rototoms, though, or David and Rick singing together.

'Great Gig In The Sky' is the greatest piece of music Erik Satie never wrote. When we started rehearsing this, it hadn't been decided how it was to be sung, though the girls all had a really good reason for why they should be the one to sing it, my favourite being: 'It has to be one emotion, one voice, *or there's no point doing it.*'

Of course, dear.

---

[*]   Bit of a muso in-joke. Refers to 'Joe's Garage' by Frank Zappa.

In the end, each girl got to sing a third of it.

'Wish You Were Here' was probably the longest I got to wait in the wings before having to come on. I can't tell you how much I love singing that harmony, even if it is right at the top of my range.

'Welcome To The Machine' was spooky and majestic. It was the only song where I thought the sound effects and film seemed dated. I had to try and be a big bad bass synth on this, which is always nice.

'Us And Them' is musically one of the all-time Floyd greats. Unless you're just playing bass on it, in which case it's actually quite dull. Well, it is over seven minutes long. I was a model of restraint, though, sticking pretty close to the part as it was played on the record, not that I had much choice, as anything else would leap out. In 1994 I was given a harmony to sing on the choruses, which changed the whole complexion and made it a song I actually looked forward to. If only they'd thought of it sooner.

Now for the money shot . . . Er . . . 'Money'. The bass is meant to come in in time with the cash registers, which would be nigh on impossible as they were all over the quad,* but luckily I had a recording of David shouting 'ONE, TWO, THREE, FOUR' etc., coming through my monitors.

A lot of it sounded great, but the reggae section will haunt me to my grave and the bass solo makes me cringe, though Chester Kamen tells me it's revered among London's Brazilian jazz community. *Muito obrigado, amigos!*

Helicopters and searchlights can only mean one thing: 'Brick'. It's phenomenal fun to play, not to mention sing, although the slap break and subsequent Chic-type bass playing are yet more moments of shame. Although over the years I've had so many bass players tell me they love that bit that I'm a little torn. I always felt for Tim, getting his second solo of the night right after one of David's most iconic ones.

Coming down the home straight and round the last corner it's 'Comfortably Numb'. I never get bored of playing this and still get tingles waiting for the first solo, and the second, of course. The fun to be had while playing it was to see how locked down you could get it in the

---

* The quadrophonic sound system, meaning half the sounds were playing at the back of the arena or stadium.

bridge sections. At first I used to stand next to Nick and hold up one or two fingers to indicate how many bass notes and bass drums were in each bar, just to make sure we were bang on, but after a while it became something of a joke between us. I used to go fairly bonkers at the end, but I figured the guitar was probably so loud in the PA by then it didn't really matter what I, or indeed anyone apart from David, was playing.

We'd then come off and mill about at the back of the stage, waiting for the encore. David and I would have a gargle of port, as we had taxing vocal duties coming up, but by the end of the tour, this had deteriorated into gulping down a huge glass of it.

With 'One Slip' it was back to the new album and a full eighties rock extravaganza. The bass solo in the middle is actually Tony Levin playing a Chapman Stick on the record. Luckily I wasn't asked to get one of those, instead I just put my bass through every effect I had and hoped for the best.

'Run Like Hell' is quite simply the most fun I've ever been paid to have. We had a whole run of shows in the States where it pissed down, so we'd all sing, 'Rain! Rain . . . !' at the beginning.

I can't remember if I did it on this one, but on the 1994 tour I changed the last line to 'They're gonna send you back to (name of town we were playing) in a cardboard box!' Cheesy? Perhaps.

On the last night at Earls Court in 1994 it was 'Send me back to Gala . . . '

24

I n the middle of the 1989 European tour we took a serious left turn at Athens and went to Moscow to play four shows at the Olympic Stadium in early June, and it was the strangest, most fascinating, moving and funny bit of touring I've ever done. Well, outside of rural Australia anyway . . .

Gorbachev was busy shaking things up with *glasnost* and *perestroika*, and so was encouraging artistic exchange with the outside world, hence the invite. When we turned up with our full whizz-bang *War of the Worlds* blitzkrieg experience, Russia's only previous experience of live Western pop music had been Billy Joel and Elton John, who'd performed solo, except for a cardboard cut-out of Ray Cooper. This was going to be interesting.

David and Nick had attended a Russian space launch some months earlier, and a cassette of *Delicate Sound of Thunder* – without case, for weight reasons – had been taken up to the Russian space station MIR. It was a comforting thought that should the world perish in the near future, our jolly little band would be amongst the few human endeavours to remain, along with the names of the Apollo astronauts, and, of all people, Richard Nixon, whose name adorns a plaque on the moon.

Our gear was flown from Greece in a Soviet Air Force Antonov An-124, the biggest plane in the world at that time, and still. Syd, my tech, went in it. He said they turned the engines on, and a couple of hours later turned them off, and somehow when they opened the doors they were in another country. He wasn't aware of the plane moving at all.

Our hotel was the National, probably the biggest hotel in the world (I see a pattern emerging, 'We were served the biggest bowl of caviar in the world', although, come to think of it, I think we were) and was extraordinary. It had over 600 rooms, with corridors so long that the crew would take footballs to practise dribbling on the way to the bar.

The rooms were tiny, bleak, but with a certain post-war charm of my own imagining. The first time I got out from the freezing drizzle that passed for a shower, I discovered that what I'd thought was a flannel was in fact the one and only towel.

There was no hotel operator, every room had its own dedicated phone line, meaning there was no buffer between you and the archaic creaking nightmare that was the Soviet telephone system. This also meant you had to make a real, outside, charged call to speak to someone on the floor below.

Beside the lift on every landing was a terrifying old woman sternly guarding a samovar of steaming Russian tea, which was so strong that taking a sip was more like hitting on a hookah pipe than having a cuppa.

There was a bar on each corner of every floor, some of them serving food allegedly, although most of it would have been better suited to building a house than ingesting. The bar we adopted was nicknamed the Star Wars bar by the crew, because it was pretty much identical to the bar in *Star Wars*, in terms of clientele anyway. The East was still shut off from the non-Communist world, so we would spend our evenings carousing with delegations of East German die-cutters and Cuban engineers *en route* to Angola. One evening, when Rick treated us all to a sing-song at the piano – which the crew had liberated from another bar – he was accompanied by a load of Yugoslavian mechanics, who happened to be a part-time brass band and had brought all their instruments along for the conference they were attending.

Although the state was all-seeing and all-powerful, it soon became clear that there was very little that couldn't be taken care of with twenty B&H. Gorby had implemented a vodka ban a few years earlier, thinking that if the country was going to pull itself together and rejoin the wider world, it might be easier if its citizens weren't paralytic. Although the ban had been lifted, vodka was still very hard to get hold of, and the only bar in town that had any was the International Hotel.

I went one night and came staggering back with some of the crew.

On our way through Gorsky Prospect we came across a gaggle of girls in two parked cars, who were playing music and, y'know, like, hanging out. The crew steamed straight in to do their selfless bit for East-West relations, and with my head swimming somewhat, I leaned back on a pillar to enjoy the scene.

Suddenly, from out of nowhere, a man was standing beside me in a crisp fifties-style suit and, I'm pretty sure, sunglasses. In a spy-movie Russian accent, he quietly said, 'Mr Pratt, I think you and your friends have had a lot of fun tonight and should now be getting back to your hotel.' Then he was gone.

It took me a second to take it in, but then my three hours in the bar vanished as quickly as the mystery man, and I felt immediately stone cold sober.

'Um, lads, er, it's a bit late, you know? Perhaps we could, um well, you know, er . . . get going?'

The lads stared at me in disbelief and bewilderment, but something in my tone made them take me seriously and so we set off for the hotel, with me furtively looking around and making sure everyone walked on the pavement, wasn't too loud and only threw up in dustbins.

The shows themselves were amazing events, tickets having been doled out to the party faithful, with anyone young and potentially troublesome banished to the back of the hall, behind rather a lot of soldiers. Apparently the tickets had been awarded like prizes. For instance, if your plant had produced the most tractor parts in Belarus, you got two tickets to the Bolshoi, and perhaps two to Pink Floyd, whether you liked it or not. This meant that the front rows mainly comprised prim elderly couples, ladies clutching their handbags and people who would much rather be at the circus. At one show, there was a bloke bang in the centre of the front row who spent the whole evening desperately trying to listen to a football match on his radio.

There are always key moments in a show which act as triggers, when you know the audience are going to go mad, such as the helicopter at the start of 'Brick' (part two), the cash registers from 'Money', the clocks from 'Time', the appearance of the mirror ball, etc. One trigger that set the audience off every night in Moscow, and which remains a complete mystery, came halfway through 'Us And Them'. We had an accompanying film that showed various people from all over the world going to work. One of the sequences showed South African diamond miners holding their boots upside down above their heads, to show they hadn't smuggled any diamonds out in their footwear. In every other city in the world where we'd played this song, the moment passed without incident. In Moscow for some reason, the image sparked a wave of recognition in the entire audience and sent them berserk. If someone could enlighten me as to the cause, I'd love to know.

Three Western albums a year were released in the USSR on the State record label, and in this particular year, unsurprisingly, one of them was *Delicate Sound of Thunder*, our then current live effort. People would bring their copies along to the show, get a bit overexcited and throw them to us onstage, which while very touching seemed a bit of a waste, as we all obviously had copies already. They also had the well-intentioned but incredibly dangerous habit of throwing money at us during 'Money' – not notes, you understand. Incoming watches proved to be something of a hazard as well. Sometimes the soldiers charged with keeping order would get carried away and run up to the stage to throw us their hats, which were great souvenirs, but probably took some nifty explaining on their part when they asked for new ones.

Buford Jones, our sound engineer, would while away the tedious hours before showtime by playing computer games on his Mac by the mixing desk. In Moscow, he'd be surrounded by hordes of fascinated fans, marvelling at this new technology, the likes of which it appeared they'd never seen. It was rather poignant and sad that at the time the Soviet Union had pretty much the most advanced and active space programme in the world, but it would seem only cosmonauts got to master Pac-Man.

There was a drinks reception held for us at the British Embassy, which was pretty impressive, I thought, the ambassador, Sir Rodric Braithwaite, being a total dude. He'd obviously done his homework, and seemed to have a prepared bit of chat relevant to each member of the party when we had our allotted five minutes of conversation, just as he no doubt would for any other visiting delegation of hungover shabby idiots. I was told about a particular Russian folk singer whose songs were both witty and subversive, which he thought I might enjoy. He even wrote his name down for me, which I lost, obviously.

I, of course, had arrived half an hour late, having slept through my alarm call – if there was one, that might have been too sophisticated a concept for our hotel – and woken up next to someone I shouldn't have, frantically tying my tie as I ran across the bridge over the Moskva to the embassy. The embassy staff were all very charming, having been picked, no doubt, for their fluency in, and knowledge of, all things Russian, and displayed what seemed to be a genuine love for the place, tense as things where. (There had just been a by then routine expulsion of a dozen or so diplomatic staff for alleged spying that was a staple of the Cold War.) We even got to see the bar where everyone who left had their farewell drink, before ritually having their tie cut off and pinned on the wall, which was by then a huge mess of snipped neckwear.

I was presented with some sort of Olympic medal by the sports section of *Pravda*, simply because they recognized me walking past their office, which is about as sporting an achievement as I'll ever accomplish.

We were warned to be on our guard against set-ups, such as changing money on the black market, as back-street moneylenders were often police plants, not that you needed to change much money really, as most of the things you'd want were black market anyway, and those people wanted dollars.

Jon and I visited a music shop, and at first found the array of shoddy and old-fashioned goods amusing – the original sixties-designed fuzz boxes were a must – until an old man came in to buy a guitar. He was obviously a seriously accomplished classical guitarist, and although he wrestled with pretty much every guitar in the shop, it was apparent that they were all crap to the point of being unplayable. He was almost in tears and it was a heartbreaking sight that certainly shut us up.

I bought an album of Lenin's speeches, which I used on a remix I did years later of an Icehouse song called 'Love In Motion' – perhaps unsurprisingly called the Lenin Mix – a Paul McCartney album made specially for the USSR, which I've never listened to so still don't know what's on it, and an album that from the cover appeared to contain fish noises. It did, although most fish don't make much noise, so half the tracks comprise a spoken introduction to the type of fish – in Russian – followed by the sound of bubbles and something knocking against the side of a fish tank. Obviously it doesn't really stand up to repeated listening, but two of the fish and one introduction formed part of my contribution to the Orb track 'Spanish Castles In Space'. So the next time you find yourself with time on your hands and have smoked an awful lot of spliff, you can dig out the first Orb album and play 'spot the fish record'.

When we got to the airport to leave for Helsinki, we were informed that our entire luggage was to be searched for items that weren't allowed to be taken out of the country. This was mainly military hats, watches and general Communist Party paraphernalia. This caused some alarm as we'd all spent most of our spare time accumulating military hats, watches and general Communist Party paraphernalia. When I asked for a stamp in my passport, I was politely informed it would cost $20, so I made my excuses and left.

We all sat waiting nervously, until Jon got his guitar out and he and I amused ourselves by singing our hastily composed country ditty that went something like this:

> 'I just gotta get my shit to Helsinki
> I just gotta get my shit over that line
> I just gotta get my shit to Helsinki
> And boy, my best girl sure looks fine.'

Of course it was a false alarm, the customs guys just wanted to see what decadent marvels Pink Floyd filled their Samsonites with, and I have a box of mouldering badges and watches lying around somewhere to this day.

I even let Billy Mackenzie borrow my Russian army hat to wear in an Associates video, for which he repaid me with a collection of Chekhov plays, sweet man that he was.

25

STADIUM ETIQUETTE

W hen you first play stadiums, the crowd is a vast, indeterminate mass, with only the first few rows being vaguely recognizable as human beings. Invariably someone catches your eye, who you keep going back to, not necessarily for reasons of attractiveness, sometimes there's just something indefinably interesting about them. This can even be the very obviously gay guy down the front who you find yourself repeatedly looking at, invariably sending the wrong signals, and then trying to somehow imply that you're not trying to send those signals, thus making it even worse.

Another good one is when you find someone you like the look of and decide you're going to share the gig with them, you know, just give them the odd smile and maybe try to let them in on some of the things going on. Maybe it's just me, but it's something I've often done, and I think it can help your performance if you're having a shared experience with at least one member of the audience.

Except, that is, at Maine Road Stadium in Manchester, where the girl I was smiling at kept looking behind her, then turning to her mate and saying, 'Is he lookin' a' me?' as if I was some nutter on a park bench rather than part of the awesome spectacle she was willingly attending.

At a show in Modena, Italy, there was a guy right in front of David who was the absolute spitting image of me, which half the band noticed and found very amusing, especially as he got more and more twatted as the show went on and had actually passed out by the encore.

In a gig in Naples, half the front row confidently mimed how I was going to invite them backstage afterwards and they were going to give me cocaine, which was odd, as I had absolutely no intention of inviting any of them anywhere.

Once, while playing 'Comfortably Numb', again in Italy I believe, I spotted a guy down the front who was obviously in the grip of a very strong acid trip. Having been in the audience at a Floyd gig on acid myself, I found myself empathizing with him, to the point where I almost felt high. The awful thing was he looked as if he was heading towards a full-on bad trip. I tried to catch his eye, but couldn't do too much as I was singing, and to make things worse it was the nasty tone of the verse that was setting him off. I tried to communicate that he should hang on for a little bit, while he slid deeper into his psychedelic quagmire. As we hit the bridge, the lush orchestra and David's heavenly 'There is no pain . . . ' grabbed hold of him and I could see him lifted up into the sky, where the sun shone and brought him back to the light. I felt incredibly relieved, and have probably never got so psychically close to a punter before or since. So please don't stand in front of me if you're tripping, it's fucking exhausting.

When you're up on stage, you're a lot more susceptible to the audience than you might think. There are 80,000 people out there who love you. Well, not *me*, the majority of Pink Floyd's audience have hardly come to see me . . . Except for three certain Japanese dwarves, but I'd rather not go into that.

If one person thinks you're not really up to it, though, they can scupper the whole illusion. At one show I had to switch basses very quickly for some reason, and in the process my guitar strap pushed up my shirt collar. As I got to the front of the stage to sing, a guy down the front tugged at his collar, pointing out my sartorial disarray. I think I even said sorry.

At a show in Kansas City there was a beautiful girl stood centre front who was entirely unimpressed by the whole show. She didn't leave, though, she just stood there looking bored. You try to reach out to people if you can – girls get longer than boys, not surprisingly – but eventually, as in this case, you give up and start to actively dislike them, which is an awful way to feel about your audience. The bass player before me once ended up spitting at a fan, running off and spending the next two years writing a massive opus about alienation and loss. Personally, I just get a bit upset.

At the climax of the final encore, 'Run Like Hell', we had a bit of a shock in store for the front few rows. The entire front of the stage was made up of sections of three-sided slats, one side black, one mirrored and the last containing 400 aircraft landing lights. These would spin, and the effect could probably best be described as resembling Satan's combine harvester. How the band never got sued I'll never know, as it basically burned and blinded the front three rows – a lot of whom, of course, would be on acid, or at least *very* stoned – although it did seem to send rather a lot of them into an epiphany of psychedelic ecstasy, it must be said.

With this particular bored-looking beautiful girl, I remember thinking, 'Right, Miss Too-cool-for-school, let's see you blasé your way out of this.' But as everyone around her screamed and convulsed in pain and wonderment, she merely reached inside her jacket and pulled out a pair of shades, which she nonchalantly popped on and carried on watching with disinterest.

The other annoying thing was the bass-playing contingent, who would stand there scrutinizing my left hand, often showing displeasure at my playing style and technique. I'm far from the most technically correct musician in the world, and can easily be made to feel self-conscious, so I tended to step back or turn away to hide my fingering.[*]

After a while, you get really good at finding your guests in the audience, which is lovely if it's someone close, or someone you haven't seen for a long time, especially when you've been on the road for a while. It's not so good, however, when you see them going to the bar. It can really ruin your evening, and they never understand why you're being all sulky and petulant with them after the show.

I'm embarrassed to say that once, only once, mind, I spotted a girl in the audience, in Austin, Texas, again, who was so breathtakingly beautiful that I sent Syd, my tech, out into the audience to bring her up to say hello between songs. He went out to roughly where I'd told him

---

[*] Someone once heatedly pointed out to me that on the whole 1987–89 tours, I'd been putting a tiny extra inflection into the 'Money' riff, which was, of course, sacrilege. I hadn't even noticed I was doing it.

she was, and moved down the row pointing at the backs of people's heads, while I frantically shook my mine, until he found her, at which point I jumped up and down to let him know he'd scored.

At Giant's Stadium, New York, on the 1994 tour, there was a girl in front of me wearing a DEA cap, which I loved. I tried to intimate to her throughout the show that I wanted it, and she said yes, but I don't think she understood the request, as when Syd went and relieved her of said cap, in exchange for a few of my guitar picks, she seemed most upset. If she's reading this, I would like to take the opportunity to unreservedly apologize, and if it's any consolation, I still have the cap, which I treasure. Well, sort of, as in I haven't lost it. Oh hang on . . . no, there it is. Phew.

Occasionally, when playing major cities where there were important people in the audience – Jack Nicholson, Jeff Beck, Ahmet Ertegun, Adrian Gurvitz –you'd get a little pep talk, or a heads up at least from David or Steve O'Rourke, asking if we could maybe give it our best shot – not that we ever didn't, Cuyahoga Falls got as good as New York or London. The only time Nick Mason ever had a word about making it a good one was when we played the Stadio Municipal in Torino, Italy. The reason for this, it transpired, was that the bigwigs from the Ferrari factory down the road were attending.

When we arrived at that particular stadium, I'd thought nothing of it – another day another stadium, so to speak – but was amazed to discover it was the home of none other than the mighty Juventus! When I was a lad, there were only a few European football clubs whose names you knew, mainly because they were the giants of the European Cup. These teams were Ajax, Juventus, Bayern München, Real Madrid and AC Milan. Realizing this was the hallowed turf, the crew had organized two teams for a kickabout, but as soon as the game got under way the polizia stationed around the pitch ran on to stop it. When asked why the answer came back, 'England! Banned from Europe!'

Admittedly English clubs had been banned from playing in Europe since the Heysel tragedy three years earlier, but a ragtag bunch of crew and musos? It seemed a bit harsh.

Mind you, the polizia got their come-uppance later on when there was a riot during the show. At one point a truce was called and the troublemakers' ringleader was summoned to have a pow wow with the chief of police. He strolled over to him, in front of everyone, went to shake his hand, changed his mind and punched him in the face. The first we knew of any of this was when a gust of wind caused the band to be tear-gassed, nearly halting the show as we frantically got our eyes dabbed with lemon-infused water. But only after the crew had melodramatically been seen to themselves, the great pansies . . . Just kidding, lads.

At Wembley Stadium there was something like twelve different types of backstage pass, something not usually of concern to band members as the laminate trumps all. Not so here, though, where I ended up with about five different passes and still found certain areas off-limits. My granny, however, managed to get right to the stage, no problem.

She had come from Cyprus for the gig, and over the last few days had endured family members patronizingly telling her, 'Now you probably won't like them, Maria, but they're the best at what they do, and you should be very proud of Guy.'

Being the contrary troublemaker that she is, she *loved* the show, and couldn't contain herself, running as fast as her seventy-six-year-old legs would carry her through several manned barriers, arriving at the back of the stage just as we were coming off. She accosted David, shouting at him, 'I didn't think it was a ghastly racket *at all!*' Accusing him of being . . . 'really good'.

David looked round at me and I got the usual, 'One of yours?'

*

As any fule kno, since 1977 the pig has been an integral part of any Pink Floyd show. In fact, Roger Waters is busy unleashing porcine inflatables all over the Antipodes as I write. So whatever happens, the pig must go on, so to speak.

In mid-May 1988, Pink Floyd played the Veterans Stadium in Philadelphia, to a much more than sold-out crowd. They were uncomfortable, drunk and rowdy – not the greatest mix, it must be said – and I found myself really disliking them, for which I apologize to any of the doubtless many nice folk who were there and may be reading this.

We had two laser tables, which were surrounded by water jackets – that is, a collection of pipes that keep them cool. Towards the end of the first half, one of these blew up, causing hundreds of gallons of water to be dispersed backstage, where all the electricity for the sound and lights is kept. Not ideal.

When we came off stage for the interval, a frantic mopping-up operation was going on, in the midst of which was the pig, being inflated in readiness for its entrance during the upcoming 'One Of These Days'.

The problem, or rather one of many problems, was that a large amount of water had somehow found its way into the pig, which by the time it was inflated had become extremely heavy. This was indeed a conundrum, as if the pig went out, the wire wouldn't be able to support the extra weight, and it would crash into the audience.

There wasn't time to get the pig deflated and emptied, so a way had to be devised of getting the pig out while emptying it. The solution that presented itself was to snip a hole in the lowest part of the pig's body, and send it out. This, of course, was its cock. I allowed myself a small chuckle, as while I was banging away on the bass, the pig proudly sailed out and pissed on the audience.

26

Venice was to be the crowning glory of the 1989 tour. The reason that most bands don't perform stadium spectaculars there is because, well, there isn't anywhere to perform. It's a stunning hodgepodge of romantic little piazzas, alleyways and canals, as I'm sure you know, but noticeably lacking in major sporting venues.

Pink Floyd got around this slight hiccup by getting hold of a North Sea oil rig, setting up the stage on it sailing it into the lagoon, flying the Jolly Roger, of course, and parking it up facing the Piazza San Marco. Simple!

It was my first trip to Venice, and I was very excited, especially as I had friends coming out for the show, plus the added *frisson* of Rick's daughter Gala attending, with whom I had by now definitely overstepped the mark.

My dear friends Andy Caine and Youth helped make the stay particularly memorable, as they got spectacularly drunk, passed out, missed the show, got chased across Piazza San Marco by Simon Le Bon, then capped it all off by missing their flight home. A stunning scorecard that even I could never hope to match. Although it did turn out to be quite a profitable trip for Youth, as he suggested to one of our backing singers, Durga McBroom, that she should come to London, where he'd 'make her a star'. She did and he did, briefly anyway. Anyone remember Blue Pearl? His pitch was that she would make a great 'deep house diva'. I remember adding that it was probably better than being a deep-sea diver, for her anyway.

We were opening the Venice Festival, and there were all manner of problems to overcome. I don't want to go into all that too much, as being a pawn in a bigger game I was only party to hearsay, so Nick Mason's excellent book is probably a better bet for all the technical stuff.

One thing that was amusing, though, was that the head of the Gondoliers' Union came to see Steve O'Rourke a couple of hours before the show to demand a massive payment, as apparently we were causing the gondoliers to lose work. This was patently nonsense as every gondola in town had been booked to park up in front of the stage for the gig. He then threatened to gather all the gondolas in front of the stage – where they were going to be anyway – and as we played they'd blow their whistles.

As we were playing about 500 yards offshore, and the sound had to reach right to the back of the square, we had something of a fearsome PA set-up.

I believe Steve's reply was along the lines of, 'OK, give it your best shot.'

Our hotel, the Excelsior, was out at the Lido, so we had to drive (sail/boat/motor?) to soundcheck the afternoon before the show. I have a distinct memory of arriving at the back of the main barge – there was another one with all the generators and TV trucks on it – and walking to the back of the stage, at which point everything became familiar. I ran up the same old stairs, past the same old backstage snug, and Syd giving me the same old bass in the same old tried-and-tested fashion. I went to my spot stage left, did the same old routine of looking left to make sure the effect units in my rack hadn't been replaced with, I don't know, venomous snakes? – a constant worry – check my tuning – unnecessary really as Syd would have tuned the bass seconds before handing it to me – looked down and clicked through my pedals as usual. Then and only then did I look up. Holy shitting Christ!

As a child, my first epiphany concerning art was the discovery of JMW Turner at the age of eleven. In my first year at school I won the art prize, and what I asked for and received was a print of Turner's fabulously evocative and ethereal painting of San Marco from the lagoon. I was standing pretty much exactly on the spot it was painted from. Probably about 50 feet higher up, but even so, it was and remains a gobsmacking moment.

The gig was extraordinary in many ways. It was being televised live all over Europe, so timing was critical, and David had a huge LED clock in front of him to keep him up to speed. It's the only time I've ever heard a trace of nerves in his voice, but only between songs, of course. Playing to a load of people in boats, with a huge crowd in the distance, was pretty disarming as well, and there was a brilliant comedy moment when a barge full of champagne-swilling canapé-nibbling dignitaries tried to muscle in and park in front of the stage. They were pelted with bottles, food and God knows what else until they were forced to beat a very undignified retreat to somewhere round the side, which we all delighted in greatly.

After the show it was back to the hotel for a grand soirée, but I had other ideas. It was only about 9.30 p.m., so I thought the best option was to head straight to the San Daniele Hotel, where all the pop stars and my mates, not to mention Gala, were situated to get some bar action and compliments in first.

As usual, our ornamental security guard – not Barry – proved totally useless and couldn't get me off the barge. After about twenty minutes I got fed up, went up to someone and said, 'Hi, I'm Guy Pratt, I'm the bass player and I'd really appreciate a ride over there.' I was immediately obliged. God only knows what he used to say to people that made them so actively do nothing. We used to stand outside nightclubs in the rain while he 'sorted things out', until one of us went up, said who we were and got us ushered in immediately.

Once safely ensconced in the bar at the San Daniele, things started to look up. Paul Young demanded to buy me a drink, which I gratefully accepted. Then about twenty minutes passed while people offered to get me drinks and I kept saying no, as Paul had me covered. I then realized that Paul, though incredibly sweet, is not the most assertive person in the world and that unless I took action myself I was going to die of thirst.

Youth and Andy had woken up by this point, and as everyone enquired, 'Wasn't that just the best thing you've ever seen?' Rather than try to explain that they'd started drinking a tad too early and missed it, they had no choice but to nod meekly.

After that, we all headed back to our hotel at the Lido, where a massive party was in full swing.

Apparently, in a moment of drunken excitement, I asked Gala to marry me, which was probably a tad flippant. We arranged to go for a gondola ride the next day, by which time I was extremely hungover and regretful. Gala informs me that I barely looked at her, didn't say a word and was very definitely not about to marry her. We finally laid the ghost of this awful trip to rest last August when, playing in Venice again with Gilmour, we went for a very funny midnight gondola ride. I'm happy to say that seeing as I did actually marry her, eventually Gala's decided to forgive me.

That night a bunch of us went looking for a nightclub, *any* nightclub, as that's what you did in the eighties. We found a bizarre little basement place, and spent the evening trying not to look at the female dwarf who was straight out of *Don't Look Now*. There was myself, Gala, Tim, Gary, Durga, Youth, Andy, Paul and Stacey Young, Simon and Yasmin Le Bon, and John Taylor, who Gala had a quick fling with when she got home as she was so pissed off with me.

We chugged home by water taxi, through the sinking city, past endless abandoned, rotting ground floors, and Andy told Paul he'd just bought a flat in Venice.

'It's a basement, it was really cheap.'

'Really, that's great.'

'No, Paul, I'm joking.'

At Piazza San Marco, Youth and Andy jumped out to go to their hotel. Just as we were pulling away, Simon realized they hadn't chipped in. 'Hey, who were those guys?' he asked, while we all made out we'd never seen them before in our lives, giving it that old line, 'I thought they were with you.' Feeling cheated by a couple of impostors, Simon jumped out of the taxi and sprinted after them, while we all collapsed in hysterics on the boat.

We were at the airport at the same time as everyone else the next morning, including a very sorry, battered-looking Youth and Andy. They'd carried on back at their hotel bar, overslept for the second time in two days, missed their plane and were waiting for the next one, having had to buy new tickets.

'I could've gone to the Caribbean for what this cost me,' moaned Youth.

I went to say hello to Simon, 'Shh! Not now! I'm writing a song!' he said.

Which was odd, as he appeared to be checking in, although the next Duran Duran album did feature a song called 'Venice In Peril'.

27

STORYVILLE

I started work on Robbie Robertson's album at Village Recorders in West LA the day after finishing the Floyd European/Russian campaign in a state best described as completely fried. It was either start then or lose the gig, and this was a prestige appointment, Robbie's previous album (the imaginatively titled *Robbie Robertson*) having been a humdinger, a classic even. Besides which, I didn't really *get* holidays as a concept back then. I thought they were just for people who didn't love their job, the idea of 'rest' being completely alien to me then. That's probably why I have so little hair left.

The only break I got was a couple of weeks in, when I spent three days on a house boat up at Lake Powell, Arizona, which was like a fey version of *Deliverance*, it being an all-male party including Jimmy Nail and legendary comedy writers Ian La Frenais and Dick Clements.

Our one moment of excitement – apart from crashing the boat practically every time we moored, despite having Ian's brother-in-law, an alleged ex-coastguard on board – occurred when we came across what seemed to be, through binoculars at least, a boatload of stranded girls. Alas it turned out to be a rather distressed bunch of LA hairdressers, who were in a complete state, having been stuck for an unbearably terrifying whole half-hour. Seeing as Lake Powell has 1,960 miles of coastline, if you do get stuck, the chances are it's going to be slightly more than half an hour before someone comes to get you. Incredibly, their main concern seemed to be that people from the same socio/political universe as them had rescued them.

'You live in Hollywood? We live in Hollywood *too*!'

Had we been from Cleveland, they may well have opted to stay and starve.

Working with Robbie was pure gravy, as Americans like to say, though I'm not entirely sure what it means, apart from 'good', for as well as being a man of incredible wit, charm and talent, he has one of the coolest histories of anyone I've ever met. He was, and still is, I expect, the most amazing storyteller, which I put down to his being half Native American, and therefore part of a rich culture of oral history.

We would toil away in the studio, while he worked on lyrics in a little office upstairs, coming down to review the day's progress at six o'clock every day. This became known as 'Rob's story hour' as he would inevitably start on some tale that would grow and meander, with us all rapt, almost but not quite sitting around his feet.

'So, Garth and I are on the run from Al Kooper, who's coming down from Chicago to kill us for stealing his weed, and we're holed up in this joint in Florida with a one-armed go-go dancer from Jack Ruby's club. Meanwhile I got Dylan on the phone asking me where the hell we are, when the ATF turn up with these dogs, which Garth nearly shoots 'cos they turned the lights out and this is just before Clapton shows up at the airport . . . ' And so on and so on, all delivered in Robbie's seductive laconic drawl. Hilarious.

He told me how he went on a year-long *Fear and Loathing*-type bender with Martin Scorsese, careering around the world, picking up awards for *The Last Waltz*, and that the guy who sells Travis Bickle the guns in *Taxi Driver* was Neil Diamond's junkie tour manager, who organized Neil's tours on crazy zig-zag routes that coincided with his 'connections'. When Neil asked how come they were flying from New York to LA via, I dunno, Kentucky, this guy would say flat out, 'That's how it is now, there are no direct flights any more.'

The producer who'd brought me in was my mate Stephen Hague, an American who lives in London and is very much in tune with the English zeitgeist, having produced New Order and the Pet Shop Boys. The engineer was another Brit, Steve Nye, himself a successful and established producer, and a very, very, very dry wit, which made for a slightly fraught relationship between them and much confusion in the control room whenever you called out for Steve or Stephen.

At one time we had yet another Steven on the session, and when Robbie had to introduce someone to us all, he said, 'This is Steve, this is Stephen, and this is . . . Stev*est*!' Steve Nye was also the first, but not the last, engineer to say that Betsy – my 1964 Jazz Bass – was the best-sounding bass guitar he'd ever recorded.

Over the next three months I got to play with a ludicrous panoply of musicians, especially drummers, as pretty much a career's worth of bashers passed through the slightly tacky art nouveau-style doors (the studio had been redecorated some years earlier to Fleetwood Mac's drug-addled specifications). Robbie wanted a then terribly fashionable New Orleans vibe on the record, and so imported players from The Meters and Neville Brothers, who I held in complete awe, owing to the fine tutelage of Robert Palmer.

There was guitarist Bill Dillon, who had an amazing ethereal style, using so many different effects and gadgets that at one point Robbie suggested he get an assistant to help him play his parts. As far as we could tell, though, in the months we worked, he never seemed to change his clothes once.

My favourite player was Zigaboo Modeliste, legendary sticksman for The Meters, who'd also played for Dr John, Lee Dorsey, Allen Toussaint and, of course, on *Sneakin' Sally*, Robert Palmer's first album. I'd always heard him talked about in such hushed, revered tones that I'd assumed he was about ninety years old, or long since dead. In fact, he was in his early forties and had the spent the last few years working in a shoe shop in New Orleans. Watching him play was incredible, as you couldn't really make out what he was doing – 'Mixing up gumbo' as Robbie used to call it.

He stuck up for me, which was really touching, as my idea of bedtime was way out of whack at this point, and I was seldom less than an hour late in the morning. On one occasion, as producer Stephen Hague was chastising me, he stood up from behind his kit, threw down his sticks and declared, 'A man with his talent is *allowed* to sleep in once in a while!'

Stephen's point being that this was far from once in a while.

It got to the point where Robbie and Stephen actually drew up a list of my ever-more-far-fetched excuses and pinned them to the wall, where people were then encouraged to add their own, such as, 'Taken hostage by Colombian drug lords', 'Obliged to go drinking with firemen after saving children from blazing orphanage.'

Ginger Baker was in for a while, and turned fifty during the sessions, which seemed unimaginably old to me back then. He was an utter sweetheart, with a surprisingly encyclopaedic knowledge of olive oil. He'd bought an olive farm in Tuscany years before, where he'd sort of retired to have a word with himself. If you wanted to get him choked up, you just had to ask about the quality of the supposedly extra-virgin olive oils on the market. This would send him into paroxysms of barely suppressed rage, bringing him almost to tears as he cursed how they had 'maybe a drop if you're lucky' in them.

Ginger told me that the night Jimi Hendrix died, he'd arranged to meet him at a nightclub, as they were going halves on a jar – *a jar?* – of pharmaceutical cocaine, which Ginger brought with him. Utterly dead-pan, Ginger said, 'It's a shame he never showed up, cos if he'd come to see me, he certainly wouldn't have fallen asleep.'

He would spend hours working out parts, including playing cymbals laid on the floor, and using all sorts of odd beaters. The only snag being, as soon as we began recording, he'd forget what the part was, and we'd have to start all over again.

Jazz legend Tony Williams came in, and I was terrified of being in the same room as him, thinking how crap I must seem next to the jazz bassists he'd played with. Weirdly, the song he was asked to do was a straight four-on-the-floor job, which he actually had great trouble play-ing. He wasn't asked back, although why you'd ask someone like him to play like that I couldn't fathom.

Then there was the legendary Ndugu Chancler, who's played for just about everyone, even supplying the pristinely perfect beat on 'Billie Jean' and he too ended up on the cutting room floor. I can't remember much about him being there, except that it was another legend to notch up.

Finally, there was Jerry Marotta, who I adored. I felt the most at home with him, as he'd played on so many records I loved, was a man of some culture, mad and a fellow drug fiend. He was the only musician on the album to ever end up back at my house, not counting the disastrous bar-becue I had one Sunday afternoon, where a load of west Londoners got completely twatted and threw water over everyone.

So ensconced was I in LA by this point that I even had a proper girl-friend, the lovely Carrie. She had two children by Emilio Estevez – a Hollywood secret at that time – who like his brother, Charlie, was per-haps somewhat lacking in the attentive-parenting department. Martin Sheen, though, was fiercely parochial, and liked to have his grand-children around him, so all the various exes and their families were put up in houses all around Malibu, from whence he could keep a kindly interfering eye on them.

Martin was quite rotund at the time, which made him pretty fear-some looking. He even had a sign on his fridge door that said, 'If you indulge, you will bulge!' I thought he was brilliant, but he viewed me with nothing but utterly justified suspicion. One morning, I was lying in bed nursing an appalling hangover, and wondering just how late I could be into the studio, when there was a commotion outside. Martin had come storming in and was yelling at Carrie, mainly about me, 'Who is this guy? What do you really know about him?', etc. I pulled the covers over my head and lay there whispering, 'The horror . . . the horror . . . '

One Saturday, Carrie invited me to a Sheen family reunion up at their house. I got there to find Martin's seven – yes, seven – brothers and their families all there. It was terrifying; they all had those intense, piercing eyes and gruff, commanding voice. I have never felt so outnumbered in my life. When I told Jerry about it he said, 'Hey, man, you should've taken me. I'm like having five people with you!'

I worked on the album for nearly three months, and they carried on for ages after I'd left. The album didn't come out for another two years. It's a great album, I think, and I did some quite nice playing on it. One song, 'Hold Back The Dawn', has four tracks of bass on it – bassline, chords, harmonics and fretless.

I'm not particularly surprised that Robbie hasn't asked me to do anything since, although if you're reading, Robbie, I do get up in the morning these days.

28

MICHAEL JACKSON

About four weeks into Robbie Robertson's album, I got a call from producer Bill Bottrell, asking if I could pop in and do a session for him that evening. 'Sure,' I said. 'Who's the artist?'

'Michael Jackson,' he replied.

I thought he was having a giraffe. You don't just casually get asked to pop in and do a Michael Jackson session. Well, I don't anyway.

I had a rather fierce hangover from the night before, having been to see The Who perform a star-studded Tommy at the Universal Amphitheatre.

There had been a huge proper Hollywood party afterwards, complete with fun fair, and quite a few Floyd mates were in town. Tim Renwick and Jane Sen with Mike + the Mechanics, and Mr Gilmour, who'd come to LA to buy a Second World War P-51 Mustang fighter. (He didn't.) Needless to say, it had been a late night, which wasn't a problem for dealing with Mr Robertson's delicious swampy grooves in a by now familiar and comfortable environment, but for a first-time gig, especially one as big as this, it ratcheted up the paranoia slightly.

I got permission from Robbie and producer Stephen Hague to leave early and arrived at Westlake Studios about half past five. I then nervously made my way into the control room to meet the moonwalker himself and was informed that he had 'just left'. This was to become something of a habit over the next week or so. It was great to see Bill, though, and quite a relief to not actually have to play in front of the man himself in my slightly fragile state.

They had a pretty basic track down – basic by Michael Jackson standards anyway, I thought it sounded fucking amazing – plus a vocal, with Michael warbling something about sunlight and trees and children, and 'what about them'. What indeed?

Bill then explained why I was there. Madonna's 'Like A Prayer' was a hit at the time, and on hearing it Michael had apparently commented on the bass, and how he'd like something like that on his record. Bill, who engineered 'Like A Prayer', had told him it was me and that I was in town. Voila!

The only snag was that the bass of mine he liked is a very particular type of bass playing, the technical term for which is 'showing off'. It's a very particular sound that involves an octave pedal – a trick I'd nicked from Pino Palladino a few years earlier – which is well suited to furious fancy-pants riffing, but not something you necessarily pull out of the bag in a ballad when the singer's asking, 'Did you ever stop to notice, all the children dead from war?'

As Michael wasn't there, I didn't feel too pressurized, so I set about laying down a few ideas for him to peruse the next day. I was a bit stumped, but had the idea of nicking the bass line from 'Bad', figuring that Michael would probably like it, he just wouldn't know why.

My friend Kevin Gilbert had been working on the sessions, and told me some quite disturbing stories, for instance, how Jackson would allegedly eat whole boxes of Kleenex every day. Not *eat* eat, but nervously tear them up and roll them into balls, then put in his mouth from whence they would never emerge.

Another odd thing was the loo. It had a door at each end, CCTV cameras over these doors, and a monitor inside, so you could see if anyone was thinking of coming in, and leave from the other end if it concerned you. This is not standard lavatory configuration for any studio – or indeed any building – I have ever visited, and was apparently done at Mr Jackson's request.

Two days later I was summoned back. Again Michael had 'just left'. Bill went through my various takes with me, explaining how Michael had liked this bit, wasn't sure about that bit, wondered if I could do something that was a cross between this bit and that bit, etc., etc. So I had a few more goes and left. This happened again a couple of days later, and I was starting to think, if Michael could just bloody well be there for once he could tell me exactly what he wanted, then I could do it for him, and that would be that.

My next visit was different. Michael had allegedly 'just left', but there was a weird vibe in the room and a lot more people, including a rather surly heavy-set 'engineer'.

I got started and almost immediately things became strange. The 'engineer' said, 'I don't think Michael would like that,' with great certainty. At first I thought, Fair enough, but then when I asked him if one particular idea was worth trying, he seemed to lean over before giving me a reply, as if he was listening to someone.

Someone hiding under the mixing desk.

That was it. Someone was hiding under the desk, telling the 'engineer' what Michael would or wouldn't like.

I couldn't believe it, and it was all I could do not to fall apart in a mixture of hysteria and confusion. This was too, too strange. Michael Jackson was hiding under the desk telling his engineer to tell me what he wanted me to do.

Once I'd got my head round the idea it became hilarious. I'd try to get to the other end of the desk to get an ashtray or whatever, only to find three people blocking my path. I started playing ludicrous things, like the melody of 'Worker's Playtime' – you know, der di der der, der di der der – and then asking the 'engineer' if Michael would think it appropriate. No matter how absurdly I played, he'd have to lean over, pause and then say, 'No, I don't think Michael would like that.'

I tried to convey my astonishment to Bill, but he was avoiding eye contact, or so it seemed.

I later found out the cause of the great man's monumental shyness. Apparently he was on nose job number twelve, or thereabouts, and his attempt at a button-like proboscis had pretty much collapsed. No plastic surgeon in LA would have any more to do with it and apparently it looked truly awful. One can only suppose that he went to Costa Rica or some other nip/tuck haven to get it sorted. But that wasn't all. At the same time there was apparently a big triangular flap of skin hanging off under his right eye, which would jiggle alarmingly when he danced, inducing those with even the strongest of stomachs to vomit.

When Michael's next album came out, the track we'd worked on was nowhere to be seen, or heard, rather, so I just thought, Ho-hum and forgot about it, until several years later when a friend phoned to tell me I was on HIStory, as he'd seen my name in the credits. I checked it out and, lo and behold, there I was, steaming my way through 'Earth Song', which subsequently went on to be Mr Jackson's biggest-ever single in Europe, not to mention the highlight of Jarvis Cocker's career when he wiggled his arse to it at The Brits.

I'm very proud to be on it, it's a great song and I think I did a great job, even if it was the most bizarre session I've ever done.

n 1990 I had a disastrous trip to New Orleans to work on a band project with Jon Carin. Part of the disaster was that it wasn't actually New Orleans at all but a slasher movie-style backwater called Reserve, Louisiana, nearly two hours' drive away. New Orleans was terribly fashionable at the time, as the Neville Brothers had a big hit album and Daniel Lanois had opened a studio there. I'd always loved The Meters and Dr John, and I'd worked with some of Louisiana's finest with Robbie Robertson the previous year.

Unfortunately, town was so far we only ever went in a few times, and I got to hate our backwater plantation house. The surrounding area comprised of fly-blown shack bars that served only piss-weak American beer, drive-thru daiquiri shops, and garages that offered a 'free cheeseburger with every oil change!'.

There was a supposedly upscale housing development being built nearby called Cretin Homes, which I thought hilarious, and about right, too. I even sent a photo of it to *Private Eye*'s 'I-Spy'. When I pointed this out to the guitarist Brian Stoltz he said, 'No, it's pronounced "Cray-Tan", it's French.' I gave up trying to explain that cretin is actually a French word (from the Latin *ChristiÇnum* (Christian), via a medieval French dialect to be precise).

We were working on Jon's songs to play for a record-company bigwig who was going to come down and see us. There were problems right from the start. One of the songs was called 'Headhunters' and was about how people are bombarded and brainwashed by advertising. I was

meant to sing a harmony on the chorus, but couldn't bring myself to sing the main line, 'Headhunters are killing the American heart.' As being the richest, greediest and most belligerent country on the planet, it's America's effect on the rest of the world's hearts that bothers me. I hope any Americans reading this will understand that it's nothing personal. Talking of hearts, mine wasn't really in it, and it obviously showed in my playing. There was a lot of muttering behind my back and I wasn't really getting along with anyone. Just before we packed up, Robert Palmer released a new single, a song I'd co-written, which went into the American Top 40, so I did what any sensible person would do and flew to Bogotá.[*]

A friend of a friend of the people I was staying with had a Sunday night classic rock show on Bogotá Radio, and asked if I'd be a guest. This was literally the day I arrived, so I had very little idea of what was going on, and of course agreed. When I got there, it turned out there was another guest, one Andrew Loog Oldham, who needs no introduction here. We spent the next three hours discussing music whether there was a record playing or not, he constantly spoon-feeding me the local export across the mic.

The next day, still in a complete daze, I was invited to an art gallery opening. I was asked if I'd mind doing an interview for one of the country's main broadsheets, to which I, of course, agreed. The journalist I spoke to was very pretty, but didn't speak a word of English, so the entire

[*]   This wasn't as impetuous as it sounds, as I'd met a lot of Colombians recently
      through my friend Chucho Merchan, bassist, arranger and Colombian.

thing had to be conducted through an interpreter, who was just another guest at the party we'd all been at for about three hours by this time.

When she asked the translator what I thought was the best thing about Madonna as an artist, the question I heard was, 'What's your favourite part of Madonna's body?' Imagine my horror when the interview appeared and I discovered that apparently I feel Madonna's greatest contribution to popular culture is her belly button.

It was a funny time to be in Colombia, as Pablo Escobar had recently absconded from his luxury prison, and was blowing up or shooting pretty much anyone he thought might want to put him back there. Being in hiding meant he'd cut back on his staff quite a lot, leaving a lot of bodyguards out of work, and lacking the necessary qualifications to earn the $50,000 a week they were used to. This meant that anyone who had a secretary, friend, or contactable family member was a potential kidnap victim.

While staying in Escobar's home town of Medellin on more than one occasion I would be at a party or barbecue and there'd be a phone call for me. This would be someone I didn't know asking if I was having a nice time and generally letting me know that they knew where I was, and that I was only at large as long as they decreed. I can only assume that a lack of consensus on who to contact to pay the ransom was why I wasn't bundled into a car.

It's also the only city I've ever visited where it is illegal to *wear* a crash helmet on a motorbike.

The reason being that with its balmy sub-tropical climes, most bars and restaurants are at least partly open air, and if the judge/MP/businessman/ex-husband you had it in for was at one, you simply rode up on a moped with a submachine-gun-toting passenger and took everyone out, in the hope that your target would be among the many casualties.

As these were the only people who ever wore crash helmets, for obvious reasons of anonymity, they were banned.

I spent some time in the beautiful town of Cali, which sadly, after Escobar's death, saw the ascendance of the Cali Cartel, making it the new coke capital. It sits in a valley surrounded by mountains, on top of one are three giant crosses. The locals joke that they were put there to stop the devil getting in, but unfortunately 'he was already here, so now he can't leave'.

I'd heard about a record shop there, which was meant to be one of the finest in all South America, and asked my friend Jorgé where it was. Apparently it was in a part of town I shouldn't visit alone, which apart from one main shopping street in Bogotá, seemed to be pretty much the case for every part of every town in the country.

We headed off into a very old labyrinthine district of twisting alleyways and howling dogs and found the shop, which was an Aladdin's cave of the Latin arts. Every mambo, bossa nova, cha cha, merengue, son, danzon, salsa, rumba, bolero, guaguanco and tango ever recorded was probably here, from Machito Live at the El Mocambo all the way to El Mocambo live at the Machito.

At this juncture, I should point out that, as it was 1990, Britain was in the grip of the whole Madchester, baggy, rave thing, and I would be lying if I said it hadn't affected my wardrobe, which meant I was probably wearing trainers that came up to my knees and some sort of surf T-shirt probably embroidered with lizards.

We walked into the record shop to be greeted by classic Wild West saloon-type suspicious looks from all and sundry. Jorgé strode up to the counter, behind which was the most fearsome patriarch imaginable, about eighty years old, all bushy moustache and eyebrows and smoking a meerschaum pipe. Proudly indicating me, Jorge pronounced, 'This is my friend Guy, from England. He play for Pink Floyd!'

The patriarch looked at Jorgé, then at me, looking singularly unimpressed.

'Pink Floyd?' he said, then shook his head. 'No, he look like . . . Manchester musician.'

The fact that deep in this temple of musical orthodoxy, a man like this had heard of the Happy Mondays, let alone knew how they and their ouevre dressed, makes him probably the coolest person I will ever meet.

30

KNEBWORTH 1990

Knebworth 1990: Pink Floyd, Paul McCartney, Mark Knopfler, Eric Clapton, Elton John, Genesis, Robert Plant and Jimmy Page, Cliff Richard, Status Quo, Tears for Fears. Attendance: 120,000. What a line-up! What a show! Although, to be honest, strangely unmemorable as a day.

It was the day classic rock started looking seriously corporate, middle-aged and somewhat middle class. A fact that's best exemplified by the swag we were given for doing the show. Rather than a tour jacket or sweatshirt, we got Knebworth '90 Barbour jackets. Seeing as it rained so much, I'm surprised they didn't do Knebworth '90 green wellies.

Pink Floyd rehearsed at Bray Film Studios, with the delectable Candi Dulfer playing sax. She was probably asked more questions about reeds, pads and the relative merits of Conn vs Selmer instruments in two days than Scott Page was in eighteen months. She certainly was by me anyway; I was quite bewitched. Even though her reedy David Sanborn style of playing didn't really suit the material.

Backing vocals were supplied by Clare Torry, she of Great Gig fame, the one and only Sam Brown and, touchingly, her mum Vicki, who'd sung with the band in the past and tragically wasn't long for this world.

During a lunch break, David took me for a spin in his new Ferrari F40. Although stupendously fast, the smell of petrol was somewhat off-putting and I still reckon that if you're paying £180,000 for a car, you're entitled to a comfy seat, a radio and an ashtray, or at least somewhere to keep your change.

Nick never used to come to anything in his sexier cars, which was somewhat disappointing. Admittedly it's probably like choosing what shirt to wear when you've got 900 in your wardrobe. You'd just give up and go for the sloppy T every time.

Talking of shirts, for the show, my girlfriend Susie had got me an acid house-style white hooded top and printed a big number 1 on it. It was my little in-joke for the band, as Roger had worn a T-shirt with the number 1 on it for *The Wall* shows. The difference being he'd meant it.

We flew in by helicopter. Not a sexy Jet Ranger or anything like that, but a big old Chinook-type army jobbie that was like being on a tube train going through an earthquake.

The Hard Rock usually does the backstage food at big charity gigs, and this was no exception. There was a rumour going around that the whole backstage area had been rejigged at the last minute because McCartney's enclave was too close to the decidedly flesh-based catering and he'd kicked off, but that was about the only rumour, which shows you how grown up and docile an event it was.

There was an extremely strict, and expensive, curfew, too, and as we were on last, it meant we were somewhat at the mercy of the acts before us. McCartney was on just before us, and unsurprisingly he went down a storm, asking the crowd after each song if they wanted some more, which of course they did. They weren't to know they were eating into the Floyd set.

By the time we went on, there was a storm of such magnitude raging that our circular screen had to have the screen removed – you couldn't just take the whole thing down as the frame contained half the band's lights. Sadly this meant we were filmless, although in the driving rain, I doubt anyone in the crowd could bear to have their eyes open for more than a few seconds at a time. The howling gale made us look like we were in a Whitesnake video, and I remember my fingers being so cold I could barely play, but the old triumph-over-adversity attitude kicked in, and I seem to recall we played a bit of a blinder.

The band's dear friend Michael Kamen came on to play on 'Comfortably Numb', as he'd written the orchestra part, which in my opinion is the finest in the history of pop music. He was going to play it on a synth, or at least augment what Jon was doing. I think the wildness of the storm got to him, though, because rather than the chords *we* knew, he went off on a mad Stravinsky-style, tonally challenging tangent that sounded very disturbing, although he did look fantastic playing it.

It was lovely to have the gang back together, and quite a big deal to headline such a stellar event, and all for charity, too, so it was only fitting that when we left, none of the principals or management bothered to say goodbye.

31

J apan in the eighties was the most exotic, hi-tech sci-fi theme park imaginable. It probably still is, but *then* it was conquering the world, practically everything we bought was made there and the economy was going through the roof.

I first went in 1984 with Icehouse, when I'd wandered around wide-eyed and open-mouthed, allocating each district points from one to ten on the *Blade Runner* scale. None was less than seven.

When you hailed a cab, it would pull up and the door would open automatically, closing once you were safely inside. The white-gloved driver would be watching a telly, and through his headset he'd be karaoke singing along to whatever video was on. Bonkers! The language barrier made things amusing, as I once had a cab driver in his sixties, who happily sang along to W.A.S.P's 'Fuck Like A Beast'.

As soon as you put your key card into the slot beside the hotel room door, the loo seat in the bathroom would start heating up in anticipation, a new film of plastic having slid around to cover it since your last use. On every street corner there were hot and cold drinks vending machines, and I became utterly addicted to the sickly sweet little cans of coffee they sold. They even had a built-in licensing function that shut down the sake section at 11 p.m.

All the office workers seemed to go and get drunk after work, the preferred tipple being whisky. This didn't seem to agree with them particularly well, as by eight o'clock, half the city was playing hopscotch on the freeway.

Everybody smoked, everywhere, all the time, and overflowing ash-trays lined the pavements. The Japanese smoked differently, only taking four or five puffs before stubbing their cigarette out, then lighting another a minute later.

We went into the record company to be shown around, and every encounter was an orgy of bowing and hand-shaking. I wandered off with Ray Hearn to have a sneaky peak. He opened a door and found himself in a boardroom with a full-on conference in progress, where someone was giving a talk with an overhead projector and everything. All eyes were on Ray, to see what the intruding gaijing (foreign devil) manager had to say. He stood there frozen, then raised a fist and shouted, 'Sell more records!' Before slamming the door and running down the corridor, both of us giggling like naughty schoolboys.

The Japanese version of the album, Sidewalk, came with a lyric sheet, which was odd, as no other version did. I asked Iva if he'd supplied them with the lyrics and the answer was no.

As it transpired, the record company boss's wife liked to translate lyrics from international releases as a sort of hobby. Iva was horrified, and rightly so, for when we checked the lyrics, she'd written down what she thought they were from listening to the album.

Here are some examples:

Iva's song	Japanese lyric sheet
'This city is the one we want tonight'	'This city is a one man woman tonight'
'So soft and warm, as only summer nights can'	'So something warm, and so is summer night's can'

I met and hung out with some really nice arty Japanese kids, and when I asked them where they learned their English, they told me partly from school, but mainly from album lyric sheets. Oh dear.

Tokyo was awash with Western models, as despite having conquered the world industrially, they seemed to find the whole consumer thing a little odd. As a result, all of their adverts for washing machines and TVs featured gaijing. The little ex-pat community I knew cruelly referred to them as FEMs and FAMs (Failed English Model or Failed American Model).

I once stopped off *en route* to Oz to stay with my girlfriend Kate, who was modelling there. She was in an apartment block stuffed full of models, mainly American and many as young as fifteen. You'd hear them on the phone at night, sobbing and pleading with their parents to be allowed to come home, only to be told, 'Now come on, honey, this is going to put you through college.'

Traditionally, Western bands hung out in the Lexington Queen, where the models got free drinks and locals were banned. It's a pretty tacky cattle market, and apart from having to go 'because the rest of the band are' I've always steered clear of it whenever possible.

Tokyo is choc-full of amazingly exotic clubs and bars, full of amazingly exotic Japanese people. Who wouldn't want some of that? The care that goes into cocktails is incomparable, and they'd even make ice for your drink by chipping away at a huge block until they'd sculpted one big perfect cube.

I was once taken to a tiny place that played the heaviest dub imaginable, and featured cocktails made with snake's blood. I was introduced to Yohji Yamamoto, then my favourite designer, and nearly fainted. Although that was probably more to do with the snake's blood.

Icehouse frequented a club called Red Shoes, next door to which was quite the most brilliant business idea ever. As you staggered out of the club at three in the morning, twatted, there in front of you was a practical joke shop. And, joy of joys, it was open. There was nothing for it but to go in and give them all your money. Every night.

With a culture so steeped in honour, the Japanese would never do anything so vulgar as check your credit card for validity or authenticity, and when I got home after my first trip I had about thirty letters from Barclaycard. The first five told me to stop using my card as I was way over my limit, and was followed by one saying, 'Oh, go on then, we've upped it,' then another five saying, 'Please stop using it,' then another, 'Oh go on.' And so it went on. This was in the days before Thatcher's deregulation made personal debt so desirable to banks.

Japanese culture traditionally dictates that they acknowledge no culture other than the one that defeats them. This is why it's a tragedy that the US beat them, rather than say, France or Italy. Everyone seemed to be dressed as a parody of an American, although with a studiousness you'd never find in Cleveland.

Ray Hearn moved to Japan – he's still there – and on one trip he took me down to the dodgy bathhouse district, where the Yakuza 'run ting'. Despite being a uniquely Japanese brand of organized criminal, even they had been infected by the Yankee bug. All of the young ones I saw had their hair permed and dressed like Robert De Niro in *Mean Streets*.

Most of the times I've visited Japan it's been to do shows promoted by Mr Udo. Traditionally, he takes the band to the same teppanyaki restaurant – I expect he owns it – which features live prawns. If it's your first time, it's pretty uncomfortable watching them being thrown onto the hot plate, where they jump and writhe while being burnt to death. After a minute or so, someone in the party will ask if they can at least be covered up. The chef then places a lid over them, and listening to the 'ping kang pong' as they bounce off the sides is even worse. Jimmy Page is the only person I've known to ask for more, wanting to see them do 'the dance of death', as he called it. I should add that once cooked, they are quite unbelievably delicious.

Going there with Pink Floyd in February 1988 was a whole different ballgame. Just before we arrived, there was a tragedy in a newly opened nightclub. An enormous chandelier had fallen onto the dance floor, killing and injuring dozens of people, and as a result, health and safety considerations – already the most stringent in the world – had gone into overdrive. All pyrotechnics were banned, and we had to lose about half of our lights, due to weight concerns. After much haggling, the flying bed and the pig were allowed to stay, but the section of the audience in their paths had to be moved out of the way first, which meant the preceding songs were somewhat disturbed by stewards getting a couple of thousand people to temporarily leave their seats.

The Tokyo public transport system is famous for its rush-hour crush, so to ease the burden, big gigs start at 6.30 p.m., the idea being that people come straight from the office, then go home afterwards, probably stopping off for a couple of Chivas Regals and a quick game of hide-and-seek on the flyover while they're at it. This meant you played to an audience comprised mainly of neatly suited men and women, with briefcases on their laps or in front of them. The absence of the smell of pot was noticeable, too.

Going on with half the show missing to a decidedly unstoned audience, at six thirty, doesn't make for the vibiest gig. It's the only place we played where there was actually a moment's silence at any point. The audience would clap enthusiastically, for about twenty seconds, then stop. Dead. Admittedly there was the occasional shout of something like, 'Lick light!', 'Girrmorr!' and even 'Bink Vroy!', but the last thing I want to do is have a cheap shot at Japanese-English pronunciation.

. . . Although I *did* once get asked to write a song for a Japanese girl group called The Body Con Girls. They were the figureheads for a girl craze at the time that involved being, ahem, body conscious. The brief was, 'Verse in a minor key, chorus in a major key and no R or L sounds.'

It's quite difficult writing a pop song without Rs or Ls. The word love is out, for a start. I enlisted the help of my friend Kevin Gilbert, and we managed to come up with a ditty called 'Make Some Time For Me' without an R or L in sight – or sound. They never recorded the song, but I still have the demo, sung rather beautifully by Kevin's then girlfriend Sheryl Crow.

Japan is the only country where I have ever taken Ice, a highly distilled form of amphetamine, which I took once out of curiosity, and a second time by mistake. I certainly wouldn't recommend it to anyone, as the only noticeable effect is to keep you awake for days on end, by the end of which there are bats coming out of the walls and your skin looks like the Dead Sea Scrolls.

I was first offered it in a bar in Nagoya in 1988, luckily at the end of that leg of the tour, so I had a month to get over it. The next time was in Tokyo with The Power Station in 1996. I couldn't leave my room for a day, and was still terribly twitchy and paranoid when we got the Bullet train to Osaka. As luck would have it, Hall and Oates were on the same train, and as well as Daryl, I knew and was fond of their bassist T-Bone Wolk. I hadn't seen him for a couple of years, so he was somewhat surprised that I didn't appear to want to either look at him or utter a single word to him.

32

COVERDALE PAGE WHITESNAKE

S ometime in early 1993 I got a call from Lionel Daniels, a delightful guitar tech who'd looked after me when Floyd played Knebworth, and who I also knew through his work for Gary Kemp. He asked if I was available for a tour. I was as it goes, but that was obviously dependent on whom it was with. 'Can't tell you that, I'm afraid. I just think you'd be good for it.'

Taking Tea with Jimmy

Right. Well it's hard to say you're available for something that might turn out to be Chris de Burgh, but still, I was grateful for the thought.

A couple of days later, after several furtive phone calls that were driving me up the wall, he fessed up. Jimmy Page and David Coverdale had made an album together and were about to embark on a tour of the US and Japan, but they were in need of a bassist. I nearly wet myself. *Jimmy Page!* Holy shitting Christ!

I went to audition a few days later, and I remember thinking how inappropriately attired I was for a monsters-of-rock gig, as having recently returned from an extended spell in LA I was all baggy hip-hop tops and Gucci loafers. Despite my clothes, we all took to each other immediately, and I was offered the gig.

The other guys in the band were a treat. Denny Carmassi, previously of rock legends Montrose and Heart, was the real deal as far as rock'n'roll drummers are concerned. Soft-spoken and thoughtful, he had a penchant for leggings that gave him a whiff of Max Wall. Brett Tuggle, David Lee Roth's keyboard player for many a year, was your classic good-time party boy and a boon to any tour bus. I could listen to his Sammy Davis Jr impressions for ever. It was a very new world, being with straightforward guys who just wanted to play rock'n'roll, with none of the judgemental airs of the planet I was from.

It's the funny thing about working with your heroes; with some of them you know you're never going to get over that hump, while with others you can after a while. With Jimmy I felt incredibly comfortable and relaxed straight away, which was all the more surprising as he had the most daunting image, i.e., the Devil, of any of my childhood icons.

David Coverdale was a rare treat, too. He was surprisingly bright and witty, very engaging and had quite the most superbly rich Richard Burton speaking voice, which made every utterance sound a grand proclamation. And what things he had to say . . .

Gala's best friend was, and still is, Sara Lord, daughter of rock legend Jon Lord, keyboard player for Deep Purple and Whitesnake, who he had left under a cloud many years before, when, amongst other things, it transpired that his tech was getting paid more than him, so David hadn't seen Sara since she was about twelve.

I mentioned to David that Gala and Sara were knocking about locally and weren't up to much that afternoon, so perhaps they should come down to rehearsals and say hello.

'Sara? That precious flower? Why bring her forth that I may rest my eyes upon her once again!'

Blimey, steady on.

I called Gala and they came down, and Sara and David had a lovely little catch-up before it was time for us to crack on.

'Girls, what are you up to for the rest of the afternoon?' boomed David.

Not much it transpired.

'Go to San Lorenzo! Use my tab!' he offered, somewhat forcefully.

Christ! I thought, I'm glad I don't have to compete with this. 'Uh, thanks, David, but I've got it covered, I've got sort of an understanding with Harlesden Kebab.'

As the girls trotted off, with David looking wistfully after them, he turned to me and said, 'You know what, Guy, I can see that you've got something particularly special to lose, but I tell ya, these days, you either catch some dreadful disease or they slap a lawsuit on ya.'

He then concluded triumphally, 'These are dark days indeed for a cocksman!'

There was meant to be an arena tour of the US, then it was sheds, then it was theatres, then it was . . . Japan in a few months' time. I love Japan so much that it seems odd and somehow rude that the last two times I've visited it was with acts that weren't selling anywhere else. Although once we got there I could see why the theatre tour had been abandoned. This sort of grand-gesture rock needs a big canvas; anything smaller and the crowd would be thinking, Ah, bless 'em for having a go.

It was the first out-and-out rock tour I had ever done, both on and off stage, as most of my previous touring compadres, myself included, had been far too genteel to spend their evenings chasing strippers. Oblivion, yes, girls even, but strippers, no. Moreover, having stood on stage next to David Coverdale dressed up like Long John Silver shouting, 'I can't hear you!' was probably the closest I'll ever come to doing panto. I also have to admit that some of those Whitesnake tunes are great fun to get stuck into, ironically or not.

The joy of the Zeppelin stuff is that hardly any of it goes how you, or at least I, think it does. Jimmy's musical brain is different from anyone's I've ever worked with. With most musicians, if you're suddenly not sure of where the beat is, you just look at their feet, and there'll often be some sort of tapping going on to give you a clue. Heaven help you if have to refer to Jimmy's feet, or indeed any part of his legs. A lot of his stuff is simply uncountable; you just jump in and hope for the best. I loved it.

He had a self-tuning guitar, a godsend for someone like him, who uses so many different tunings (I used to jokingly refer to him as the thief of DADGAD). This technological marvel was a Gibson Les Paul, with a built-in computer and motors to tune each string. The first time I saw it I was amazed, and Jimmy was more than happy to show it off to me. There was an LED display panel in the side of the guitar: 'You press this button here, and it tells you what tuning you're on, then you press this and it tells you, oh dear . . . ' The panel read, 'Call factory.'

The tour certainly kept me on my toes, playing wise, and by the end of it my right wrist was probably more toned than it has ever been. I was required to play with a pick, something I haven't done by choice since I stopped trying to be Bruce Foxton. I use one for a lot of the old Floyd tunes, but 'Money' is hardly as taxing as 'Still Of The Night'.

My tech was incredibly attentive, unsettlingly so, as he even tailed me when I went out. Admittedly, with the excellent Brett as a drinking partner, I was on a bit of a bender, but I thought that's what you did in Metal World. When the tour ended, one of my beloved Spector basses never made it back from Japan, so maybe he would've done better to keep an eye on that instead.

A few years later I got asked to play on a Whitesnake album. I can honestly say I never saw that one coming. I was quite excited, especially as it involved flying to Nevada to record it, and I was going to stay at David Coverdale's Lake Tahoe home. Come on! It was October, a tricky time of year wardrobe wise, being so trans-seasonal – I am being sarcastic, dear – so I called David and asked him what the weather was like, so I could pack accordingly.

'Guy, I can always lend you a sweater,' he boomed.

I thanked him for his kind offer, but politely informed him that being thirty-five, I tended to dress myself. Habit really.

'Well, we keep the house pretty warm, so it's basically jammies and a robe!'

They did, and it was, although I must confess to borrowing a rather spiffing pair of jammies off him.

Denny was on hand to play drums, with long-time 'Snaker' Adrian Vandenberg on guitar. A very civilized Dutchman – all ginseng and alfalfa sprouts – I was surprised and impressed to learn that he was good friends with photographer Anton Corbijn.

With America still in the grip of grunge, a Seattle producer was brought in to 'contemporize without compromise', as David put it. This translated as getting in someone who was familiar with the current milieu and then either disagreeing with or just ignoring everything they suggested. David wasn't going to make a grunge album in a million years, and it would've sounded ridiculous and forced if he had.

We were recording at Sierra Sonics down in Reno, which was a beautiful but slightly too long drive away and hardly the sexiest of towns. It was like Vegas, but without the money. Johnny Cash may as well have sung, 'I shot a man in Reno, just to keep busy.'

David's house was spectacular and obviously the property of someone who's spent a lot of time in the nicer Four Seasons hotels – he even had their 'Do Not Disturb' signs – and he looked after me ridiculously well, to the point of being overbearing. Who would've thought that this giant, thrusting rock figure would turn out to be the Jewish mother I never had?

One Sunday he asked me, 'Guy, do you like fishing?'

'Er, not really, David.'

'Well there's a fantastic spot a few miles away, I can have you taken!'

'Um, well, I don't fish really.'

'It's famous and renowned, Guy, be a shame to not see it.'

'Well, I suppose I . . . '

He called his tour manager, who was just thrilled at the prospect of taking me fishing on his day off, and we went and sat in a boat out in the middle of a lake.

Like so many things in America, it wasn't *really* fishing; it was all done for you. The fish were a long way down, so rather than relying on skill or technique when laying a line down that far, the boats had motors and weights that zoomed your bait about 300 feet down in a second. The bait was probably a mixture of fillet steak and crack, so even if the fish got off the hook, he'd have to come back for more.

David called a couple of times to make sure I was all right/having a good time/warm enough/had a hanky/been to the loo.

It was a very temperate few weeks, spending eight-hour days in the studio, then heading back up the hill and into our jammies for dinner, then watching a movie or two in the downstairs cinema with our teddies and Ovaltine. Well, almost. The world of 'cock rock' had a surprisingly fluffy lining. David's taste in film was very eclectic and wide-ranging, as was his taste in music – lots of African stuff and obscure European choral music – perhaps surprisingly.

In the studio, David would do what a lot of singers do: 'saving their voice'. This entails singing the song softly until they're ready to record, so as to guarantee its freshness and vigour for the take. For rock singers, the higher and more glass-shattering the pitch the better, something I've never understood. Isn't it more macho to have a low voice? Would Richard Burton have got as far as he did if he'd squeaked like a deranged mouse? Anyway, for run-throughs David would often sing an octave lower than he intended to when recording. I'm not a fan of high-end screeching myself, and thought it a shame he didn't do the actual vocals the same way as he did in rehearsal. He's got such a great rich timbre when he sings low. But what was I going to say? 'Hey, David, you know how that ball-busting heavy-metal singing's all bollocks, yeah?'

In the end, rather than being grungy, this album marked a return to his blues-rock roots, including a very fine version of 'Stay With Me Baby', rather than the MTV pop-metal that had bought him his house. Talking of which, he very graciously lent me his Jag – you know, the one from the video. I only took it out once, and called up all my mates to say, in full Rik Mayall voice, 'You'll never bloody guess what bloody car I'm in!'

Talking of which, David's Bentley had the licence plate B'STARD, so top marks for that.

One evening as I was dressing for dinner – or undressing more like – there was a knock at the door. I opened it to reveal David offering me a shot glass of what looked like brandy. It was Starka, a Polish aged vodka that tastes like a sweet but very fine cognac, and it's delicious. It's a favourite tipple of his, and he offered it to me often. I was always happy to join him in a glass, but it was his passion rather than mine, so it came as something of a surprise when the album came out and I was credited as Guy 'Starka' Pratt, as if I'd been necking bottles of the stuff every day. I would have been happier if I had a single recollection of someone calling me 'Starka' even once. Though I did appreciate the case he sent Gala and I as a wedding present – probably more than Gala did anyway.

'I can't hear you!'

33

REHEARSALS

A h, rehearsals. This is the period of time spent in a rehearsal studio or sound stage – or aircraft hangar in the case of Pink Floyd – getting your show together before taking it on the road. I haven't done much off-the-peg touring, probably because in my youth I always assumed that this time – usually between two and six weeks, depending on the stature of artist, complexity of the show and the artist's commitment to their audience/album/VAT bill – was to be spent learning the songs and knocking them into shape as a band. Wrong.

The general idea is that the musicians learn the required songs *before* going into rehearsal, so the time rehearsing can be spent ironing out the kinks and technical glitches and getting a feel for playing together as a unit, while perhaps learning which bits of the stage are going to explode when, so as to avoid standing on them.

As a result, I would turn up on day one, chirpily saying how much I was looking forward to learning the music, and when everyone else grumpily informed me they already had, I'd quizzically enquire, 'Well what are you going to be doing for the next few weeks? Aren't you going to get bored?' Like I said, I didn't do much off-the-peg touring.

The touring musician is a different beast to the studio musician. While it's worth paying a bit for someone to come in and give your record that million-dollar pocket, once they've done it all you need for the tour is someone who's capable of playing it, or something approximating it anyway. That person tends to be cheaper and more malleable than the person who played on the record. I'm not being disparaging, though, because unlike the studio guy, they do actually have to be a reasonably decent human being. The ability to get along with a load of people you don't necessarily know, or even like, whilst spending months living closer to them than anyone apart from their family when they were a child is an essential part of their make-up.

A top studio musician can be a complete arsehole, as usually they're in and out in a matter of hours and no one has to deal with their problems, or smell their socks, or listen to how demanding their girlfriend is or how undervalued they are and don't really need this shit for that matter.

Rehearsals are the absolute proof of the equation: 'Time expands to fill the amount you have to do any set piece of work.' If you have a month, you'll do precious little for the first three weeks, then go into a blind panic for the last week. You also discover that songs you thought you knew you don't, and songs that you don't . . . you do . . . somehow.

When rehearsing with Coverdale Page, for example, apart from their album, obviously the show was going to consist of quite a lot of Led Zeppelin and Whitesnake. I sat up all night learning one tune, and when I went in the next morning I was told by Jimmy 'That's not it, it's this.' I watched his fingers, thinking, It can't be, that would sound horrible! But it bloody was.

In the studio there was a big pile of Zep and Snake CDs for us to refer to. It was almost embarrassing that every time a Zeppelin number was mooted we'd all stand there going, 'OK,' and waiting for the count in, whereas as soon as a 'Snake' number came up, I had to dash for the pile and listen to the thing, often for the first time in my life. I must say, though, it was great fun to play those songs that I never envisaged myself doing.

When I did David Gilmour's tour in 2006, we had two weeks to rehearse. It was terrifying, as my experience of working with David live, i.e., with Pink Floyd, has been the most time-rich, slow and considered I've ever known, which is something only music of that stature can buy. Admittedly we didn't have the huge production and logistical elements of a Floyd tour. But we did have a whole new album, some new musicians, my first attempt at playing double bass, plus a set list of about forty undecided songs to get through in ten days at Chiddingfold Servicemen's Club (sadly causing at least one Girl Guides event to be cancelled). As it turned out it was one of the most engaging and fruitful rehearsals I've ever done, because, well, it just had to be.

I've done two tours with Roxy Music, and one with Bryan Ferry, and have never rehearsed with them for more than two days. A record for me, and I think quite possibly for most people. Admittedly, they have the advantage that most of their songs are indelibly etched into my brain from childhood, so they only have to be activated rather than learned. Also, the fact that I've worked with Bryan for twenty years makes it easier somehow.

Annoyingly, I've done several Bryan Ferry solo gigs, and despite having appeared on four of his albums, I have yet to perform a single song I actually played on, although that will hopefully have changed by the time this is published.

Back in the eighties, rehearsals were split into two camps. There was Nomis in Olympia (posh), then a load of places around Pentonville Prison (make of that what you will), John Henry's (credible, with a fine canteen), EZ Hire (a bit tawdry but drug-soaked and the only one you'd still be in at five in the morning), the Depot (kinda groovy but way too many stairs) and various other wall-carpeted hellholes. Here are some titbits from them.

I turned up at John Henry's one day, only to be informed that Womack and Womack would be at least an hour late, so being in possession of the most fearsome hangover I repaired to the local pub, which was a scary sawdust-on-the-floor Irish fighting pub, beloved of relatives of the Pentonville detainees.

I went to the bar and ordered my customary double Bloody Mary, instructing the barman to 'make it a hot one', and as they do, or certainly should, take a couple of minutes to prepare, I went to make a phone call. When I returned to the bar, my Bloody Mary was sitting there waiting for me. With steam coming off it. My instruction had been taken literally, so rather than being liberal with the Tabasco, the barman had popped it in the microwave. I couldn't be arsed to wait for another, so shovelled in as much ice as I could and drank it anyway. It was like tomato soup with vodka in it.

While rehearsing at the Depot with Jimmy Page, I was making my way up one of the myriad endless staircases when I bumped into the lovely Justin Welch, then drummer with Elastica, who dragged me into a tiny room, gave me an enormous line of coke, and enquired who I was there with. When I told him, being chemically emboldened, he insisted I took him up to our studio and introduce him to the great man, so he could get an autograph for his uncle. Somehow I agreed – Jimmy's rehearsals were strictly off limits to *anyone* – and luckily enough, Jimmy was charmed by Justin, as opposed to sacking me on the spot. Unfortunately there was no paper to hand, so Justin got his autograph on a brochure for Eric Clapton's Antigua rehab centre.

In 1991 I did some ramshackle gigs with Nigel Kennedy, whose classical musician booker obviously didn't have the hang of this rock music thing. I was called and told there would be a day of rehearsal at Nigel's flat, and then . . . 'A day at John Henry's flat . . . '

I was in the house band for a Kosovo charity gig in 1999, featuring Jimmy Page, Gary Kemp, Nigel Kennedy, Boy George, Midge Ure and an auction presided over by, ahem, Jeffrey Archer. It was in the banqueting hall of Whitehall Palace, right next door to the Ministry of Defence. While we were rehearsing, someone came over from the MoD to tell us to keep the noise down, which seemed a bit rich as they were busy dropping cluster bombs all over the former Yugoslavia at the time.

34

GOODS TO DECLARE

The tour of Japan had been a great success. It had been an absolute joy playing Zeppelin with Mr Page, and I had developed a great fondness and respect – if that's the word – for Mr Coverdale.

As the main party, composed entirely of American residents, left for the LA flight, there was the usual end-of-tour ritual of lying about staying in touch and collaborating on numerous non-existent future projects, accompanied by some genuinely emotional lobby farewells.

Jimmy, Lionel (Jimmy's tech), Jimmy's then manager, photographer Ross Halfin and myself left for the airport after breakfast. Realizing he would be all alone up the pointy end, Jimmy magnanimously stamped his feet and got me upgraded from Club. He's not a great fan of flying, our Jim, a few nights previously in a club a girl had jokingly tried to take his scarf, which prompted him to explode, spluttering about how it was his lucky scarf and he couldn't get on a plane without it.

We then repaired to the First Class lounge, where Jimmy ejected the charming hostess from behind the bar, insisting that only I was fit to prepare his Bloody Marys. Those who know me may be inclined to agree with him, although this being Japan, one can only guess at the enormous shame and dishonour we were heaping upon, not only the hostess, but her entire family and the families of everyone who had ever worked at Nagoya Airport.

By the time we boarded the flight at about eleven thirty, we had managed to morph our hangovers into something more pleasant, going from abject terror at the certain knowledge of hitting the ocean at 600 mph to not particularly minding if three out of the four engines packed up. This may also have had something to do with where I was on the plane. I don't know if it's because you're more comfortable and get smiled at a lot, but I've always felt completely at ease in First, a tad anxious in Business and numb with fear in Economy, as if the back end of the plane could crash without trolley service so much as being disrupted up front. I'm over it now, probably due to the resigned acceptance that I never get to fly First Class.

We settled ourselves in, which took a while, as Mr Page doesn't travel light at the best of times, and after three weeks in Japan, even the most ascetic of Zen monks would find themselves carting home a trailer's worth of talking, bleeping, flashing rubbish. Jimmy's luggage proper was a marvel of accumulation. He had so many cases I felt compelled to take a picture of them, lined up in all their glory at check-in.

It was to be eleven hours back to Heathrow, but I was actually looking forward to it, what with being half-cut, in the posh seats and sitting next to an all-time hero I'd come to know and love. Back then, of course, there was also the knowledge that about a minute after take-off there'd be the heavenly 'ping' that accompanied the 'No Smoking' sign going out.

It was then that Jimmy uttered what were to be fateful words, 'Right, Guy, I reckon we do three hours power-drinking, then sleep the rest, what do you say?'

As suggestions go, it seemed eminently sensible, though 'tis a far better man than I who has the power to predict his slumbers on a long haul, no matter how far back the seats go.

We embarked upon the first part of Jimmy's plan with verve and gusto, and what little I can remember would have left the most casual of Zeppelin anoraks begging God to strike them down, so full would be their cup.

You see, we'd been to a bootleg record/video shop, deep in the bootleg quarter of the bootleg district of Tokyo. Everything has its own district in Tokyo, and if you ever find yourself in need of pruning shears at midnight, you'll have no trouble getting a kindly Japanese person to direct you to the late-night gardening implement district.

While in this shop, the owner had instructed us to pretty much fill our boots. This was probably because upon finding every note he'd ever played anywhere on anything blatantly and illegally for sale, Jimmy had been delighted. Which is just as well, as he could have amassed the legal firepower equivalent of Dresden and taken the man and his shop down.

His attitude to bootlegs is very different to certain other guitar legends I know, in part because he rarely plays things the same way twice, so he's quite grateful if someone gets it down, so he can hear what he did.

Armed with a huge stack of soon-to-be brandy sticky and very probably ruined CDs, and some of the finest booze available to mankind, Jimmy proceeded to take me through Zep's career, gig by gig. I mean, this is supposed to be a tour story, but his . . . I got the lot, What really went on on the Starship, irate Texan hoteliers shooting up the bath, the night Bonzo died, how many people Peter Grant had killed – well, maybe not that – though what still puzzles me is how we got through so much material in such a short space of time, as things degenerated rather rapidly, and I have the photos to prove it.

Me in the galley, Jimmy in the galley, me in Jimmy's lap, him in mine, hanging off the wing, etc., and we couldn't have been at it that long, for true to his word, pretty much bang on three hours into the flight, Jimmy suggested we go to sleep.

'All right,' I said.

'Good,' he said.

'How do I do that then?' I said.

'Take this,' he said. So I did.

When I woke up I was somehow already in Customs at Heathrow.

Signing a cheque.

In a wheelchair.

Apparently on our arrival Jimmy had tried to rouse me, but to no avail, so he'd left me in the care of the cabin crew. Lionel recalled that when he heard, 'Wheelchair to First Class, Wheelchair to First Class,' coming over the PA, he'd thought to himself, 'Pratty.'

What is extraordinary is that enough of me had been functioning to clear Passport Control and demand to be taken through the red channel and then, in an inexplicable fit of madness, insist that I had purchased everything, both in my bags and on my person, in Japan. And I mean everything: 'See these socks? Osaka!'

It was a pretty big cheque and I was actually halfway through writing the amount when I regained consciousness.

I've never asked Jimmy what he gave me, and I doubt I ever will.

When I got home, things didn't get much better. I opened the door and Gala took one look at me and said, 'Oh dear.' I looked like death cooled down, and had got it pretty much 100 per cent wrong on the present front. She hated the pearls ('old Sloane!'); the Issey Miyake jumper ('orange tie dye?'), and as for the pièce de résistance, my beloved perma-boil water heater (Tea! Coffee! Instant! And fun!), well, that sits forlornly at the back of my lockup, gathering dust to this day, although I do still have a fabulous collection of Led Zeppelin bootleg CDs, and the ones that aren't stuck together bring me great joy.

Jimmy's luggage

35

DIVISION BELL

The *Division Bell* was the first, and I fear only, Pink Floyd studio album I have ever been involved with. The mop tops had decided to revert to their old practice of setting up in a studio – their own, Britannia Row in this case – and jamming for however long it took to amass enough material to sift through and work into an album. As they were but three, a bass player would be required, and seeing as I'd taken care of those duties for the last six years, I was called upon to provide the low end. I had a manager of sorts at this point, who when I suggested he speak to Steve O'Rourke about my fee, told me not to worry, as he 'knew how to handle it'. He duly called Steve and rather than suggest a rate for my time and playing said, 'So, about Guy's travel expenses.'

'Travel expenses?' said Steve. 'Well, let's see, the bus from Notting Hill to Islington is what, seventy pence?'

Thrilling as it was to be asked aboard, it couldn't have come at a worse time, as I had literally just returned from my first holiday with Gala, a magical three weeks exploring Mayan ruins in Mexico.

We hadn't been a proper item for very long, and the general assumption was that going on holiday would enable us to get whatever it was out of our systems, after which we'd split up and life would go back to normal. Subsequent events have shown this wasn't the case. I was very aware that the knives were out for me, as everyone in and around the band had known Gala since she was born, and I was the band's resident disaster-waiting-to-happen Byronic wastrel.

I was designated to be Rick's driver, as I only lived round the corner from him – at Gala's, in fact, as I'd rented my flat out to Tony Howard's son Felix – and the first day's drive in to Britannia Row felt like the longest car journey ever. I loved Rick, and knew that carrying on with his daughter was way beyond the pale, not to mention the stick he must've been getting from the others, and I felt awful for him. When he was asked how long it took to properly accept Gala and I being together he said, 'About six years.' By which point we'd been married for two.

Work was measured, nay, leisured, nay, unhurried, nay, just slow, as David and Nick both had new Mac laptops, and seemed far more interested in shuffling around their address books and choosing new alert sounds than writing an album. As a result, I spent most of my time in the studio with Rick, who didn't have a laptop and so was forced to pass the time playing music, which he appeared quite keen to do.

When the three weeks were up, there was actually a fair amount of material and my services were dispensed with as operations moved to David's studio for sifting. When the album proper was recorded, David handled most of the bass chores and I ended up playing on just three tracks. One because I'd had a hand in writing it and the others because I pleaded with David that if I wasn't on the new Pink Floyd record, I'd look a bit of a twat. Although I *did* get to look a bit of a twat at one of the sessions, at David's studio when I forgot to zip up my gig bag on the way out, so my bass fell out and broke in two on the footpath.

The tour was a very different kettle of fish to the previous ones. There was no ambience coordinator this time round, but the band was much the same, except for the very welcome addition of Dick Parry, who had originally played on *Dark Side of the Moon* and *Wish You Were Here* and is quite simply one of the finest sax players I have ever heard.

The girls were Durga McBroom again, but with new additions, the staggeringly chilled Claudia Fontaine and the one and only Sam Brown. Sam, despite having the voice of an angel, had the filthiest mouth imaginable, and a very hardcore taste in jokes. I called her 'the girl who makes roadies blush'.

David was now very ensconced with Polly Samson, and she came along with son Charlie, while Nick and Nettie brought their two boys, Cary and Guy.

I was entering uncharted territory with Rick, seeing as I'd been living with his daughter for a year and a half. He brought along his soon-to-be-wife Millie; Tim Renwick and Jane Sen were an item; Sam Brown came complete with husband, child and nanny, and even Jon Carin's girlfriend Brandy came along, so he was hardly going to want me in his room all night off my nut going through gig tapes. Obviously I wasn't going to be chasing models with Gary Wallis, so I decided I needed an interest of some sort.

There is no way of saying this without sounding stupendously pretentious, so I won't bother with excuses. Over the previous couple of years I'd bought a few pre-Colombian textiles, which I'd got to know about because I had a larger-than-life Irish mate, Paul Hughes, who dealt in them. From him I got a list of every museum and private collection in the US that had any, and sought them out everywhere we went. The band's studio engineer Andy Jackson was doing our live sound, and together we became momentarily expert in the field of ancient Nazca, Chimu and Paracas ceremonial dress. As a by-product of this, we could talk a pretty good game on Inuit and Aztec carvings, should the need arise. Sadly it never did.

There was a fair bit of tension, as we were no longer the Four Musketeer-type gang of rogues conquering the world together, more like a travelling version of *Cheaper by the Dozen*. As a result, musically it was infinitely better than the preceding two tours. Pre-1987 the band had been riven with tension, both live and in the studio, which before it got too much probably helped them achieve the artistic heights they attained. We'd been having far too much fun.

Mind you, the fact that we had a very good and genuinely Floydy new album to play probably didn't hurt. I've always loved songs that are written with live performance in mind, my two favourite examples being when Roger Daltrey sings, 'You know that the hypnotised never lie' in 'Won't Get Fooled Again' and Pete Townshend spits, 'Do ya!' And Jarvis Cocker's immortal, 'Common people . . . like YOU!' So the first time we stood in front of 80,000 people and David belted out, 'WHAT DO YOU WANT FROM ME?' was a bit of a tingler.

There was a sponsorship deal with Volkswagen, and relations with them tended to be very strained. Nick had jumped at the chance of designing a signature car, enlisting the help of his friend designer Peter Stevens. I don't think he really got what he wanted, as the resulting purple – purple? What do you think this is, Prince? – Golf wasn't much of a statement. If they'd listened to me, of course, it would have been very different. My suggestion was a black Beetle with enormous quadrophonic sound system, on-board mirror ball, inflatable pigs that grew out of the side-view mirrors, which were prisms, obviously, spinning headlights and reinforced bumpers for knocking down 'The Wall'. With an optional extra of the lower half of a mannequin diving into the roof. Who in their right mind wouldn't want one of those?

Production rehearsals were at Norton Air Force Base in San Bernardino, California.

It was a vast place with a five-mile runway, built to accommodate the old SR-71 spy planes. If you stood at the edge of the hangar, the tarmac stretched for miles, with the entire decommissioned Pan Am fleet lined up almost as far as the eye could see.

In order to accommodate the younger members of the party, we stayed an hour and a half's drive away, in a family-friendly resort in Palm Springs. You'd get up in the morning, have a quick swim, sprightly breakfast, then jump in the van, full of beans and raring to go. After a seemingly endless drive through the baking desert, barren but for wind farms as nothing else could grow out there, you got to work wilting.

The show was truly spectacular, setting the benchmark for all stadium tours that followed. To the extent that the stage design and screen have been nicked by practically every major tour since. Our lighting designer Marc Brickman got free rein and as much smoke as he wanted.

Particularly thrilling was that the show was to open with 'Astronomy Dominie', complete with psychedelic oil lights, and us playing it as a four-piece. As soon as I heard about this, I commissioned Scott Crolla to make me a 1967-style nehru suit of blue brocade. The only snag being that whilst it looked great as a suit, I was usually too hot to keep the jacket on for more than a couple of numbers. So most pictures, and indeed all of *Pulse*, feature me wearing what appear to be flock wallpaper leggings and a T-shirt. I never get it right.

The first show was at Joe Robbie Stadium, Miami, about which, of course, I remember little. We had a promotional airship announcing the band and album and were all promised a go on it, but alas, one of the engines packed up and we never got asked again.

Our transport was a Boeing 727 again, but rather than the Liberacetype opulence of the previous tour, this one belonged to a basketball team, and not one of the bigger ones. Granted it had nice big comfy seats, but there was a pressure leak in the back door, which is exactly the sort of thing I don't want to know about a plane I'm flying on. It was generally a bit ragged, and had a video library consisting of *Boyz n the Hood*, *Cleopatra Jones* and other blaxploitation classics. Not that we got to watch them, though, as the TV would invariably be used as a child pacifier, forcing me to have my headphones on as loud as possible in order to drown out *Aladdin* or *The Lion King*.

The Boeing was soon replaced by a Scandinavian Airlines 767, which had the most brilliant and devoted crew, but alas Economy seats. Admittedly we had about three rows each, even after we'd insisted they take half of them out.

The third show was in Mexico City, where they built a whole load of stadium-type seating – or 'bleachers' as they're known in the US, apparently because the boards get bleached by the sun. Christ I'm dull – which looked like they would support the audience for about a song and a half. Behind the stands a whole shanty town sprung up overnight, as people moved in to be close enough to hear the gig if they couldn't get in. I think the tickets were punishingly expensive, which would explain the decidedly Euro trash look of the first few rows. Rather than the type of wave one presumes was invented here, the audience did the single most impressive thing I've ever seen done with lighters. On the beatier tunes, like 'Brick' they would flick them on the snare beats, two and four of every bar. Not only was it an amazing sight, it was also an excellent practical physics demonstration, as a wave of light swept through the audience at exactly the speed of sound.

The stage had been designed so that the giant circular screen could be hidden behind it, making a dramatic *Close Encounters*-type entrance, rising and curling round behind the stage, at the start of the second half. When some of the early reviews weren't all that flattering, they decided to rejig the set list and have it in place for the start of the show. This was more than a little annoying, as not only did it mean a lot of design and equipment went to waste, we also had to now perform on an incredibly narrow, cramped stage for no reason whatsoever.

We played at the fantastically named Sun Devil Stadium in El Paso, Texas. But sadly no one challenged any of us to a shoot-out, we weren't forced to circle the wagons and the sheriff didn't get together a posse and run us out of town. Although the first time the lights came up, the stage was bombarded by the most extraordinary and frankly terrifying assortment of insects imaginable.

The Division Bell was released on 30 March, going straight to No 1 in the UK. Primal Scream's Give Out But Don't Give Up went in at No 2. They had a party to celebrate being No 1, and when someone pointed out that actually Pink Floyd were, they replied, 'Pink Floyd don't count!'

It was knocked off the top spot by Parklife a month later, thus heralding the dawn of Britpop.

I remembered Blur from their 1991 hit 'There's No Other Way', which was essentially a baggy-style reworking of 'See Emily Play', and liked the fact they'd titled their second album after my favourite piece of graffiti that was sprayed on a wall at Marble Arch, 'Modern life is Rubbish'. Stephen Duffy was matey with them at that time, and I drunkenly berated him once in a Sydney hotel room for hanging around with 'a bunch of Syd Barrett wannabes'. When we played Rick Parklife, his only reaction was 'Why's that bloke singing like Syd?' We were in Birmingham, Alabama, at this time, and a few of us convened in David's suite to listen to the album and see what all the fuss was about. Probably because we were a bit scared of going out in Alabama. The general consensus was that they were pretty good.

It was the first time Floyd had played in Nashville, Tennessee, and the audience, although appreciative, weren't a whoopin' an' a hollerin' like we were used to. Until we played 'Wish You Were Here', that is, when they went berserk. Probably because it was the nearest thing to a country and western tune in the set.

There was much to enjoy in Nashville, not least some amazing guitar shops, although as a retail outlet, what could possibly compete with Barbara Mandrell's Christmas Shop? Oh yes, my friend, country and western-themed Christmas knick-knacks available fifty-two weeks a year. Although it did also stock such non-Yule items as a model Billy Ray Cyrus tour bus. I must confess to being momentarily intrigued by the lap-dancing club that called itself 47 Beautiful Girls and 2 Ugly Ones! I think that was it, although I can't remember the exact numbers.

We had a whole run of shows that were absolutely deluged by rain. In Dallas we had to cut the set short as one by one the lights, effects and instruments went down. The guitars were all on radio rather than leads, so there was no risk of electrocution, but when Tim's packed up he thought about plugging into his back-up lead. This would not have been a good idea. The *Pulse* booklet has a great picture of a sodden David contemplating his dead Telecaster as, despite our most valiant efforts, 'Run Like Hell' just sputtered out.

We went straight to Europe from the States without a break, not that I minded as Gala had just got a job working on a film in New York, so I would only have been moping about. A lot of the shows were in famous places, such as Cinecitta studios in Rome, rather than stadiums. Impressive as a lot of them sounded, it usually entailed the audience paying $50 to watch the band while standing in a car park. I didn't really like that, especially as, to be honest, a fair portion of the audience were starting to get on a bit and probably could've done with a nice sit-down.

Prague was a very special gig, and none other than Václav Havel invited us to a drinks reception. Obviously he wasn't really that interested in meeting the hired hands, and doesn't speak a word of English anyway. As it was a no-smoking palace, I nipped out through the kitchen for a fag, only to be joined a moment later by the president himself. I gave him a light and got a smile that signified our bond as smokers, if nothing else. We went out for dinner with some government ministers, which was most enlightening. It was as if a load of student activists who sat around in cafés arguing politics all day had suddenly been told, 'All right then, smarty pants, *you* do it! You're now Foreign Minister, and you, you're Minister for Defence, let's see how well you get on.'

The gig was at Strahov Stadion, which was quite the biggest stadium I've ever seen. So big, in fact, that we had to cordon off a third of it as we were only playing to 150,000 people and it seats 360,000. It had been used by the Communists for mass public gymnastics displays, which would take place once every four years. They could have built ten smaller ones and had a show every few months rather than have so many people spend quite so long perfecting their routines.

It had also been home to the biggest KGB listening post outside Russia, and for this reason it didn't appear on any maps. It made things slightly awkward for the crew, who were driving around looking for the biggest stadium in the world that apparently didn't exist.

We played the Hockenheimring in Germany, two days after the

Grand Prix, where a car had burst into flames in the pits. Apparently the heat was so intense that someone's whisky caught fire in the club bar above. We ran around looking for burn marks, but they'd already cleared them up. Boo. It was also the only time my suit paid off, as Emma Kamen was having a sixties costume party back in London. David was flying home, so I cadged a lift and was in Holland Park still in my stage gear less than three hours after finishing 'Run Like Hell'.

When we played in Lyon, half of London seemed to be on holiday nearby or have driven down specially. Keith Allen came with his mate Charles Fontayne, then chef at Le Caprice. They'd been drinking solidly all the way down, and were a little the worse for wear, to say the least. Charles was having a pee up against one of the trucks when we came off for the interval, and when Barry Knight suggested he might want to get out of the way to let the band through, he exploded, deciding no one had ever been so rude or treated him so badly in his life. He stormed off and apparently was next seen about six hours later having walked all the way to a remote village.

Famed twee comedy vicar Derek Nimmo was also there – I believe Nettie Mason used to be in his touring company – to whom Keith delivered the classic line, 'What you doin' ere, you old drug dealer?'

36

EARLS COURT

T he last shows I played with Pink Floyd – apart from an incredibly emotional rendition of Great Gig in the Sky in Chichester Cathedral at manager Steve O'Rourke's funeral, or Nick Mason joining David's band for 'Wish You Were Here' and 'Comfortably Numb' at the Albert Hall – were at Earls Court in 1994, when we basically plotted up for most of October. The first night was a well-documented calamity, as one of the stands collapsed, injuring tens of people, and causing the gig to be called off, while Rick was playing the opening strains of 'Shine On'.

None of us was aware of what was happening, as we couldn't see what was going on from backstage. We had a tape that started playing twenty minutes before we went on that comprised of thunder, birdsong, rain, church bells, babies crying, telephones, helicopters and a random cross-section of every type of sound on earth, so the groaning of tortured metal collapsing would hardly have registered with any of us.

There was a lot of running about and general kerfuffle backstage, by which time Rick and Jon were already onstage. Robbie Williams, our production manager, barked at me to get Rick to stop, but he wouldn't say why. I went up the stairs, trying to keep out of sight, and hissed as loudly as I could, 'Rick! Stop! Come back!'

He looked at me, puzzled, then, hardly surprisingly, very annoyed. 'Why, what is it?'

I didn't know, and all I could think of to say was, 'Bad thing!'

Obviously it's awful that people were hurt, although it could have been a lot worse, as no one was *really* badly hurt, or died, although apparently a guide dog disappeared in the mêlée. I'm not quite sure what he was doing there . . . describing the show for his owner? 'Woof!' (blue) 'Woof woof!' (thinly veiled reference to another band member).

I was back home by 9 p.m., being all domestic and changing light bulbs as Gala had found us a new home while I'd been on tour, but I remember that our disaster was the lead story on the *News at Ten*, ahead of the Unionist ceasefire in Northern Ireland. Personally, I would have seen it the other way round, but maybe that's why I'm not a TV journalist.

An extra date was scheduled, and anyone who'd been injured was invited to come to another show and given a backstage pass. As a result, over the next couple of weeks, backstage looked like a scene from a David Lynch movie as various unfortunates in neck braces and all manner of surgical supports availed themselves of the buffet and bar.

I decided to smash a guitar at the end of the last show, as I had previously on the last show of the 1987/88 tour, which had prompted David to come over and remark, 'What a violent little boy you are.'

Obviously I didn't want to smash one of *my* guitars, as I was rather fond of them, and had actually paid for a couple of them. Rob Green of Status Graphite, whose basses I used a lot, kindly furnished me with a bodge job he had lying around, and wasn't too upset to see destroyed rather than played. Word of my little scheme got around the crew, in particular the pyrotechnics guys responsible for all the fireworks and explosions. These blokes are basically ex-NASA sociopaths, and when they heard, their natural response was, 'Oh, Guy, I think we can do a little better than that, don't you?'

I agreed to their idea, which seemed pretty amusing to say the least. They strapped a giant firework to the back of the bass, which had two wires coming out of it that I had to, at the appropriate moment, touch on the terminals of a battery, which was also attached to the back of the bass. This would cause my bass to shoot flames about 50 feet into the audience for a minute or so, after which I could take it off and smash it.

What could possibly go wrong?

On the final furlong of 'Run Like Hell', I switched basses and went into my running-on-the-spot routine – the one dance move Floyd had, David joined in sometimes, not often, decorum you understand – and then tried to touch the two wires to the battery. This turned out to be a lot trickier than I'd envisaged, but eventually I managed it, only instead of the wall of flame I'd been assured of, there was just a 'Fooomp', followed by nothing. Great, I was now holding a bomb. I continued running on the spot while trying to hold the bass as far away from me as possible, expecting it to explode at any moment. Luckily we made the end of the song without me being blown up, so I took it off and started smashing it sledgehammer-like into the stage.

There was another snag. Most basses have a 'bolt-on neck' construction, which meaning that the body is one piece of wood and the neck another, held together by bolts. There is therefore an inherent weakness at the point where the two bits are joined, so with enough force they can be rent asunder.

The other type of bass construction is what's called a 'thru body neck'. This is where the neck is one piece of wood that runs the whole length of the bass and the body is essentially two bits of wood stuck on either side. This is a far more resilient type of bass construction, and unfortunately what I'd been supplied with.

I swung and I heaved, again and again, but to no avail. Practically weeping with frustration, not to mention exhaustion, I gave up on the idea and decided instead to throw the bloody thing into the audience à la Pete Townshend at Woodstock.

Unfortunately, the bass I had was a lot heavier than the Gibson SG favoured by Pete at that time, especially with a bomb strapped to the back. Also, I'm not entirely sure what the fire regulations say with regard to throwing a bomb into the audience at Earls Court, but I've got a feeling it's probably not encouraged.

Unluckily for my grand gesture, but extremely luckily for the audience, the other snag was just how far away the audience are at a Floyd gig. I threw the damn thing with all my might, and all I managed to do was nearly decapitate one of the security guys at the front of the stage, who looked at me as if to say, 'What the fuck?'

He also very kindly brought the guitar back to me in the dressing room afterwards.

37

THE CASE OF THE MISSING CAR

The names and locations in this sorry tale have been changed to protect the guilty, innocent, and just plain confused, if indeed this story even happened at all . . .

There comes a time in any long tour when you've had quite enough of some people, and they've probably had enough of you, too. It's then that the band party is in danger of splitting into more factions than a radical 1960's student-led political movement.

This happened in Europe with Pink Floyd once, so as we had a couple of days off, myself, 'Jimmy' and 'Colin', who hadn't yet fallen out with each other, decided to take a road trip to a beautiful and famous town about 100K from where we were staying in order to regroup and recharge. (Mysterious enough for you? As long as it is for the lawyers that's all that matters.)

We rented a brand-new top-of-the-range Mercedes and set off, with visions of culture, art and early nights in a charming if down-at-heel pensione in our heads. Once there, of course, the Pink Floyd gene kicked in and we found ourselves unable to resist booking into the presidential suite at the smartest place in town.

We had a delightful dinner in one of the town squares and were full of plans to get up early and take in the many museums and historical attractions on offer. I even remember repeating, 'It's not a night-time town, man, there's no point in even looking for any action.'

Unfortunately our good intentions were scuppered by one brandy too many, and we were straight on the phone to find the hippest club in town and demand VIP treatment. Colin was management rather than a musician, so he was well versed in such matters.

Having visited the club and been very well looked after, we decided it was time to leave after being caught trying to kidnap two of the club's rather lithe go-go dancers, along with the cage they were dancing in.

We headed back to the hotel, loaded the entire contents of the very substantial far from minibar into our car and decided to put it through its paces.

Colin was first up, and took us on a screeching imaginary car chase through the labyrinthine medieval streets, ending up at the bus station.

That was Jimmy's cue to take the wheel and use the huge expanse of empty tarmac as a skid-pan, which unsurprisingly caught the attention of the local constabulary, who pulled us up and asked if we could explain what the fuck we were playing at. Jimmy did a fabulous job of explaining that although we appeared to be in a £50,000 brand-new Merc, it was in fact a complete jalopy with knackered brakes, and he was merely doing his best defensive driving to bring the unwieldy beast under control. We were duly ordered out, and the police gave the inside of the car a once-over with their torches. We stood in awful silence as only the truly busted do, the solitary sound being the ghastly 'glug, glug, glug' of an upended magnum of champagne emptying itself over the rear seat.

'OK, vamoose,' they said.

What?

I was reminded of the scene in *Life of Brian* when the Romans search the house and find a spoon. This was unbelievable. We'd got away with it and were free to carry on our rampage, driving our now booze-sodden car with the blessing of the local police.

That was my cue to take the wheel.

Tragically emboldened by our scrape with the law, I drove at breakneck speed out into the countryside, screaming the incredibly stupid line, 'This is our Karma! We're indestructible! Nothing can stop us now!'

Bang. Bang. Screeeeeeeech. BANG.

As it turned out, there was something very capable of stopping us: a very old and solid stone bridge, to be precise.

I'd hit the end of said bridge, causing the car to bounce from side to side, finally coming to rest at the end of it. All four tyres were shot and the front of the car was now V shaped, with rather a lot of steam emanating from the engine.

We sat in stunned silence for a minute, none of us having sustained any injuries, incredibly enough, but then I'm a great believer in the old maxim that God protects children and drunks.

We were out in the middle of nowhere, stunningly pissed, and had trashed a rental car with no other party than a somewhat inanimate bridge involved. This was not going to be easy to explain to the hire company.

Our immediate problem, though, was how to get back to civilization. We noticed a string of fairy lights way up the hill, and decided to risk driving up there.

The car made the most God-awful groaning and screeching noise, and was only capable of about three miles an hour, driving as it was on it's rims. Apparently what happens when you do that is the wheels become unbearably hot, transferring heat through the axles and causing the engine to explode.

As we edged closer it became clear that what we were seeing was a restaurant, which would at least have a phone, although quite who we were going to call and what we were going to tell them, we had no idea.

It might just have been late, but it's more likely that the demonic howling of our fatally wounded car is what caused the proprietor to suddenly turn off all the lights, making it very clear that we weren't welcome at their establishment. Oh dear.

Somehow wrestling the beast through a three-point turn, we then tried coasting downhill, and actually made it to the outskirts of town, by which time even the interior of the car was toasty. God only knows how near we came to turning into a fireball.

We decided to abandon the car and worry about a story once we got back to the hotel.

As we tiptoed off, I noticed someone looking out of a window. A witness! This was terrible. 'Speak French,' I whispered imploringly to my co-conspirators.

'Sacre bleu!' 'Arc de Triomphe!' 'Jean Paul Gaultier!' we shouted unconvincingly for the benefit of anyone in earshot.

Back in our suite we did the only sensible thing when confronted with a huge and potentially life-changing calamity: we had another drink and went to bed.

The next morning we awoke to a hangover almost, but not quite as awful as the realization of just how much trouble we were in. We needed a plan, and the best we could come up with was to brazenly say the car had been stolen and hope it wasn't found before we skipped town.

This was awful in so many ways, but it was either that or chip in the £50,000 needed to replace the car. Although thinking about it now, it was *me* who'd crashed it, though luckily not me who'd hired it.

We then played out the most ghastly scene, as I faux chirpily paid the bill, while the others went through the motions of taking our bags to the car.

'Man! The car's gone!'

'No way!'

'Yes, really. It must have been stolen.'

'Gosh, how terrible.'

Our acting was on a par with the worst seventies porn movie, and only the fact that none of the staff spoke English as a first language stopped us from being seen for the dreadful charlatans we were.

What made things worse was that the staff had been so wonderful and forgiving of our appalling, childish, drunken behaviour, and were terribly upset at the idea of our car being nicked, something that had never befallen a guest at the hotel since the advent of the petrol engine.

We went to the police station to report the theft, hoping beyond hope that no one from the bus station incident the night before would be on duty. Luckily they weren't, but neither was the relevant officer apparently, so we were told to come back that afternoon to fill out the necessary forms. That would be a catastrophe, as the longer we stayed in town, the more likely the police would be to put two and two together, although judging by their incompetence the previous night that could take months.

Colin then played the Pink Floyd card, insisting that we had a show that night several hundred miles away – we didn't – and that unless the police wanted to be responsible for cancelling it, they would have to take our word, give us the appropriate papers and let us go on our way.

It was with great sighs of relief that we sunk into our seats on the train back to rejoin the band, but our troubles weren't over yet, as we would still have to square the insurance with the hire company when we got to a town big enough to have one of their offices.

When we did, two countries later, I was amazed by how casual they were about it. Jimmy even got a bit cocky and questioned a $50 excess that appeared on the bill. I kicked him repeatedly while aggressively whispering, 'Just pay the fucking thing, you idiot!'

38

LOS ANGELES

I have so many little bite-sized pieces of fluff from my encounters with the lady that is LA that it seems only fair to give her her own chapter, wound-up, phoney, drop-dead gorgeous, two-timing, pre-menstrual whore that she is.

I first went there in a professional capacity in 1986 to work with Bryan Ferry, who was recording there with his new producer Pat Leonard. I even had a suite at the at the time new Le Mondrian, which I thought rather swish.

On my first night, Bryan invited me to accompany him to dinner, which was at the then compulsory restaurant Helena's. When famous people dine in LA, they tend to do it in packs, I don't know if it's for defence or fear of being in a minority, but whenever you get invited to a restaurant out there by someone celebrated, the chances are it'll be a table for at least twenty, with several other well-known faces in attendance. Quite how this works I'm not sure, as half the time no one seems to know anyone else, so who organizes these orgies of mutual self-congratulation is a mystery.

It came as quite a shock to me when we arrived and I discovered that amongst the eighteen or so other diners, and seated right across from me, was one Madonna Ciccone. To her right was her then husband Sean Penn, who had been in the news only the day before for beating up a photographer at the very same establishment. What fun!

Much as I admired him as an actor, and still do, it was a rather tense dinner as he was in a somewhat ornery mood, scanning the table for any signs of interest in his wife. This meant that whenever Madonna was holding forth, which was frankly for most of the meal, you had to keep your head down. This made me feel incredibly rude, as it's very hard to show someone you're paying attention to what they're saying when you're too scared to look at them.

I made one pathetic attempt at a joke when Madonna said she liked my watch and asked to see it, which obviously required me to take it off and slide it across the table, as proffering a body part would be tantamount to rape and incur a near fatal drubbing from Mr Penn. It was a religious souvenir a friend had given me, featuring the face of Christ with the apostles' names used for each of the hours. I suggested it would have been better if he was actually on the cross, his stigmata'd arms being the hour and minute hands, which was greeted with a stony silence, while Sean glared at me in a way guaranteed to notch up the fear-o-meter a couple of degrees.

Bryan spotted Timothy Leary and went to say hello, but as soon as he opened his mouth Mr Leary suddenly and manically grabbed his arm and pointed up the skylight, exclaiming 'Look! It's Venus!'

By now I was in a state of total fear and bewilderment, wondering if the whole place wasn't just clinically insane, when suddenly into my lap jumped the delightful Katie Wagner, daughter of Robert, who I'd had a crazy crash-bang two-week fling with the previous year in London. She was a welcome relief, and it certainly changed my standing at the table when it transpired that I actually knew someone in the joint.

Katie and I arranged to go out the following evening, when she introduced me to a make-up artist who ended up in my suite at about 4 a.m., where I pathetically tried to impress her – I thought the suite would be enough – by playing the unfinished tracks I was working on with Bryan. This proved to be a colossal mistake, for, as luck would have it, the next day she had a job on a photo shoot, doing make-up for none other than Bryan Ferry. Deep Joy! When she casually let slip that she really liked his new album he, quite understandably, hit the roof, and I was promptly put in the doghouse and threatened with being stripped of my rough-mix cassette privileges. This was in the comparatively innocent days before MP3s and the Internet, when it was common practice to have 'work in progress' tapes. Nowadays anyone taking a copy of an unfinished, or finished *anything* out of a studio would be vaporized before they reached the door.

Restaurant culture in LA is completely star driven, and half the time you find yourself dining at God-awful places with the most appalling food, service and décor, just because it's been deemed hip. This can last for several months, maybe even a year, by which time the management might even have got themselves together. Alas, it will all be for nothing, as fickle mistress fashion decrees that restaurants must be abandoned with all the vigour they were originally embraced.

Once I was having dinner at just such a place, with a friend and a load of Disney executives, for some reason, where the service was beyond rubbish, as in waiting for over two hours for a bowl of pasta rubbish, so when the bill came, my friend and I, being English, elected to show our displeasure by not tipping. The Disney execs all agreed in principle, but when it came to filling in their Amex slips, sweating and straining with the pressure of the momentous decision, they all cracked and added their usual gratuitous gratuity.

As we made our way down the road, or rather across the car park – the only people who walk anywhere in LA are either homeless or just off a plane from London, jetlagged and dementedly wandering in search of the bacon sandwich they will never find – we were chased and accosted by the manager who, apoplectic with rage and incomprehension informed us, 'When you stiff the staff, you stiff the whole restaurant!' When we replied that that was the whole point, she practically combusted in front of us.

I seemed to spend pretty much all the time I wasn't on tour between 1988 and 1990 in LA, as for some reason I was fêted as a player out there, which seems odd as they already had most of the world's top bassists, and no one in London seemed to reckon me that much. Not that I'm complaining, of course. Hey, I was living the dream.

I stayed with my friend and one-time manager Tarquin Gotch, on Benedict Canyon up in the Hollywood hills, just down the road from the Manson House and, I recently discovered, Heidi Fleiss's house o' sin. D'oh!

We were surrounded by various ex-pats, the focus of whose lives was the house of the wonderful Ian and Doris Le Frenais, whose seventies-style brown shagpile carpet was a constant source of wonderment. It was out here that I got to know Jimmy Nail properly, as he was there a lot, writing Spender with Ian. I thought it extraordinary that anyone could write a gritty Newcastle cop show in Hollywood, but that was nothing, as I discovered that the mighty Auf Wiedersehen Pet had gestated and been born in this opulent fantasy land.

Tarquin and I founded the Fat Intellectual Society of Beverly Hills, or FISBH, whose activities consisted of fine dining, late-night drink and imbibing drugs, tempered by going to see at least one art-house movie every couple of weeks, then talking about it. A bit. Sadly its membership never seemed to expand beyond the two of us, which was probably down to the taxing regime.

If you're in LA, and in showbiz, literally every area of your life is infected by it. You need a dentist. Suddenly everyone's telling you, 'Hey, you gotta go to my dentist, man, he's the best. He does Streisand and Willis. You're gonna love this guy.'

Yes, in LA, people even love their dentist, that's how nuts it is.

I did need a dentist at one point, just for a check-up and a clean, you understand, so I got a recommendation from Jon Carin. For some reason I felt safer taking advice from a New Yorker, even if he did live 3,000 miles away.

He did not disappoint. The surgery I was sent to had more platinum discs on the wall than most record companies I've visited. The high-heeled hygienist in a slightly-too-small white coat who cleaned my teeth looked as if she'd come straight from an Aerosmith video rather than any dental college.

As I lay there, helpless, my mouth a seething fountain of water jets, the dentist came to check on me. More to the point, to show me his pictures of him backstage with Dylan and Chrissie Hynde, pointing out various people and asking me if, and how well, I knew them. All I could do was nod ever so slightly and say, 'Gggssshhhhwhh.'

When I was working on Robbie Robertson's album, I got one of my nasty ear infections and asked Robbie if he knew an ENT guy, and boy, did he. I was sent to Joseph Sugerman, brother of Danny Sugerman, Doors manager and author of No One Here Gets Out Alive – there really is no way of getting away from it out there.

He did some tests and gave me the odd news that, 'You actually have very good hearing for a musician.'

Which just meant I hadn't yet deafened myself from being on loud stages.

Dean Markely, whose strings I'd endorsed back in the 1980s but had never met, had a beach house about seven hours' drive up the coast in Santa Cruz. I was informed through my contact Brad that Dean wanted to offer it to me for a weekend, complete with hovercraft. *Hovercraft?*

We arranged a date, a couple of weeks hence, I was given instructions and keys, and promptly forgot all about it.

About two weeks later I was at a party, somewhat the worse for wear, talking to a rather enchanting girl, when at about 3 a.m., I suddenly remembered that I had the keys to a house in Santa Cruz in my car, and was expected to use it . . . Now.

What the hell, I thought.

'Would you like to come to Shanta Cruz for the weekend?' I asked. 'I've got a housh on the beach an' a hovercraft.'

'Cool, I'd like that sometime, when were you thinking?'

'Um, well, sort of . . . now?'

'What? Like this weekend?'

'Well, yes, but leaving sort of . . . now.'

'OK.'

Blimey! This girl was mad. My kind of mad.

We headed off up the Pacific Coast Highway, stopping to get beers and, well, beers.

After about an hour, the initial thrill of our impetuous adventure began to wear off, as we realized we were in for a very, very, long drive.[*]
She was smoking joints, which I declined, but in the confined area of my Ford Probe – the official car of proctology! – it was bound to get to me, and it wasn't until I woke up that I realized I'd fallen asleep. What had startled me was a siren, which, as I opened my eyes and looked in the rear-view mirror, I could see was accompanied by flashing lights. We appeared to be in a desert, with the blazing sun just up and me driving, asleep, at about 100 mph. Oh dear. We were on a deserted stretch of impossibly straight highway, so I could've actually been going like that for miles.

I pulled over, spilling beer on my lap from the can between my legs.

---

[*] Rather like the scene in *Swingers* when they drive to Vegas, only worse.

Could I *be* more illegal? The grim realization of just how much trouble I was in was tempered by the thrill of being pulled over by real live CHiPS! with the bikes! the uniforms! and everything! How cool! How gay looking! Well, not really.

I wondered what I was going to say to Pat Leonard when I called him from jail. Could he maybe stump up bail? Sorry I can't finish the album but I'm being deported?

They saw the can and the bag of weed, for which my companion took the rap – I'm ashamed to say I can't remember her name – as being a California resident she only copped a ticket. They took my wallet and found the little packet in it, then they gave it back.

'Now you want to drive a little more carefully, sir, I want you to promise you won't be drinkin' in the vehicle no more, and you have a good day now.'

That was it. In the space of three minutes my life had completely fallen apart and then pulled itself back together, something I was going to have to do as well.

We were miles from anywhere, and from what people have told me, providing you're not a murderer or doing something really bad, if you get stopped in a barren enough place, they'd rather let you off, as they'd have to spend the rest of their day doing dull paperwork, rather than cruising butchly up and down, lookin' for mean no-good low-down motherfuckers. Personally, I can't think of a better reason for letting me off. There was some sort of citation to be dealt with later, I believe, but Pat's office made it magically just go away.

As we drove through Carmel, we couldn't get a single station on the radio, and I wondered if this was because the town's then mayor, Clint Eastwood, had never worked in radio and so banned it.

At one point the cliffs and coastline became so beautiful there was nothing for it but to stop, get out and have a look. There was a stunning beach hundreds of feet below us, and as I looked up and down, I was sure there was no way to get to it, and wondered if perhaps no one had ever been down there, except by boat, of course. That was before my eye was taken by the biggest smiley face I have ever seen, drawn in the sand.

Sadly, when we got to Santa Cruz, delightful as Dean's house was, the hovercraft was 'in the shop' and the rest of the weekend was, perhaps unsurprisingly, a very low-key and sober affair.

*

On 23 August 1989 David Gilmour took me as his 'date' to a dinner at Timothy Leary's house. I remember the date because halfway through dinner we got word that the great and controversial psychiatrist R. D. Laing had died. I couldn't think of a more apt place to be, as he and Leary both represented, to me anyway, the more cerebral end of the psychedelic pantheon. Incidentally, Andrew Crawford, who I'd lived with in Queen's Park, was the son of Hubert Crawford, a partner of Laing's, who'd tragically killed himself, as Andrew would too.

It was a pretty stellar table, thus ensuring that I spent most of the evening trying in vain to remove my foot from my mouth.

Timothy's wife, ex-Helmut Newton model Barbara, was a ball of energy and fun, who allegedly kept sending poor old Tim out on the lecture circuit to maintain their Hollywood lifestyle. David Byrne was most charming and Bianca Jagger seemed very keen to put some moves on David. I will forever cringe recounting that on being introduced to Mr Leary's goddaughter Winona I asked, 'Is that one careful owner?'

It was the last thing I ever said to her. Fair enough, it's a bit much to expect a Hollywood actress to be up to speed with *Exchange & Mart* jargon and how it may relate to her name. Still, I bet I'm the only person who's tried that gag on Ms Ryder.

Mr Leary's *other* goddaughter was one Uma Thurman. He was certainly at the front of the queue when the goddaughters where handed out.

Apart from all that, it was a pretty straightforward dinner party, and a real privilege to hear Mr Leary wax lyrical about his old peer, until at the evening's end, when he very politely enquired if anyone fancied some 'hot chocolate with heroin in it'.

39

THE MEDICAL

The Power Station had made a lot of sense in 1984. Two guys from the biggest band in the world, (John and Andy Taylor), one of the coolest yet-to-peak singers (Robert Palmer) and a drummer who'd segued seamlessly from Chic to Madonna via David Bowie's all-conquering *Let's Dance* (Tony Thompson). Add the unstoppable mix of godlike Bernard Edwards in the producer's chair, the fearless Jason Corsaro engineering, and sparks were definitely going to fly.

However, in 1996 the reformed Power Station didn't make much sense at all, except perhaps to Tony Thompson and Andy Taylor, who'd been a little light on the employment front for a while. Robert was always happy to do anything that involved getting on planes and singing.

With Britain in the grip of Britpop fever and America gangsta rap and Marilyn Mansoned up to the eyeballs, quite who EMI thought was going to rush out and buy an album by a bunch of guys flogging some 1980s in-flight magazine lifestyle is anyone's guess.

John Taylor had bailed out during recording, perhaps wisely, although I don't think it was a happy time for him personally, so Bernard had taken over bass duties. On completion of the album, while in Japan for a Chic reunion, which strangely didn't include Tony Thompson, Bernard tragically succumbed to Tokyo flu and died. This was a terrible shock, and is well documented on the resulting live album, which was recorded on the actual day he died. He cuts short an interview saying he wants to go and rest.

The album was about to be released, and there were promotional duties and a tour of Japan to be honoured, so a bass player was required, and Robert suggested his old mate, me. It was a dire project, but any chance to hang out and play with Robert was to be welcomed, plus, if you're asked to stand in for your idol, how can you refuse?

For the Japanese tour, the promoter required that all band members have a medical check-up, for insurance or something. The management had asked that I see my doctor to get a clean bill of health, but I refused, saying it was their problem and they could sort it out. I figured it was my chance to get a free examination from a la-di-da Harley Street practitioner, rather than further burdening my sterling but hopelessly overstretched local NHS practice.

An appointment was made for me at 6 p.m. in two days' time, the venue Robert Palmer's suite at the Landmark hotel. Excellent, I thought: two days for a mini detox, see the doc and be already at Robert's in time for early-evening drinks, ideally leading into Gala joining us for dinner. Perfect.

I arrived at the hotel, made my way up to Robert's suite at about ten to six and rang the bell. No answer. I rang again. Nothing. I went down the corridor, found a house phone, and asked to be put through. It rang for about three minutes. Now I was getting concerned. I went back and hammered on the door, still nothing. Shit. I went back to the phone, not quite sure what I was going to do. Get someone to break the door down? Call an ambulance?

Just as I picked up the phone, a familiar tousled head leaned out of Robert's door wrapped in a bathrobe. It lives!

'Bob, man, what the fuck are you playing at?' I yelled in a mixture of relief and annoyance as I ran back down the hall. 'Are you all right?'

He thought about this for a second and said, 'Um, yeah, sure, I guess.'

I entered the room. Oh my God. It was twatted. Every inch of the deep-pile carpet and executive reproduction furniture was covered with bottles, glasses, CD cases, overflowing ashtrays and unconscious Japanese people. There had been one hell of a party and it had ended about twenty minutes ago.

I was agog. 'Robert, you are forty-seven years old and about to have a medical! Are you mad?'

He looked at me, puzzled, 'I never get ill,' he said with utter conviction.

I was livid, basically because at the relatively tender age of thirty-four I'd spent the last two days being nervously health-conscious, not to mention slightly apprehensive at what the doctor might find, whereas Robert plainly didn't care. This was made all the more annoying by the fact that in the end he sailed through the medical while I had to confess to having gout.

The phone rang, it was the doctor apologizing that he was going to be late. Thank Christ for that. Mary, Robert's girlfriend, surfaced and we made a start at getting rid of the empty glasses and confused karaoke bar owners littering the room.

Robert muttered something about getting himself together and called room service. 'I'd like a cappuccino, please,' he asked. Good, I thought, now we're getting somewhere. Then he turned to me and said, 'Guy, you like Martinis, don't you?'

'Well, yeah, you know, but, I mean I do, yes, but maybe not . . . ' I spluttered, but it was too late.

'A cappuccino and two Martinis, please. Thanks.' He put the phone down and turned to me with a huge grin.

'Cappuccino and a Martini?' chimed Mary. 'That sounds disgusting!'

'Whaddya mean?' replied Robert, triumphantly.

'It's the breakfast of idiots!'

40

LADBROKE GARDENS

Thirty-four Ladbroke Gardens was the first home that Gala and I set up together, first renting, then owning, then selling. Gala took up residence in July 1994, and I joined her when Pink Floyd began the residency at Earls Court that ended *The Division Bell* tour in October.

It was a beautiful apartment on two floors, with bay windows and madly camp rococo doors in the dining room, leading into a drawing room that featured an original Wedgwood fireplace. We only found this out when a workman from upstairs came round one day and said that if we left the door open he'd have it away for £15,000, 'Not a word to anyone.'

I had my studio downstairs, the idea being that 'the road' was now essentially behind me and I would earn my crust through writing songs, composing scores for film and TV, and embarking upon that most ambitious of enterprises, a musical, which Gary Kemp and I had decided to undertake together. They all happened over the next few years, with varying degrees of success.

This was back in the glory days of the Groucho Club, which I had become a member of back in 1988 after David Gilmour walked into the dressing room one night and enquired, 'Does anyone fancy joining the Groucho Club?' He was a founder, and only I took him up on it.

From 1994 to about 1999, it was a maelstrom of madness, the eye at the centre of which was the unholy trinity of Keith Allen, Damien Hirst and Alex James. Keith I knew from way back, and Stephen Duffy introduced me to Alex. He was well read, scruffy and genial, and had a

Fat Les

tremendous knack of falling down stairs without getting hurt. Alex also had a genuine love of pure pop music, and whenever you ended up round his kitchen table, out would come 1,000 *Pop Hits* or other books of a similar standard. We'd spend whole nights with guitars working out 'Up, Up And Away' or 'Eternal Flame' – more complicated than you'd think – that probably wouldn't have taken so long if we'd started at a more reasonable hour.

I got to know Damien in the snooker room the Groucho. He designed a bass guitar, or came up with a rough idea anyway, that was headless, oval-shaped and had a little see-through compartment containing, naturally, a fish in formaldehyde that lit up. Unfortunately we never got round to finishing it, although when he made his film *Hanging Around* for 'Spellbound', the Hayward Gallery's celebration of 100 years of film, he asked me to do some of the score. I did, and as a thank-you he spin-painted a bass for me. Cheers!

Gala and I went on a canal holiday – *canal holiday?* – with the three of them, accompanied by Damien's missus and son Connor, along with Keith's children, Lily and Alfie, and girlfriend Nira. This was in 1995 at the height of Britpop mania, and as we coasted gently around the Stratford ring, Alex and I would sit on the stern with our guitars, trying to perfect the harmonies on Laurel & Hardy's classic 'Trail of the Lonesome Pine', occasionally passing young girls with puzzled, 'Is that him?' expressions on their faces.

Most evenings Keith, Damien and I would purloin firewood, or indeed any wood, from whatever source presented itself and build a campfire, something Joe Strummer would later make a lifestyle choice bordering on a cult. I had my new and very posh Taylor acoustic guitar, and Alex had a workable if somewhat less valuable Fender. One night he got sulky with me because Gala and I had retired early and I wouldn't let him play my guitar, which I thought was fair enough seeing as he'd just given his one a Townshend makeover, smashing it repeatedly into the fire. Although he did utter the immortal line, 'Oi, Pratty, come out here now with your £2,000 girlfriend! I mean, er, guitar.'

One evening, Gala, Alex and I were holed up in a rather dull canal-side pub, getting quietly sozzled, when Alex observed, 'There's nothing better than being in a shit place with great company.' This I have found to be true on many occasions.

We were trying to ignore the group of eight girls and a dad giggling in the corner. Eventually the dad came over with the inevitable question, 'I'm sorry to bother you, but the girls would never forgive me if I didn't ask, it is, isn't it?'

Alex nodded his head and was about to speak when dad continued, 'You really are Colin from Menswear?'

'No!' spluttered Alex.

'Oh well, never mind, you were famous for a minute, the girls will be disappointed, sorry to bother you.'

Keith liked to persuade passing ramblers that we were a bunch of travelling evangelical Christians, and as I played the guitar he'd sing:

> 'Jesus is my saviour
> He brightens up my life
> He brings me only goodness
> He's been sniffing round my wife.'

After the holiday, I became Alex's musical toy boy, and we wrote several songs and TV themes together, some good, some not so, but we had a lot of fun doing it. The first thing we did was a song for Marianne Faithfull called 'Hang It On Your Heart', for which we enlisted the help of my mate, film composer Ed Shearmur. The only time we could get to record Marianne was in early January while she was on tour in America, so we flew to Miami, with Alex's girlfriend Justine. It was a long plane journey, and we went straight to the airport from the night before. Alex was bemoaning the fact that you couldn't smoke on the plane, so I told him how you could go to the loo, hold open the plug and smoke into the basin – something you'd never do now, gentle reader. This was a challenge he readily took up, although he blew it completely when he burst out of the loo, right into the path of a very suspicious stewardess, shouting, 'It works!'

We were extremely tired and emotional by the time we got to the endless immigration queue that is a prerequisite of travelling to the States. Having ticked off the list of ridiculous questions regarding soil samples, pigs and molluscs, Alex declared to customs, 'I'm just here to see the snails!' Although seeing as he now does a farming show on Radio 4, maybe he really was.

For Keith's forty-third birthday, he and a few mates went to a Fulham game somewhere in Wales or God knows where. On their return, he and Alex were all fired up about doing a football song. Alex kept trying to explain the feel he was after, albeit not very well, as the first attempt at 'Vindaloo' featured the same drum part as Amii Stewart's version of 'Knock On Wood'. He had an idea for a terrace chant, but it was slightly too long. Whenever I've heard it sung at football matches, which admittedly isn't very often, the crowd seem to get lost after six bars and veer off into 'My Darling Clementine'.

The song came together over a few very funny drunken evenings round at my basement. One time Keith called a football club score line for some results and ended up on the phone for nearly two hours, getting the operator to pour her heart out about the trouble she was having with her wayward kids.

Damien also got involved, doing the artwork and I think funding the recording. The day before we were due to record it, Alex, Keith and Roland Rivron came round to put the final touches onto the track before we went into the Townhouse to make the record proper. They turned up early, and I was having a meeting with an old magician friend, regarding a music idea he had. I told them to wait in the pub, as I'd only be about twenty minutes. Unfortunately, the magician received the very upsetting news that a close friend had died, so downed two bottles of brandy in quick succession and kept me prisoner in my house for the next two hours, threatening me with the brandy bottle and scaring the daylights out of me. I eventually got out, and ran to the pub where the lads were still waiting. I wasn't going to be at the studio till the next afternoon, so I gave them the disk with all the computer information on it. When they tried to load it the next day, it was blank. 'That'll be the magician,' suggested Roland.

Keith got asked to do a song for his beloved Fulham FC and asked, or rather told, me to produce it. Despite being an Arsenal man myself, I agreed, partly because my dad had supported Fulham, but mainly because the chairman, Mohamed Al Fayed, was going to do a vocal, so the comedy potential was enormous.

We knocked up a demo in my room at the Townhouse and booked Studio 4 to finish it. The day before we recorded, Al Fayed's head of security came in to check out the studio. I guess he needed to make a note of all the exits, potential sniper vantage points and make sure that Prince Philip wasn't hiding in the kitchen in order to poison the deluded shopkeeper. When he asked me where the gents' was, I didn't know if he needed the loo or was trying to ascertain whether it had a direct line of fire.

I was at a loss as to how I should address Al Fayed when I met him, as everyone I spoke to at Fulham or his office referred to him as 'the chairman', which was hardly going to work in the studio: 'OK, Chairman, that was great, can we go for another one?'

The first person to arrive at the studio the next day was his personal cameraman, who films pretty much everything he ever does. He immediately got up everyone's nose by demanding coffee and power points, as he was 'going to be really busy'. Yeah, of course, we all had nothing to do.

Keith had enlisted a load of his Fulham-supporting buddies to be in the chorus, plus the fan who bangs a drum at all the games. He'd had his entire back tattooed with the Fulham logo, which he proudly showed Al Fayed, who asked him how much it cost. When he told him, Al Fayed said to a flunky, 'Pay him that amount,' which I think is Fayed-speak for, 'Kill him, he knows too much.'

The chairmen went into the studio, where everything had been set up to make it as effortless as possible: microphone, headphones, a little table, baffles arranged nicely. He stood about 6 feet away, until it became clear that the mountain would indeed have to come to Mohamed, so everything was reassembled around him. Keith had written him a little speech to go at the start of the song, which opened with the line, 'Life is about choices, we have chosen Fulham!'

Unfortunately, with his accent, no matter how many times we did it, it sounded like, 'Life is about choices, we have Jews in Fulham!' Which though potentially helpful for any Middle East peace initiatives, didn't really help the song.

I only went out on the road twice in the eleven years following the Floyd tour. Once was to Japan with The Power Station in 1996 and the second time was around Europe with Gary Moore in 1997. This was to promote his album, *Dark Days in Paradise*, which I'd played on. The title, I believe, is inspired by a quote that appears elsewhere in this book. It was all very jolly, being a compact band comprising Gary, myself, Magnus Fiennes on keyboards and Gary Husband on drums.

Gary had his own car, so it was just the three of us, plus our brilliant tour manager Robbo, in a full-size tour bus with bunks, lounge, the lot. Scandinavia and northern Europe are riddled with blues festivals, some of which border on village fêtes, and it often felt like a gentle potter rather than a tour. Almost the sort of thing you'd find an advert for in the back pages of *The Lady*: 'Wanted, companion for summer blues excursion, taking in the Jotunheim Mountains and fjords of Norway. Working mojo essential.'

Gary is, of course, a phenomenal guitarist with a very open ear, and as a result, he flirted with the then-fashionable oeuvre of drum and bass. This didn't go down particularly well with his fiercely blues-based audience. At the Montreux Jazz Festival one of the more experimental tracks was greeted with near silence when we finished, until someone in the audience shouted in a thick German accent, 'No, Gary, blues and rock-'n'roll!' This got my back up a bit, so I shouted back, 'Yeah! Rock me Amadeus!'

We also played the Hell Blues Festival – I kid you not. It's actually a town in Norway. Funny really, I always thought hell would be an accordion festival.

The lairiest gig we did was a Hells Angels festival in a wood near

Lyons. Magnus was more of a studio bod, and would get rather carried away on stage. During the first song he pointed manically at the audience and somehow managed to dislocate his shoulder. He froze, grabbed his arm, screamed and ran off stage, leaving us to carry on without a clue as to what had happened. Magnus figured that as these guys were Hells Angels, they probably popped each other's shoulders in every day, for fun even. Although when he indicated his arm and what needed doing, apparently they all recoiled like big Jessies. This left him no option but to wade through the battlefield of the audience and find the Red Cross tent, which was apparently full of people suffering the consequences of falling off motorbikes or making narcotics at home, as well as raving, flipped-out, bleeding greasy bikers. Nice. He managed to find a medic, who popped his arm back in, and he was back on stage in time for the third song, although he looked about twenty years older. We finished and got the hell out, narrowly missing The Stranglers arriving tour bus. They were on at 2 a.m. Rather them than me.

*

One December afternoon, mooching around Portobello Road looking for a Christmas tree, I happened across Joe Strummer and his wife Lucinda. 'Hey, Guy, I've got to write a song for a movie with Alex James, can we come and do it at your place? You should get on board, man, we'll do it together!' I didn't really know Joe that well, and still held him in awe. Now he wanted to come and write a song in my house. Blimey.

They came to the house, we had a couple of bottles of rioja and Gala knocked up pasta for everyone. It was the most perfect, warm and convivial vibe in which to work.

Alex had one of his tum-ti-tum Syd Barrett- type tunes, and Joe set to work immediately transforming it into a *Paris, Texas*-type tale of desertion and misunderstanding. He lay on the floor frantically scribbling, just like I'd seen in so many photos, and then it was time for him to sing it.

We did a level check, got a rough sound for him and hit record. Everything went out of the window as that famous leg started pumping manically, he closed his eyes, cupped a hand over his ear and belted out the song as if his life depended on it. Just like Joe Strummer. It was like having Elvis come to your house, 'Tunesmiths, man, that's what you guys are. Tunesmiths!' He even gave me a nickname 'Doc Fender', I think for no other reason than it was a spare nickname he had hanging about. The film was called *Divorcing Jack* and the song was called 'Divorcing Jack', not an easy title to write a song with, and they never even used it, the idiots. Still, at least I got to do something with the great man.

In 1998 I moved my studio into a room at the Townhouse, where I spent the next few years writing songs, playing sessions and doing music for telly, something that can be fantastically good fun, like *Spaced* for instance. The series contained endless movie in-jokes, for which I had to supply parody music, a brilliant challenge in itself. I still pride myself on my John Carpenter.

When the producers of *Linda Green* told me they wanted a sort of Latin feel, I thought, Sod it, let's do it properly, and went to Havana. For *The Young Person's Guide to Becoming a Rock Star* I had to invent a band, and a sound for them, so I was quite chuffed when my little non-existent creation was awarded Album of the Week in *Melody Maker*. Not to mention an Ivor Novello nomination for a song called 'Why Won't You Shag Me?' Which was worth it just to hear the title being read out . . .

41

In early June 2005 we were enjoying a family holiday in Formentera when the *Sunday Telegraph* broke the news that Pink Floyd might be reforming for Live8. I didn't believe a word of it, not least because we were on holiday with the Gilmours, and they didn't believe a word of it either.

I was going on tour with Roxy Music the following month, and got a concerned call from Levi, their tour manager. Bryan was worried I might jump ship for this mythical gathering. I told him not to worry, as I was with David and he was having a jolly good laugh about it. I think my exact words were, 'It'll take a bit more than Bob Geldof's ego to get that lot back together.'

Luckily for the world, as so often, I was wrong.

A couple of days after returning home I got a call from David.

'Are you sitting down?'

It was on. Roger had picked up the phone and called him, that's all it took.

They'd need an auxiliary bassist for two songs, and David – and hopefully Rick and Nick – wanted me. I did know the songs after all, although I'd somewhat blotted my copybook a few nights earlier in a bar in Formentera. Under the influence of tequila and egged on by Polly, when the band played 'Wish You Were Here', I'd gone up and grabbed the bass, insisting that I was Pink Floyd's bass player and that there was nothing to worry about. It was a five-string fretless bass, and I was really quite pissed, so I made a terrible hash of it. Even worse, the press got hold of it and a few papers ran the story that David had got up in a bar and played his own song appallingly.

Nevertheless, I was going to have to choose between Roxy and Floyd. Infuriatingly, Roxy weren't even *doing* Live8, they just had a gig booked in Germany that day. Just who the promoter thought was going to turn up remains a mystery.

I spent the next two hours pacing up and down, up and down, until the phone rang. It was Phil Manzanera.

'You must be pacing up and down, up and down,' he said.

I doubt I'll ever receive such an accurate or intuitive phone call in my life. Certainly not from a man anyway.

He said not to worry; they'd sort something out. Comforting as that was to hear, I knew it was utter tosh. Short of doing a Phil Collins at Live Aid, I was never going to be able to do both shows, and let's face it, I don't have his sort of billing.

Before I'd had to make my final decision, Roxy's gig got changed to Live8 Berlin, so if I was going to have to bail on Floyd, at least it wasn't to play some empty *Musikhalle*.

My mind was finally made up a few days later when Roxy played the Isle of Wight Festival, and Neil Warnock, agent for both acts, pulled me to one side and helpfully suggested, 'You're not doing Hyde Park. No way. Can't be done. Forget it. Not a chance. But I promise you'll be able to do both David and Roxy next year.'

I thought I'd made a pretty wise decision.

The gig in Berlin was chaos, as was only to be expected. The stage was in the middle of a road going through the Tiergarten, and you had to mind yourself so as not to bump into a traffic light when you made your way up the stairs. There were no proper dressing rooms, so we had to go dressed for the gig and hang around in the backstage bar. By the time we went on, four hours late, our suits were positively wilting, and the dancers' feathers had drooped. It was pretty rammed backstage; we had to take turns on the sofa and it took a lot of willpower to spend six hours resisting the seriously good German beer that was on tap. Not to mention trying not to stare at Brian Wilson too much.

We went and waited at the back of the stage for the last twenty minutes before we went on, and I noticed a gaggle of people, some of whom I recognized as Faithless, who were on after us. I quite like their music but don't know that much about them. I know there's Maxi Jazz, Sister Bliss, and Rollo, Dido's brother, but that's about it. Coincidentally enough, I'd played bass on their version of 'Reasons To Be Cheerful' a few months previously, although none of the band had been in the studio at the time. Thinking that was a pretty fair opener, I went and introduced myself, saying how much I'd enjoyed playing on their new record. There were some muttered thanks, but it felt a bit uncomfortable, then someone proffered a hand and said, 'Hello, Guy, I'm Aubrey, Faithless's bassist.'

Well, how was I supposed to know? I'm sure I was only brought in because the band weren't around, and they probably didn't even know till after I'd done it. Still, I made my excuses and ran up the stairs sharpish, narrowly missing the traffic light.

We all had to use whatever gear they had, and the amp I'd said yes to was right at the back of the stage, so whatever it sounded like, and however loud it was when I plugged in that was how it was going to be for the whole set. Luckily it was all right, not great but all right. The audience looked like they'd just about had enough; they'd been there for over twelve hours, poor loves. Bryan managed to rouse what little spirit they had left, although it looked a bit odd, playing on a road to a quite narrow but very, very long audience.

We went out to dinner afterwards, when of course all I wanted to do was get to a TV and watch a certain reunion, but that wouldn't have been very sporting. I'd called Gala to ask about The Who's performance, what Pete was wearing and whether he was playing a red Strat etc., still the schoolboy fan. She told me she'd got a bit tipsy and stood on a flight case at the side of the stage doing windmills all the way through 'Won't Get Fooled Again'. That's my girl.

My phone nearly melted with running commentary texts from practically everyone I know when Floyd played. '"BREATHE" GOOD.' 'WHY RICHARD GERE ON BASS?' 'NICK SOUNDS GREAT.' 'CAN'T SEE RICK.' 'OH MY GOD, THAT SOLO.' 'THEY'RE ONLY BLOODY HUGGING.'

Much as I'm sad I wasn't there to see it, I'm glad I had another gig that day. I obviously would have done it, but then my last memory of playing with Floyd would be tucked away at the back behind the real talent, an eternal reminder of just how little a part of it I really was.

42

VENICE 2

August 11 2006. 10 p.m.

I am having a piss behind the stage in Piazza San Marcos in front of which four thousand soaking wet people are roaring their approval as the last notes of 'Fat Old Sun' fade into the brickwork. That I'm here at all is a wonder. David Gilmour was booked to play the previous weekend, but as we were leaving the hotel for soundcheck news came through that the roof of the stage had partially collapsed, and we were to await further instruction.

Both that show and the following night's had to be cancelled, as the whole stage would need to be pulled down and rebuilt.

In classic 'the show must go on' style, David decreed that the gigs should go ahead the next weekend.

We were booked to fly out on August 10th, coincidentally the same day that British air travel went into meltdown over the discovery of an alleged plot to blow up airliners using liquid bombs. That really should have been the end of it, but no, David simply ordered up a private jet and so here I am.

It's stopped raining at least and we're heading into the home stretch of the second half. I hear a familiar bass rumble from the stage, announcing the start of 'Coming Back To Life'. No sweat, there's about two minutes of guitar solo followed by a verse before I'm needed.

But rather than the usual soaring tones of David's black Strat, the next thing I hear is David himself, singing.

'On the turning away . . . Of the pale and downtrodden . . .'

WHAT!!!!

I haven't played this song since 1990. (Apparently this is untrue, as I am later assured that we played it on several occasions in 1994, so that's just twelve years then.)

I frantically get myself together and run back up to the stage, luckily avoiding a *There's Something About Mary* type mishap. Mike my tech hands me a bass and I try to saunter nonchalantly onstage. I walk to my mic and have a quick peek at my setlist to make absolutely sure 'On The Turning Away' isn't mentioned and it's not me who's got muddled. It isn't. Phew. I start thinking about how the song goes, as I've got about thirty seconds before I come in – that's the beauty of Pink Floyd, half the time the bass doesn't even *begin* until about the time most pop songs have finished – then check around and realize that my two stage left partners, Steve and Phil, have never played or rehearsed the song *ever*. Great. I'm going to have to try to coach them through the song whilst trying to remember it myself, and it's the full eighties fretless rubbery type bass playing as well.

FUCK! Fretless!!! I've got the wrong bass on!!

I dash to the back of the stage shouting to Mike to get the fretless, we do a hasty guitar change, and I'm all plugged in and ready to go about two bars after I was supposed to come in. Ho hum.

We soldier on, and as the song picks up pace it all becomes rather thrilling. I then check with Steve and Phil, who I see are looking to me for guidance; I alternate between shouting chords at Phil and miming drum beats to Steve whilst trying not to get tripped up myself. The song only has five chords in it, but they don't necessarily show up where you think they will. I realize I'm in a triage situation and will have to leave a man down. I decide to let Phil fend for himself as the drums are more crucial than the rhythm guitar. I manage to cue Steve into the breakdown where everything stops until a rather nice bass figure brings the last verse in. I get through it OK and we're on the last few furlongs as David puckers up and gets down to what he does best. The song ends in a train wreck as Steve misreads both David and my signals to slow right right down as meaning don't really slow down at all, but we're through it, the audience love it, and David is beaming at having put his band totally and utterly on the spot.

I walk over to him, feeling I've handled the whole thing pretty well, and mustering my best hysterical Withnail scream at him: 'Monty, you terrible cunt!!!'

He smiles back and says simply, 'You were terrible.'

Praise indeed.

43

ON AN ISLAND

D avid Gilmour's solo tour of 2006 was just heaven. We had all the good bits of being inside the Floyd cocoon, but with the cosy lightheartedness of a small band.

Most of the old faces were there. Syd was my tech, Marc Brickman was doing the lights, Colin was mixing, and Rick, Jon and Dick were in the band. Phil Manzanera, who I'd toured and recorded with in Roxy Music, was my stage-right partner. The only new face was our drummer, Steve DiStanislao. I'd met and played with him before when the Black Crowes flew me out to New York to audition drummers for a *week* without paying me for the privilege. When his name came up, I'd wholeheartedly recommended him.

I had a nice bit of resolution as well, when Jon and Stevie got to be in Icehouse for a day. A German TV show was doing an eighties special and as 'Hey Little Girl' had been voted best song of 1983, Iva had been asked to do it. He asked, could I put together a band to mime two songs in Munich? We were starting our tour in Dortmund two days later, so I asked if David Gilmour's band would suffice. We went and it was a hoot, I even bumped into Womack and Womack, who were charm itself. It was a great little awayday before starting the *On an Island* sojourn.

It was strange playing the songs I knew so well from stadiums in small theatres. Kicking into the solo in 'Comfortably Numb' with people right in front of you rather than 30 feet away, with no giant mirrorball or lighting histrionics, was weird but nice. Especially as since Live8 the solo out of 'Comfortably Numb' has become almost a physical thing.

The Croz

It's practically a *place*, like Lourdes or something, where people go to worship and be cured of their ills.

It was a family-structured tour, so when we were in Europe we played mostly around the weekend, so David could go home to be with the kids. Mind you, it was a very short tour, so that meant we just had a few days off in Paris and Amsterdam, which suited me fine. Well, I had a book to write.

I like touring as an adult, as I appreciate the things I took for granted when I was younger, like staying in nice hotels, although I have to watch it at the breakfast buffet now that I actually get up in the morning.

The shows were wonderful, warm, shared experiences between us and the audience, and I even got involved in the blog on David's website. The internet makes time in hotel rooms infinitely more tolerable.

A real bonus was having David Crosby and Graham Nash come along on some of the dates to sing with us. It was great to see Crosby having made it out the other side. When I told him we'd shared the bill several times in 1983 he said, 'Oh, bad days. I probably had a freebase pipe glued to my mouth the whole time.'

I told him yes, but there were one or two amusing incidents as a result, to which he replied, 'I bet! Just don't tell anyone!'

'Don't tell anyone? David, I'm charging people money!'

Gig nights were a couple of drinks in the bar, and nights off were usually some fabulous restaurant of David's choosing. If Jon Carin and I were found wandering the streets at 9 a.m., we were looking for children's clothes rather than the way back to the hotel. Understandably, this doesn't make for great anecdotes, but I can tell you where to find the most darling little pyjamas. In Paris.

Although perhaps that's another book.

APPENDIX

TRAIN SETS

Throughout this book I have tried to steer clear of most technical stuff to do with playing the bass, for fear of alienating the general reading public or, more precisely, girls.

I feel it only right to redress this balance by giving any bass players, musos or general tech heads a complete, unexpurgated, non-bowdlerized orgy of kit. Over the next few pages I will give you the low-down on pretty much every bit of music-making equipage I can be bothered to recall.

As previously stated my first bass guitar was a Grant (I think) Jazz copy. It was finished in two-tone sunburst, with a maple-type neck and rosewood-type fingerboard (I say type, because God knows what wood it actually was) with dot markers. In 1981 I stripped off the paint, revealing the incredibly cheap but visually pleasing plywood body beneath. I took off the fingerboard, replacing it with a fretless one made of ebony. (Posh, eh?) I also replaced the bridge. It has a Judge Dredd badge that came free with a 2000AD comic stuck on the body, and comes out of its case for a quick run up and down and nostalgic sigh about every two years.

My first amp was a WEM Dominator, costing the then astronomical sum of £75 from Ivor Mairants in Berners St. I taught myself six-string guitar on a nylon string Spanish job that I inherited from my godfather, Sean Lynch, and still have.

The next bass to come my way was a see-through plexi-glass Dan Armstrong with sliding pickup, given to me by a friend of David Malin's.

I returned it when it became apparent he expected sexual favours in return, and I haven't named him here because I still might report the old nonce to the police one day.

The first 'designer' bass I bought was a 1969 Gibson 'Recording' Les Paul, sometimes known as the 'Triumph'. It had a short scale neck, and was made of mahogany. (Obviously I would never buy a mahogany guitar now, rainforest etc.) It had more knobs and switches than any bass I have ever seen (except one that we'll come to later) and was unbelievably heavy.

Throughout my time with Speedball I played this through a God-awful OMEC amp, with a 2 by 15 cabinet about which I can remember very little except, again, its weight.

I swapped the Les Paul for another Dan Armstrong (I liked them because they were short scale, and Mick Jones played Dan Armstrongs) but forget what happened to it.

Next up was my Aria Pro 2, which I bought from Tom Dixon (it was the Funkapolitan spare) and stayed with me through my first two Icehouse tours. I also by now had a Trace Elliott GP200 amp, which I played through a Yamaha 8 by 10. I had my first effects as well, which were a Mu-Tron Bi-Phase and a Boss chorus pedal.

In January 1983 I bought my 1956 Framus Triumph electric double bass from Andy's. It saw very little action until 2006 when Mr Gilmour told me I would be playing double bass on his tour.

I sold the Aria to Rik Kenton (formerly of Roxy Music, then of Savage Progress) and in May 1983 moved up to a Steinberger L2. It was stolen in 1992 (I know who by) and taken to Paris, and had the serial number 712. There is a reward for any information leading to its return.

I got my first proper fretless not long after, a Status 2, built specially for me by Rob Green, as I wanted a lined fretboard and the phenolic fingerboards he used made that very difficult. I dusted it down and used it for the first half of David Gilmour's 2006 tour, and it still sounded great, but looked preposterous.

In 1983 I also got my first home recording setup, a Teac 3440 four-track reel to reel, Klark Technic twenty-four channel graphic equalizer, a borrowed Linn 2, and Prophet 5. I forget what the mixer was.

In 1985 I bought a stupidly big Trace Elliott 400-watt rig, with angled 2 by 10s and an enormous 2 by 15 reflex cabinet. I last saw it at a Bobby Womack gig I did.

I upgraded my recording setup with a Yamaha RX11 drum machine, and a lovely Suitcase Fender Rhodes, which years later I sold to Andy Caine, I still don't know why.

As for guitar, I had a Gibson Les Paul Standard, double cutaway with P90 pickups.

On hearing Pino Palladino's absurdly brilliant bass on 'Tear Your Playhouse Down' I ran out and bought a Pearl octave pedal, even though the Boss OC2 is the correct one. I bought another instrument from Tom Dixon, a ginormous bass balalaika, which I still own and love.

I also bought a Hamer twelve-string bass; I have absolutely no idea why, which had three strings per string, with volume, bass and treble for each group, meaning sixteen knobs! Then master pickup volume and tone as well! It never made it onto a record. I sold it to Killing Joke's Paul Raven, more his speed really. I also had a Roland D50 synth and the exciting new Yamaha SPX90 by now.

In 1987 Johnny Marr introduced me to Pete Townshend's tech Alan Rogan, who was busy selling John Entwistle's guitar collection. It was Johnny's horror at me not owning a Fender that made me go perusing. I picked up 'Betsy' and that was the end of that. She is a 1964 Fender Jazz in burgundy mist (one of only three made that year) with maple neck and rosewood fingerboard. The pickups were very quiet and yet noisy, so I replaced them with EMGs, and so she remains to this day.

For the 1987-88 Pink Floyd tour I purchased a midi programmable Trace Elliott MP11 pre-amp, which was to run a Ureii JBL 1500-watt power amp into two JBL 2 by 15 cabs. I was playing a load of Boss pedals through an NCC 700 controller, and had a Pete Cornish board for other effects like the tremolo unit I used for the middle section of 'One Of These Days' (you know, the Dr Who bit). After it had become apparent that I needed to stand half a mile away from the cabs in order to hear them, I swapped them for six Hartke 4 by 10s.

I then got a Kramer Spector NS 2, black, which a cherry red shortly joined and then a natural bird's eye maple model. (The last never made it back from Japan after the Coverdale Page tour, so again, any information . . .)

I also picked up a Black Ernie Ball Musicman Stingray, which I had fitted up as a midi bass. To plug it into, I purchased a Valley Music midi moog, a complete waste of time and money as it turned out.

I was given a five-string Stereo Kramer, which had pan pots for each string. This was used to some effect on the songs 'Toy Matinee' and Madonna's 'Till Death Do Us Part'.

I was also mucking about with a Guild Ashbory weird rubber-stringed mini bass.

At my funny little mews studio I had an Atari PC running C-Lab, an Akai S1100, Allen & Heath Desk and a Kawaii K4 synth along with lots of other stuff.

In 1992 Status made me two five-string headless jobbies; one fretted, one fretless, which I used extensively on the Division Bell Tour, along with a Blond Musicman Stingray, and two Precisions. A blond 1951 early slab model (serial number 0011) and a 1959 sunburst with anodized scratch plate.

On my wedding day, 11 October 1996, David Gilmour gave me the 1961 Stack knob sunburst Jazz that I'd lusted after since 1987.

I have a Fender Custom shop reissue 61 Jazz, the body of which has been spin-painted on both sides by Damien Hirst. Despite the half-inch thick coating of surfboard paint she actually sounds pretty good, and can be heard on the soundtrack to Johnny English.

Since then the only new basses I've picked up are two Status GP Vintage (named after me I believe, at last, a signature bass!), which are my workhorse touring basses, a Ned Steinberger EU double bass and a gorgeous Lakland Stack knob Jazz fretless.

On the Gilmour tour I was also playing a borrowed reissue 61 Precision, and Rickenbacker 4001, plus one of David's modded Strats for 'When I Close My Eyes'.

My full rig for that tour was . . .
2 Ashdown ABM 900 Heads
2 Ashdown 8 by 10 Cabs
Avalon DI
Ernie Ball Volume Pedal
Demeter Compulator Compressor
Ashdown Bass Overdrive Plus
MXR Phase 90
Boss CE-2B Bass Chorus
Boss OC-2 Octave

Boss DD-5 Digital Delay
Boss CS-3 Compression Sustainer
Boss T4-2 Tuner (2)
Boss SCC-700 Pedal Controller
Roland SDE 3000 Digital Delay
Melody Evidence Audio Guitar Cables
Elite 40-100 Stadium Strings

Other guitars I have or had include:

Levinson Blade Strat
Steinberger Six-string
Steinberger Bass (with body, yuck)
Taylor Acoustic
Fender Telecaster
Fender Stratocaster (custom shop, built for Clapton)
Rickenbacker Twelve-string
Fender Jazzmaster 1959
Danelectro Electric (the one with the amp built into the case)
1850s French parlour guitar

Even if I could remember all the gear I had in my Townhouse studio, it's too tedious to recall and I've got rid of pretty much all of it anyway. It was various Macs running the current versions of Logic with Pro-Tools, and video synch stuff that was at first very expensive but over time got cheaper until becoming redundant.

I now just use a Mac Book Pro running Logic, with a Focusrite Saffire DA Converter and Avalon 737 mic pre-amp.

At the time of going to press I have just discovered Bill Nash guitars and they are amazing.

THANKS

T hanks to all the musicians, producers, engineers, programmers, tape ops, tour managers, techs, boffins, luthiers, amp makers, nice girls from the record company, publishers, agents, maybe one or two managers, blaggers, chancers and ne'er do wells I've had the honour of serving with these last twenty-eight years.

Matt Johns, for his stupendously helpful Brain Damage website, and being my researcher for a day when it crashed.

Wikipedia, which I shall blame for the doubtless countless inaccuracies.

Richard Wright, for so many things, like having a daughter, and letting me use his house in France as my lonely garret to write in. Also surprisingly useful for Floyd reminiscences.

David Gilmour for all sorts of things, although surprisingly useless for Floyd reminiscences.

Nick Mason for letting me access his picture archive, and writing his fabulous book, which saved me having to bother him for Floyd reminiscences.

Polly Samson for constant encouragement, and the immortal line 'A book is for life, not your publisher's Xmas.'

Tessa Clarke for tons of great stories and being my mum.

Iva Davies for pictures, memories, and getting me into the Aria Hall of Fame.

Kate Robbins without whom etc . . .

Jon Carin, Johnny Marr, Youth, John Lloyd, Andy Qunta, Gary Kemp,

Oct Thanks | 293

Steve Dagger, Jean Marie Carroll, Louise Allen-Jones, Juliette Wright, Emma Kamen, Pat Leonard, Bill Bottrell, Nick Llaird Clowes, Mark Gooday, Scott Crolla, Alex Paterson, Tom Dixon, Barry Moorhouse, Rob Green, Lloyd Stanton, Andy Caine, Jimmy Nail, Phil Taylor, Ian Preece, Mark Stay, Angela McMahon, Danny Schogger, Brian Macleod, Richard Bucknall, Nic Watson, Jamie Wright, Martin Clarke, Karin Pratt, Manfred and Hanna Nedwed, Google Earth. David Malin and Susie Griffiths for taking me to see The Wall at Earls Court, and countless others.

Thanks to everyone who supplied the photographs, particularly Ross Halfin (Speedball and tea with Jimmy Page); Johan Ödmann (Icehouse, Sylvain, Sylvain); Dimo Safari (Pink Floyd); Brian Rasic (Bowie, 2006), Sasha Gushov (my wedding pictures); Isaac Ferry (Roxy Music) and Polly Samson (David Gilmour).

Dear Pratt
Welcome to
Preston Marriott